THE ESSENTIAL
ROOT
VEGETABLE
COOKBOOK

THE ESSENTIAL ROOT VEGETABLE COOKBOOK

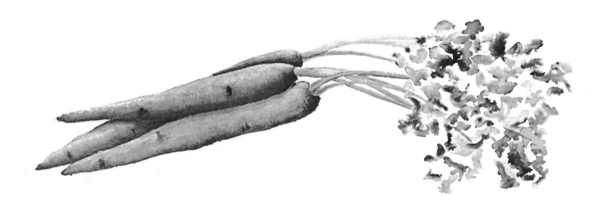

a primer for choosing and serving
nature's buried treasures

BY SALLY AND MARTIN STONE

CLARKSON POTTER/PUBLISHERS
NEW YORK

Published by Clarkson N. Potter, Inc., 201 East 50th Street, New York, New York 10022. Member of the Crown Publishing Group.

CLARKSON N. POTTER, POTTER and colophon are trademarks of Clarkson

Manufactured in the United States of America.

Library of Congress Cataloging-in-Publication Data

Stone, Sally.
The essential root vegetable cookbook / by Sally and Martin Stone. — 1st ed.
p.   cm.
1. Cookery (Vegetables) 2. Root-crops. I. Stone, Martin.
II. Title.
TX801.S763 1991
641.6'51—dc20   90-7521
                                                         CIP

ISBN 0-517-57623-6
10 9 8 7 6 5 4 3 2 1
First Edition

Designed by Barbara B. Kantor

*Again, for Abby in New York and Matt
in Los Angeles.
And for everyone in our family—especially
all the recent arrivals.
And for our mothers, who, in their
eighth and ninth decades currently and respectively,
must have eaten something right.
And, of course, for our friends, our agent,
and our editor.*

CONTENTS

INTRODUCTION · *ix*

BEETS · *1*

BURDOCK · 16

CARROTS · 22

CASSAVA · 42

CELERIAC · 48

CHIVES · 58

DAIKON · 62

GARLIC · 67

GINGER · 84

HORSERADISH · · · · · · · · · · · · · · · · · · · 103

JERUSALEM ARTICHOKES · · · · · · · · · 114

JICAMA · 124

KOHLRABI · 129

LEEKS · 135

LOTUS ROOT · · · · · · · · · · · · · · · · · · · 152

ONIONS · *157*

PARSNIPS · · · · · · · · · · · · · · · · · · · *176*

POTATOES · · · · · · · · · · · · · · · · · · · *187*

RADISHES · · · · · · · · · · · · · · · · · · · *232*

RAMPS · *239*

RUTABAGAS · · · · · · · · · · · · · · · · · *243*

SALSIFY · *252*

SCALLIONS · · · · · · · · · · · · · · · · · · *261*

SHALLOTS · · · · · · · · · · · · · · · · · · · *269*

SWEET POTATOES · · · · · · · · · · · *278*

TARO · *294*

TRUFFLES · · · · · · · · · · · · · · · · · · · *300*

TURMERIC · · · · · · · · · · · · · · · · · · · *307*

TURNIPS · *312*

WATER CHESTNUTS · · · · · · · · · *324*

YAMS · *330*

INDEX · *333*

INTRODUCTION

Of the more than 300,000 plant species on the earth, almost 6,000 are edible. Of these, perhaps only 150 have ever been consumed widely enough to be considered viable products in the world's agricultural marketplaces.

Of that relative handful of farm products, about one-third grow underground (or, in the case of corms, underwater). Only half of these, about twenty-five, find their way into food markets or greengrocers' food bins across the country, and even fewer end up on the nation's tables.

That is a shame, and something that we aim to rectify. It's time that the lowly (pun intended) root vegetables at last rise up to take their rightful places within the reaches of gastronomy. Root vegetables have received some bad press over the years, but in fact they are not fattening—one makes them that way by adding too much fat in their preparation or at the table. They are, however, full of fiber, vitamins, minerals, proteins, and other indispensable nutrients. And why not—each and every one has been designed by nature to be a miniature utility company that manufactures, produces, and stores up energy and nutrients for their stems and leaves. Consequently, they're enormously important to us nutritionally, for the well-being and support of life—human as well as plant.

Some of the bulbs, corms, roots, rhizomes, fungi, and tubers we write about and give recipes for have yet to become universally popular. They're relatively unknown, except to ethnic cooks. But there is much that remains unknown about even the best-loved stars of the underground American kitchen.

Did you know, for instance, that the great potato famine in Ireland might never have occurred if Pizarro had not explored the rarefied atmosphere of the Andes Mountains four centuries earlier? That's where he discovered South American Indians cultivating a plant in the Equadorian and Peruvian highlands 10,000 feet up or more, whose roots (read: tubers) were about the size of a peanut.

First fed to pigs after being introduced to southern Europe, then grown as ornamental plants, potatoes eventually became known for what they are: a plant that provides, per land unit, more energy and more protein for the human body in a shorter time than any other crop (five times more than soybeans, corn, *or* wheat). Even in poorly irrigated or arid soil, potatoes yield about 10,000 pounds of food per acre.

Advanced civilizations such as ours consider root crops "inferior food of inferior peoples," and deem grains superior. Yet we forget that the most expensive, glamorous, exotic, rare, and idealized foodstuff of all, the truffle, is truly a buried treasure. And when "foodies" want a snack, something viscerally satisfying, do they reach for a box of wheat germ? They do not. They go back to their roots. They pour a bag of old-fashioned potato chips into a bowl and crunch away. Loaves of batter-fried onions, deep-fried turnip or sweet potato chips, threads of daikon radish, roasted heads of garlic, grilled scallions, sautéed leek ribbons, and even lumpy mashed potatoes are the darlings of the *nouveaux gourmets* who have discovered that peasant food, down and dirty home cooking, the stuff from mama's kitchen ain't so bad after all. As a matter of fact, these days they have real panache. Root vegetables have come out of the closet—or, in their case, out of the cellar.

Although one might call this book a meat and potatoes cookbook—mostly without the meat—let us confess right off the burner that although this is a vegetable cookbook, it is not a vegetarian cookbook, because some of the recipes do use chicken, beef or fish stock, bits of fish or meat (especially in some classic ethnic dishes). Vegetarians of a more liberal bent will discover, however, that about 75 percent or more of our recipes will not break any of their rules.

Fitness and health? We believe in it and promote it in this book with good nutritional advice on how to eat healthily and yet voluptuously from the underground. But if a reader is on a restrictive diet we recommend sticking to it. Adapt our recipes, making judicious choices, modifications, and substitutions that conform to your diet.

One thing we *have* cut down on is fat—in our kitchen and in our recipes. Grease isn't glamorous. The amounts specified in most cookbook recipes really aren't necessary. Our recipes contain only enough fat to do the job, no more. We use olive oil often because it actually lowers cholesterol—but we use it sparingly because it also contains calories we don't need. Desserts are something else. They're rich, they're sweet, and they should be. They're treats. They're rewards. They're to indulge in once in a while, or just to taste or share.

What readers need to know and most doctors won't or, more to the point, can't tell them, is what foods contain that's good or bad for us. We've listed the nutritional content of all our underground vegetables. This isn't a diet book, however, and the information is there *only* for those who need it—and maybe to make others a little smug about eating healthy and loving every bite.

All vegetables, the subterranean varieties being no exceptions, belong to many different botanical families. Knowing to which family a vegetable belongs may seem superfluous information to a cook, but it is not. If you happen to be allergic to one family member, there is a strong possibility you will be allergic to every member of that family. For instance, potatoes are in the nightshade family (as are tomatoes); sweet potatoes and jicama are in the morning glory family; carrots, parsley, celery, and parsnips are in the carrot family. The rutabaga is a member of the mustard family, along with cabbages, turnips, cauliflower, radishes, and, of course, mustard itself. Peas and beans are in the legume family, as are peanuts. If you are allergic to peanuts, you'll most likely be allergic to beans and peas—but *not* to walnuts, filberts, pecans, cashews, and almonds, all of which belong to a completely different botanical family. We think this information can come in handy, especially if you have an allergic child in your household.

Almost all the vegetables found in this book have been consumed for thousands of years, at first through foraging and gathering and eventually by cultivation. They are native to vast areas of the world, each native being indigenous to a different area. Once man took up agriculture— about ten thousand years ago—roots became common crops wherever he settled. They moved with him when he pulled up stakes. When man made his voyages of exploration, he brought home new, exotic foods that turned out to be more precious than the spices and gold he originally sought. These foods, many root vegetables among them, often took well to soil and climates in other parts of the world. They survived displacement and thrived.

The history of underground vegetables is fascinating, so each, in its alphabetical turn, will be traced to its native habitat and its story told before its recipes (where appropriate) are given. (We like to give you something provocative to say when you serve our food at a dinner party.)

As for the recipes, we don't think just good is good enough. We haven't made most of our recipes deliberately "light." They just are because, as we've researched food and cooked more and more over the years, we've come to the conclusion that simple is better, quicker is better, international is better. Life is complicated enough, cooking doesn't have to be, too. So we have tried to make each recipe an overachiever when it comes to flavor, texture, nourishment, color, new approaches and techniques, and surprises. If some of these recipes become old friends in your kitchen, we will have triumphed.

We Call Them Root Vegetables, but Are They Really Roots?

Those plant foods commonly known as root vegetables are often not roots at all, but really swollen stems and food storage organs that grow beneath the earth (or water).

We will try to define those we are concerned with, the ones most of us use as foods, by their designated anatomical types—tell you which is which—just because it's nice for you to know what you're eating and to be able to call it by its rightful name, if you should want to.

The same confusion exists here that exists in trying to differentiate between vegetables and fruits. What is a fruit? What is a vegetable? It's complicated. It's technical. And it all depends on what our language calls it, and what we are used to.

It plays absolutely no part in our gustatory enjoyment.

If we refer to them as roots, treat them as roots, that's what they are to us.

That with which we dig up roots is a spade. And we call it a spade. But here is what these "roots" are to botanists:

Bulbs are subterranean buds consisting of both stems and leaves, with flattish, elongated, or round fleshy bodies that have roots growing from their undersides and spiky leaves or branchless shoots growing from their tops. Some familiar bulbs are: chives, garlic, leeks, onions, ramps, rocambole, scallions, and shallots.

Corms are really underground or underwater stem bases, enlarged and fleshy, that store food to supply nourishment to roots below and stems above. The water chestnut is a corm.

Rhizomes are parts of a plant that happen to look like roots, thick roots, but are actually underground swollen stems that can give birth to both new roots and to stems, as well. Arrowroot, ginger, lotus root, galangal, and turmeric are all rhizomes.

Roots are typically those parts of a plant that grow downward in the soil and absorb nutrients and moisture. They can be hairlike or fleshy or anything in between. You've probably eaten roots in the form of beets, burdock, carrots, celeriac, horseradish, kudzu, parsnips, parsley root, radishes (daikon, red, white, and black), rutabagas (Swedes), salsify, turnips, and wasabi.

Tubers are the swollen tips of underground stems that store energy in the form of starch to support new stem growth from their "eyes." You may or may not be familiar with some of the following unless you frequent ethnic markets—breadroot, canna, cassava (manioc), chufa, coleus, groundnut, Japanese artichoke, Jerusalem artichoke, jicama, Chinese mustard, potato, sweet potato (boniato), taro, water parsley, yam, kohlrabi.

Fungi are primitive plants that live on the decaying remains of other organisms. The truffle is the one edible fungus that grows beneath the earth in symbiosis with the roots of a few kinds of trees—oaks, hazelnuts, and lindens, mostly.

We've done biographies of many of the vegetables listed above but some have such local constituencies that they are rarely available in the majority of the nation's markets. Some may not be included at all because they may be marketed in such limited quantities. Others, at the moment, may only be found in home gardens.

You now know what you have been eating all these years or what you might be eating in the future after you've thumbed through our book. Thumbing, we trust, will turn into reading. Reading should start you cooking. Cooking is preparation for eating. And eating—perhaps dining—is what this book is all about.

BEETS

[*BETA VULGARIS*]

beetroot

remolacha (Sp.)

runkelrube (Ger.)

betterave (Fr.)

bietola (It.)

Beets are a two-part vegetable—the eminently edible leaves and the familiar ruby root. A fresh young bunch of beets with the tops still attached offers you two distinct tastes and textures that can be served at the same meal or at two different meals.

Fresh beets used to be very popular. They've lost some of their market share, we believe, because in this era of fast, fast food they take too long to cook. But canned beets (almost instant food—open, heat, and serve), although not as earthy and fresh-tasting, are one of the few vegetables that are almost as good as fresh. They're not only more than passable, they're usually much less expensive than those at the green market—you just don't get the added bonus of the tops.

Maybe canned beets are so good because there isn't much you can do to beets to ruin them. There isn't much you can do to them to make them into something other than what they are either. The only thing that makes them taste different, it seems, is pickling; beets just don't absorb flavors like other vegetables do.

Man has eaten beets since prehistoric times. They are native to a vast area of the world from Britain to India. At first beets were grown only for their tops. The Greeks ate only the leaves and so did the Romans. The root was relegated to medicinal uses until the final centuries of the Roman Empire. Pliny, who called the roots "those crimson nether parts," left the beetroot to physicians, surgeons, and prophets. Recipes for cooking the beetroot are first encountered in Roman records from the second and third centuries A.D., when some epicures heralded it as a better vegetable than cabbage—high praise, indeed.

The sugar beet, a white variety developed from the beet's close cousin, chard, began to be cultivated in the eighteenth century. When the Napoleonic Wars cut off much of Europe's supply of imported sugarcane, a French banker named Delessert saw the possibilities in the process perfected by François Achard in 1793 for producing sugar beets, and thus breaking the sugar blockade set up against Napoleon.

In two years Delessert's factories, replete with James Watt's steam engines to process the molasses and crystallize the sugar, produced more than 4 million kilos of sugar from beets grown in northern France. Then came Waterloo. Renewed trade with the West Indies dropped the price of sugar by half, and Delessert's sugar-beet industry went bust. It wasn't until the 1870s, when more efficient processing methods were developed, that sugar making from beets again became practicable. Today, almost half the world's sugar is produced from the sugar beet, the only major food crop developed by modern man.

The beets we eat, however, are the dark magenta roots that thrive particularly well in cooler countries and appear in one form or another at almost every meal in northern Europe. At tables in the Eastern-bloc countries you'll find infinite varieties, both hot and cold, of that inspired and justly famous soup made with beets—borscht or borsch.

Beetroot can be sliced or julienned for salads, dressed with yogurt or sour cream and quantities of fresh dill, marinated in a vinaigrette and served cold or warm, combined with potatoes and green beans as a variation on German potato salad, hollowed out and stuffed, or served simply with butter and lemon juice. Their sweet flavor and brilliant color can lend a dramatic contrast to many dishes, both classic and invented.

Varieties

There are green-leaf beets and red-leaf beets, the only difference being in the color of the leaves—the root is pretty much the same. The red-leaf beet has greenish leaves with red veining and a red stalk, while green-leaf beets have no red veins. Golden beets, somewhat orange in color, are a comparatively recent variety, and are grown mainly in kitchen gardens. If you do find them at your greengrocer, try them. They have a sweeter, more delicate flavor than red beets.

Availability

Fresh beets are available all year long, although the best ones according to our tastes arrive in late spring and are on produce stands until October. These are the smaller so-called beet thinnings, which have ruby-green leaves and tender roots the size of jumbo marbles. They usually come from local growers. As the season goes on, the beet roots get larger, and whereas a spring bunch might have contained 7 to 10 roots, in fall it yields only 3. Some beets are shipped to market with their greens removed; these are called *clip tops* and most likely have come out of storage and are not nearly as tender as those with their leaves intact.

Storage

If you must store fresh beets, cut off the tops and use them in salads or as a cooked vegetable. The roots last longer in the refrigerator without their tops. Just wash the roots, put them in a plastic bag in your crisper, and use them within a week or two at the most, as they lose their tenderness and can become soft.

What to Look For

Select fresh beets that are smooth-skinned, hard, and dark red with crisp green or reddish leaves (neither wilted nor yellowed). The globes should be free of cuts or bruises. Even if the still attached tops are wilted, the beets themselves can be firm and bright-looking. They will of course be of acceptable quality—you just won't be able to use the leaves as a separate vegetable.

Basic Preparation and Cooking Methods

To retain their color, beets are best when cooked whole. Leave 1 or 2 inches of stem attached (otherwise they bleed their color into the cooking water), scrub them, put them in a heavy saucepan of cold water, and bring to a boil. Reduce heat and simmer for 30 to 40 minutes. Refresh the beets under cold water, cut off the stems and root tails, and slip off the skins.

As for the greens, they should merely be wilted in the water that clings to them after they are washed. Cook them quickly in a skillet or sauté pan.

nutrition

Beets contain about 10 percent sucrose carbohydrates, a source of quick, nonfattening energy many times that of any other vegetable. Beets also have a diuretic action, nice to know when you are troubled with water bloat. As for vitamins and minerals, here are the figures: In 100g you find 44 calories, 1.48g protein, 9.9g carbohydrates, 16mg calcium, .91mg iron, 21mg magnesium, 48mg phosphorus, 324mg potassium, 72mg sodium, .37mg zinc, .083mg copper, .352mg manganese, 11mg vitamin C, .05mg thiamine, .02mg riboflavin, .4mg niacin, .15mg pantothenic acid, .046mg vitamin B_6, 92.6mg folacin, 20IU vitamin A, plus all the amino acids and no cholesterol.

SWEET-AND-SOUR BEET SOUP WITH CARAWAY AND YOGURT

Serves 6 to 8

It's odd how some vegetables that are sweet to begin with, like beets and sweet potatoes, are traditionally sweetened further in the cooking. Most of the time we don't particularly like the idea, but often we'll taste a dish, like this soup, at someone else's table or at a restaurant and discover that sugar in one form or another has been added. We then have to reassess our prejudice.

1½ pounds beets (3 pounds with leaves and stems), peeled

2 tablespoons unsalted butter

2 medium onions, finely chopped

1 tablespoon minced garlic

2 teaspoons caraway seeds (Russian black caraway seeds, if available, or Indian black onion seeds)

3 tablespoons firmly packed dark brown sugar

¼ cup plus 2 tablespoons balsamic vinegar or red wine vinegar

4 cups homemade chicken stock or canned broth

½ teaspoon salt, or to taste

½ teaspoon freshly ground black pepper, or more to taste

2 cups water

¼ cup plain yogurt or sour cream, or more if desired, for garnish

2 tablespoons minced fresh parsley

In a food processor, grate the beets coarsely and reserve.

In a soup pot or large sauté pan, melt the butter over moderately low heat and, when the foam subsides, cook the onions until they soften, stirring occasionally. Add the garlic, caraway seeds, and brown sugar and cook the mixture, stirring, for 3 minutes.

Add the beets and cook, stirring, for 1 minute. Add the vinegar, stock, ½ teaspoon salt, ½ teaspoon pepper, and water and bring the mixture to a boil. Reduce heat to a simmer and cook the mixture, stirring occasionally, for 20 minutes, or until the beets are tender. Taste and add more salt and pepper, if desired. Ladle the soup into bowls and top each portion with about 2 teaspoons yogurt and a sprinkling of parsley.

UKRAINIAN WINTER BORSCHT

Serves 6 to 8

Borscht is the old Slavonic word for beet, although it has come to mean "beet soup" in this country. Actually, in the USSR the ingredients for beet soup vary from region to region; sometimes the borscht will have a lot of meat in it and becomes almost a stew, and sometimes it will have a good deal of cabbage. Our version is Ukrainian-based and has a larger proportion of beets because the Ukraine has a huge beet crop.

beef stock

3 pounds beef flanken, shin of beef with the bone, or lean ham hock

2 bay leaves

1 large onion, peeled and studded with 5 cloves

1 celery stalk with leaves

1 large carrot, peeled and cut into 2-inch pieces

1 tablespoon coarse (kosher) salt

1 teaspoon freshly ground black pepper

3 quarts water

borscht

4 tablespoons unsalted butter, margarine, or vegetable oil

1 medium onion, minced

2 tablespoons minced garlic

2 medium carrots, peeled and sliced into ¼-inch rounds

1 medium turnip, peeled and cut into ½-inch dice

1 parsnip, peeled and sliced into ¼- inch rounds

1 small celeriac, peeled and cut into ½-inch dice (about 1 cup)

1 cup diced canned imported Italian tomatoes (about 4 or 5)

1 tablespoon coarse (kosher) salt, or to taste

1 teaspoon freshly ground black pepper or more to taste

2 tablespoons red wine vinegar

2 tablespoons sugar

2 quarts plus 2 cups beef stock

1½ pounds beets (about 3 pounds with the leaves), trimmed, scrubbed, and coarsely grated

1 pound cabbage, shredded

1 pound boiling potatoes, peeled and cut into ½-inch dice

3 tablespoons minced fresh parsley

⅓ cup snipped fresh dill, plus additional for garnish

1 cup sour cream for garnish

In a large soup pot or kettle, combine the beef, bay leaves, onion with cloves, celery stalk, carrot pieces, salt, pepper, and water and bring to a boil over high heat. Reduce heat to a simmer, skim off the froth, and cook the mixture, covered, skimming occasionally, for 1½ hours, or until the meat is tender. Strain the stock through a sieve and chill, reserving the meat; discard the vegetables. When the meat is cool enough to handle, remove all the meat from the bones and shred it with your fingers or cut into small dice; discard the bones and any fat. Reserve the meat in the refrigerator, covered. At this point the beef stock can be refrigerated for 2 to 3 days, or frozen for up to 3 months. Before you use it, remove the solid white layer of congealed fat from the top.

To make the borscht, melt the butter in a soup pot over moderate heat. When the foam subsides, add the onion and garlic and sauté, stirring occasionally, until just transparent, about 5 minutes. Add the sliced carrots to the onion mixture and sauté for 2 minutes more. Add the diced turnip, the sliced parsnip, and the diced celeriac and sauté, stirring occasionally, for 5 minutes more. Add the diced tomatoes, salt and pepper, vinegar, and sugar and sauté for 2 minutes, stirring. Add 2 cups of the beef stock and the beets to the pot, stir to combine, and bring to a boil over high heat. Reduce heat to a simmer, cover, and cook for 15 minutes.

Meanwhile, in a large saucepan set over high heat, bring 2 quarts of the beef stock to a boil. Add the shredded cabbage and diced potatoes, return to a boil, then reduce heat to a simmer and cook, stirring occasionally, for 5 minutes. Transfer the cabbage, potatoes, and beef stock to the mixture, which should have finished cooking by this time. Stir in the parsley, ⅓ cup dill, and the reserved shredded or diced beef and simmer the soup, partially covered, for 15 minutes. Taste and adjust the seasonings, adding more salt, pepper, and vinegar as needed.

Serve from a tureen, or divide among heated bowls. Garnish each serving with a dollop of sour cream and sprinkle with some of the additional dill.

CREAMED BEET AND CORIANDER SOUP WITH ORANGE JUICE

Serves 6 to 8

The addition of orange juice to this recipe offers a slightly offbeat flavor note. If you are watching calories, use lowfat milk to replace the cream or half-and-half (the soup will be less rich, of course, and the flavor a little less subtle). You may also substitute yogurt, sour cream, or buttermilk, but watch carefully that the soup does not boil or these ingredients will curdle.

3 pounds fresh beets with stems and leaves	1¼ cups freshly squeezed orange juice
2 tablespoons unsalted butter	½ teaspoon salt, or to taste
1 large onion, thinly sliced	½ teaspoon white pepper, or more to taste
1 tablespoon minced garlic	
1 teaspoon ground coriander	⅔ cup heavy cream or half-and-half
1 boiling potato (about ¼ pound), peeled and cut into coarse dice	¼ cup minced fresh coriander leaves, or more to taste
5 cups homemade vegetable stock or prepared vegetable bouillon	

Separate the greens from the beets, discarding the stems. Wash the greens and peel the beets. Chop both coarsely. In a large saucepan or soup pot over moderate heat, melt the butter and, when the foam subsides, add the onion and sauté, stirring, until it is softened. Add the garlic and cook the mixture, stirring, for 2 minutes. Add the ground coriander and cook, stirring, for 2 minutes more.

Add the beets, beet leaves, and potato and cook the mixture, stirring, for 2 minutes. Add the stock, orange juice, salt, and pepper and bring to a boil. Reduce heat to a simmer and cook, covered, 20 to 30 minutes, or until beets are tender. In a blender or food processor, puree the mixture in batches, transferring the puree to a bowl.

Return the puree to the saucepan, stir in the cream, and heat the soup over moderate heat until it is heated through (do not allow it to boil). Taste for seasoning and add more salt and pepper, if desired. Ladle the soup into heated bowls and sprinkle with fresh coriander.

GRATED RAW BEET SALAD VINAIGRETTE WITH DILL

Serves 4

Raw beets are delicious, and when served this way they are the perfect accompaniment to boiled beef, cold roast chicken, poached fish, and dozens of other dishes we're sure are in your repertoire. This salad also makes a great first course or light lunch with the addition of drained pickled herring tidbits in wine sauce or a can of sardines in oil that have been drained and coarsely broken and then tossed with the beet salad. About 2 tablespoons of minced onion would also add a nice bite.

¼ cup red wine vinegar
1 tablespoon powdered mustard
1 tablespoon Maggi seasoning
½ teaspoon salt, or to taste
½ teaspoon freshly ground black pepper, or more to taste

¾ cup light Tuscan olive oil
1½ pounds beets (3 pounds with leaves and stems), trimmed and peeled
1 tablespoon snipped fresh dill
4 large lettuce leaves

In a small bowl, whisk together the vinegar, mustard, Maggi seasoning, and salt and pepper. Add the oil in a thin stream and whisk the dressing until it is combined and emulsified.

Cut the beets into small chunks. In a food processor fitted with the shredding disk, grate the beets coarsely.

In a bowl, combine the beets, dill, and about ½ cup of the dressing, reserving the remainder in the refrigerator in a jar with a tight-fitting lid for another use. Toss the beets to coat them well (at this point the salad may be chilled until serving time). Place the lettuce leaves on 4 salad plates and divide the beet salad among them.

Parslied Sweet Beets with Two Piquant Flavorings

Serves 4

This is a quick and convenient recipe for beets. It uses canned beets so you know it's easy. The addition of lemon juice and capers makes the beets taste even sweeter—and look much more festive. Try this if you're having guests for dinner and you've been kept late at the office. It's elegant, unusual, and fast!

1   16-ounce can sliced beets with their liquid (see Note)
3   tablespoons unsalted butter, 1 tablespoon cut into pieces
    Salt and freshly ground black pepper to taste

2   tablespoons minced fresh parsley
2   tablespoons chopped drained capers
3   teaspoons freshly squeezed lemon juice

In a large sauté pan or skillet over high heat, combine the beets with their liquid, 2 tablespoons of the butter, and salt and pepper to taste, and bring to a boil. Reduce heat to a simmer and cook, uncovered, for 8 to 10 minutes, or until most of the liquid has evaporated. Add the parsley, chopped capers, lemon juice, and reserved butter pieces. Stir several times until the flavors are combined and the butter has melted into the sauce. Add more salt and pepper, if necessary, and serve.

NOTE: This recipe can also be made with fresh beets. Although it takes more time some cooks think it's worth it because of the earthy flavor. If you are one of those purists, as we are, and have the time, this is how you do it.

Start with ¾ pound fresh beets without the stems (about 1½ pounds with the stems and leaves). Peel the beets and slice them into ¼-inch rounds. In a large sauté pan or skillet, combine the beets with 2 tablespoons of the butter, 1 cup water, and salt and pepper to taste and bring the liquid to a boil over high heat. Reduce heat to a simmer and cook the beets, covered, for 10 minutes. Remove the cover, add more boiling water if necessary, and cook 10 minutes more, or until they are tender and almost all the liquid has evaporated. Continue the recipe as above. If the beet leaves are fresh and bright-looking, you can add these, chopped, all stems removed, along with the remaining ingredients.

BEETS AND PEARL ONIONS PICKLED IN RASPBERRY VINEGAR AND WINE

Makes about 4 cups

Raspberry vinegar is one of the few ingredients to emerge from nouvelle cuisine that we find useful. It has a nice fragrance and flavor and it works especially well with these pickled beets. Serve them with grilled fish, with roast pork or chicken—or whatever you like.

1 cup red wine
3 tablespoons sugar
1 teaspoon whole allspice, lightly crushed
1 teaspoon salt
¼ cup water

½ pound tiny pearl onions (about 2 cups), blanched and peeled
8 medium beets (about 1½ pounds without stems and leaves), peeled and cut into ¼-inch slices
¼ cup raspberry vinegar

In a medium stainless-steel or enameled saucepan over moderately high heat, bring to a boil the wine, sugar, allspice, salt, and water. Add the onions and beets, return to a boil, then reduce heat to a simmer and cook, partially covered, about 15 minutes, or until the beets are just tender.

Transfer the vegetables and their liquid to a bowl and add the vinegar. Let cool. When at room temperature, cover the bowl tightly with plastic wrap and refrigerate for at least 1 hour or overnight before serving. Pickled beets will keep, refrigerated, for a week or more.

CHILLED BEETS AND GREEN BEANS WITH SCALLION VINAIGRETTE

Serves 4 to 6

For this salad we use oven-steamed beets. The vegetables are wrapped in foil and baked, which is an easy and convenient way to cook beets, especially if you are using the oven for another purpose like baking or roasting. It saves fuel and produces a tender, flavorful product. If you think ahead, the beets can be steamed along with another meal one day and used for this salad a day or two later.

1 pound beets (about 2 pounds with stems and leaves), trimmed and scrubbed	1 tablespoon Maggi seasoning
¼ cup balsamic vinegar, preferably, or red wine vinegar	¾ cup olive oil
	3 scallions, white and green parts minced
1 tablespoon Dijon mustard	1 pound green beans, preferably young and thin, trimmed and cut, if necessary, into 3-inch lengths
½ teaspoon salt, or to taste	
½ teaspoon freshly ground black pepper	

Preheat the oven to 400° F.

Wrap each beet separately in foil (or together, if they are of uniform size). Bake in the middle of the oven for 45 minutes if small, 1 hour if large, or until tender when pierced with a knife. Open the foil and let the beets cool completely, then slip off the skins. Thinly slice the beets.

In a medium bowl, whisk the vinegar with the Dijon mustard, salt and pepper, and Maggi seasoning. Add the oil in a thin stream, whisking, and whisk the dressing until it is combined and emulsified. Stir in the scallions, add the beets, toss the mixture well, and let the beets marinate, covered and chilled, overnight.

In a medium saucepan of boiling salted water, cook the beans for 4 to 6 minutes, or until just crisp-tender. Drain and plunge them immediately into ice water to stop the cooking. Drain the beans once more and pat dry with paper towels. (The beans may be prepared 1 day in advance and kept wrapped in damp paper towels inside a plastic bag and chilled.)

At least 30 minutes before serving, remove the beet and vinaigrette mixture from the refrigerator, combine with the green beans, taste and adjust the seasoning, and toss well. Toss again just before serving.

NOTE: Because there is plenty of dressing in this recipe, it can be expanded to serve 8 without additional vinaigrette by adding 8 cooked and halved small new potatoes in their jackets.

FRESH BEETS IN LIME BUTTER

Serves 4
- - - - - - - - -

Here's another instance where grating the fresh root cuts cooking time and preserves the just-picked flavor. The lime adds a sharp undertone that cuts the sweetness of the beets, and the butter brings all the flavors together.

1½ pounds beets (3 pounds with leaves and stems), trimmed, peeled, and quartered

3 tablespoons unsalted butter, softened

½ teaspoon freshly grated lime zest, or more to taste

1½ tablespoons freshly squeezed lime juice, or to taste

Salt and freshly ground black pepper to taste

¼ cup sliced scallion greens

In a food processor fitted with the shredding disk, grate the beets. In a heavy saucepan or skillet melt 2 tablespoons of the butter over moderately high heat. When the foam subsides, cook the beets and lime zest, stirring frequently, for 4 to 5 minutes, or until the beets are crisp-tender. Reduce heat to moderately low, stir in the remaining butter, lime juice, and salt and pepper to taste. Remove from heat and stir in half the scallion greens. Transfer the mixture to a serving bowl and sprinkle with the remaining scallion greens. Serve hot.

BEETIFIC CHOCOLATE-NUT TORTE

Makes a 9-inch torte, serves 10

Beatific means blissful, and blissful is an apt description of this chocolate dessert. It bakes into a torte with a vaguely rosy glow, as if coated with a thin raspberry glaze. The beets make the torte both moist and smooth-textured, and they also give you a nutritional bonus that won't interfere with the dark chocolate taste. One caveat: Grind the nuts very fine but short of becoming a paste (almonds are preferred but you can substitute pecans, walnuts, or cashews). A nut grinder is best for this purpose, or use a completely dry food processor or blender and pulse, stopping and scraping the sides down often.

1 16-ounce can whole or sliced beets

4 ounces semisweet chocolate

5 large eggs, separated

¾ cup sugar

1½ cups finely ground unblanched almonds

⅓ cup fine dry bread crumbs

Grated rind of 1 lemon

chocolate glaze

2 ounces semisweet chocolate

2 tablespoons rum or strong coffee

6 tablespoons unsalted butter, at room temperature

Preheat the oven to 350° F.

Drain the beets and puree them in a food processor. Transfer the puree to a fine sieve and set aside to drain again (you should have slightly more than 1¼ cups).

Butter a 9-inch springform pan and line the bottom with a round of wax paper or parchment cut to fit. Butter the paper and dust lightly with flour. Set aside.

Melt 4 ounces chocolate over very low heat and, when partially melted, stir with a rubber spatula until smooth. Remove from the heat and set aside to cool.

Place the egg yolks and ½ cup of the sugar in the bowl of an electric mixer and beat at high speed for 2 to 3 minutes, or until the yolks are a pale lemon color and creamy. Set the mixer on low speed and add the chocolate, mixing just to combine. Still on low speed, add the ground nuts, bread crumbs, pureed beets, and lemon rind and mix until well blended. Set aside.

In another clean bowl, beat the egg whites on high speed with a dash of salt until they hold soft peaks; do not overbeat. Still on high speed, gradually add the remaining ¼ cup sugar and beat until the whites hold a shape but are not stiff and dry.

With a spatula, gently fold the whites into the chocolate mixture in several additions, mixing only to incorporate, without overfolding. Pour the batter into the prepared pan and bake in the center of the oven for 1 hour, or until the cake begins to shrink away from the sides of the pan.

Cool completely in the pan. When cooled, run a thin spatula or sharp knife between the cake and the sides of the pan to release it. Remove the sides of the pan and invert the cake onto a rack. Remove the pan bottom and the wax paper. Cover with a serving plate and invert cake again, leaving it right side up.

To make the glaze, melt 2 ounces chocolate with the rum or coffee in a small saucepan over very low heat. Remove from heat and beat in the butter with a wire whisk until thoroughly blended. Place the pan in a bowl of cold water and continue beating until the mixture is completely cooled. Spread the glaze over top and sides of the cake with a metal spatula. It can be served immediately or chilled.

BURDOCK

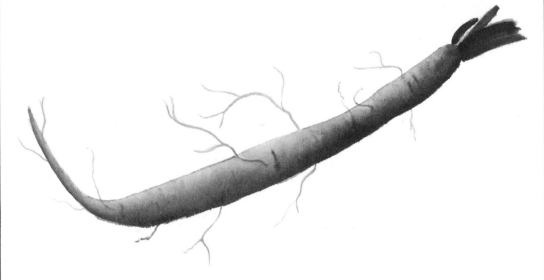

[*ARCTIUM LAPPA*]

beggar's button

gobo (Jap.)

ngau-pong (Ch.)

*B*urdock, a member of the daisy family, is almost completely unknown as a food plant in this country, but it is certainly recognized as that pesky weed whose sharp, prickly burrs are hell to remove from pants and socks.

Although it grows easily and often in profusion in temperate climates, burdock is not often cultivated here. We have seen it more often in the past few years at our local farmers' markets, however, and on Oriental produce stands.

The narrow, pointed burdock taproot, which usually has a brown to grayish hairy skin encasing white flesh, can grow to 4 feet in length. It is usually sold in bundles of 3 or 4.

The Chinese probably introduced burdock, a Siberian native, to the Japanese as a medicine about a thousand years ago. It is still used in China (where it is called *ngau-pong*) primarily as a folk medicine, but it is well loved as a vegetable in Japan and Hawaii. Added to soups, slowly simmered in dishes, or sautéed in oil, then seasoned and served at room temperature, *gobo* is a staple of the Japanese diet. Looking very much like stalks of white asparagus, canned *gobo* sometimes tastes strange to Western palates and can be searingly hot like fresh horseradish. We find fresh burdock delicious and somewhat neutral in flavor like salsify or potatoes.

Varieties

Most fresh burdock, if your greengrocer has it, is grown locally. It is the same no matter where it's grown.

Availability

Look for it in late summer and throughout the fall and early winter. Like some other roots, burdock can be left in the ground to be pulled when needed.

Storage

The fresh root will keep well in the refrigerator for several weeks, if placed in a brown paper bag.

What to Look For

Choose long, slender roots—about 12 to 14 inches in length and 1 inch in diameter. The skin should be free of bruises or cracks and dirt-brown or dark gray in color, with as few root hairs as possible to facilitate paring.

Basic Preparation and Cooking Methods

Scrub the root with a stiff brush to clean away clinging dirt. Once scrubbed, peel and cut into 2-inch lengths and drop immediately into lightly acidulated water (water with a few drops of lemon juice or vinegar added) or it will quickly discolor. Cook by steaming, braising, simmering in salted water to cover, or blanch for 5 minutes, drain, and sauté in a little oil with a sprinkling of black or cayenne pepper and, perhaps, some garlic. Burdock works well in any of the recipes suggested for salsify; substitute equal quantities.

nutrition

In 100g of burdock there are only 88 calories, 21.15g carbohydrates, 1.83g fiber, 49mg calcium, 39mg magnesium, 93mg phosphorous, 360mg potassium. Its vitamin levels are modest: only .039mg thiamine, .058mg riboflavin, and .320mg niacin. Not even a trace of vitamin C, alas.

Burdock Sautéed with Chicken Breasts, Black Sesame Seeds, and Apple

Serves 4

With this recipe plus a green salad you can put dinner on the table in under 20 minutes. The calories are kept to a minimum, nutrition to a maximum (about which no one's the wiser because it all tastes too good to be considered diet food), and, if you trim the chicken breasts of any streaks of fat, no measurable cholesterol. The burdock, to the uninitiated, will taste something like artichoke hearts.

1½ **pounds burdock**
2 **tablespoons freshly squeezed lemon juice**
1 **teaspoon salt, or to taste**
2 **tablespoons light olive oil**
4 **chicken cutlets (about 2 pounds), cut crosswise into ½-inch slices**

1 **tablespoon minced garlic**
1 **tablespoon black sesame seeds**
½ **tart apple, peeled, cored, and minced**
Freshly ground pepper to taste

Trim the burdock, scrub well, peel, and cut into 2-inch lengths, dropping the pieces immediately into a large saucepan with 1 inch of water, the lemon juice, and 1 teaspoon salt. Cover and bring to a boil over high heat, then reduce heat to moderate and cook for 5 minutes, or until just tender. Drain.

Meanwhile, in a sauté pan or large skillet, heat the oil to rippling over moderately high heat. Salt and pepper the chicken pieces and sauté them, stirring, for 2 minutes. Sprinkle with the garlic and sesame seeds and continue to sauté, stirring and turning the chicken, 2 minutes more. Add the burdock, the minced apple, salt and pepper to taste, stir to combine well, and cook for 2 or 3 minutes more, or until the chicken is springy to the touch. Transfer to a heated serving platter and serve.

NOTE: Although we sometimes call this dish Black-and-White Burdock and Chicken, a little color can be added by sprinkling with snipped chives, minced fresh parsley, or thinly julienned sun-dried tomatoes.

BURDOCK AND MUSHROOM PÂTÉ WITH YOGURT-DILL SAUCE

Serves 8 to 10

Vegetable pâtés are wonderful buffet food. This one is particularly good and can be used as a first course or served, as we often do, with drinks before dinner. Because it should be made a day before serving, you're free to be with your guests instead of in the kitchen. For a buffet, slice it ahead of time and arrange overlapping slices on a rectangular serving dish or fan them on a round platter, accompany with a bowl of the sauce, and let guests serve themselves.

1½ pounds burdock	1 cup ground blanched almonds, lightly toasted
3 tablespoons freshly squeezed lemon juice	½ cup freshly grated Parmesan
1 tablespoon salt, or to taste	½ cup grated Gruyère
3 tablespoons unsalted butter	⅓ cup minced fresh parsley
1 cup minced onion	1 teaspoon dried thyme
1 tablespoon minced garlic	½ teaspoon dried basil
1 pound mushrooms, minced	½ teaspoon dried marjoram
Freshly ground black pepper to taste	1 bay leaf
4 large eggs, lightly beaten	2 cups Yogurt-Dill Sauce (recipe follows)

Trim the burdock, scrub well, pare, and cut into 2-inch lengths, dropping the pieces immediately into a large saucepan with 1 inch of water, 2 tablespoons of the lemon juice, and 1 tablespoon salt. Cover and bring to a boil over high heat, then reduce heat to moderate and cook for 5 minutes, or until just tender. Drain and set aside.

Preheat the oven to 350° F.

Generously butter a 9 x 5 x 2¾-inch loaf pan. Set aside.

Melt the butter in a skillet over moderate heat and, when the foam subsides, cook the onion and garlic, stirring, for 3 minutes, or until they are softened. Add the mushrooms and salt and pepper to taste and cook the mixture, stirring occasionally, until almost all the liquid evaporates from the mushrooms.

In a food processor or blender, puree the mixture with the reserved burdock until it is smooth, and transfer it to a large bowl. Add the eggs, almonds, Parmesan, Gruyère, parsley, thyme, basil, marjoram, the remaining tablespoon of lemon juice, and salt and pepper to taste. Combine the mixture well.

Spoon the mixture into the prepared loaf pan, place the bay leaf on top, and cover the pan with a triple layer of buttered foil. Set the loaf pan in a baking pan and pour enough boiling water into the baking pan to reach two-thirds of the way up the sides of the loaf pan. Bake the pâté in the middle of the oven for 1½ hours, or until a skewer or cake tester inserted in the center comes out clean. Transfer the loaf pan to a rack to cool, then refrigerate overnight.

The next day, remove the foil and run a thin sharp knife around the edges of the pâté to loosen it. Place a platter over the pan and invert the pâté onto it. If it resists coming loose, tap the pan lightly on the platter until it is released. Slice the pâté and serve it with Yogurt-Dill Sauce.

YOGURT-DILL SAUCE

Makes about 2 cups

1 cup plain yogurt
1 tablespoon Dijon mustard
¼ cup snipped fresh dill

Salt and freshly ground black
pepper to taste
¼ cup light olive oil (optional)

In a bowl, combine the yogurt, mustard, dill, and salt and pepper to taste. If desired, add the oil in a stream, beating until well combined. Transfer the sauce to a serving bowl.

CARROTS

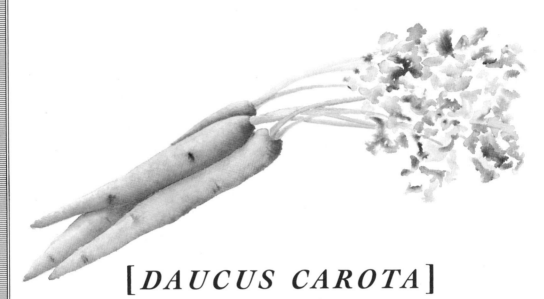

[*DAUCUS CAROTA*]

carotte (Fr.)

safranories, zanahoria (Sp.)

karotte, mohre, mohrrube (Ger.)

carota (It.)

*T*he first carrots, more than three thousand years ago, were natives of Afghanistan. Early varieties were red, purple, black, yellow, and white; the popular orange variety known all over the world today (except in Egypt where they still grow purple ones) has only been around for a few hundred years.

From Afghanistan, the carrot moved to the west into the Mediterranean area and eastward to India, China, and Japan, places where, unlike Europe, it was used as a food crop as early as the thirteenth century. The ancient Greeks called the carrot "Philtron" and used it as a love medicine, beneficial to virility in the male and as an aphrodisiac said to loosen the morals of the female. No doubt it was the carrot's phallic shape that gained it a reputation for libidinousness that continued with the Romans, especially among their more lascivious emperors. Caligula reportedly force-fed the whole Roman Senate carrots so that he could see them "in rut like wild beasts." While we doubt he saw them in this state, we can guarantee they saw *him* more clearly, especially at night, because carrots prevent night blindness.

In the Middle Ages, physicians prescribed carrots to cure everything from sexual maladies to dizziness to snakebite. In fact, until the Renaissance only the Asians seemed to serve them as a food, with no other ulterior or interior motive but to enjoy their flavor. When they were first introduced into France, only the feathery leaves were used—to decorate coiffures, hats, dresses, and coats.

Sixteenth-century French and German horticulturalists who rid the carrot of any residual poisons (carrots in their wild state are somewhat poisonous) allowed it to become an accessible, cultivated food plant. The pale yellow strain they developed became popular because it would flavor, but not color, soups, stews, and sauces. In seventeenth-century Holland, the bright orange variety was finally hybridized and took over as the favored type. This strain is rich in beta-carotene—from which the body manufactures vitamin A—which has been discovered by some university scientists to play an important role in the prevention of some types of cancer. Happily for carrot lovers, they contain more beta-carotene than any other fruit or vegetable, and the deeper the orange color the greater the beta-carotene content. Oddly enough, older carrots, rather than fresh young ones, offer more beta-carotene. These mature, deeply orange carrots are preferred by food purveyors, who consider them more attractive to consumers. This accounts for the high beta-carotene content of frozen, canned, and dried carrot products.

Because beta-carotene is converted into vitamin A by the body, just one intensely orange carrot can supply enough beta-carotene to provide an adult's total daily vitamin A requirement. There is an important difference between this naturally occurring beta-carotene and vitamin A supplements. Beta-carotene, as supplied by carrots, spills into the bloodstream from the digestive tract, then some of this is deposited in epithelial tissues (our outer skin and inner linings) and in body fat, or stored in the liver, where it remains dormant until the body needs it. It is then converted into vitamin A. The body will keep a backup supply of beta-carotene and eliminate any excess through normal bodily functions.

"Preformed" vitamin A, however, which we receive when we take vitamin A supplements or eat the flesh or dairy products of animals who ingest plants containing beta-carotene, is not the same. Megadoses of the vitamin can cause side effects ranging from mild to severe. Taking too much beta-carotene is harmless and can only cause yellowing of the skin, an impermanent disorder normalized when the diet is readjusted.

Prudent ingestion of vitamin A or beta-carotene helps in the formation and maintenance of healthy, youthful-looking skin; prevents split, peeling, and ridged fingernails; promotes lustrous, healthy-looking tresses; aids in the ability to see in dim light and helps prevent night blindness; helps prevent infections of the mucous membranes and drying of the eyes; and promotes healthy tooth enamel and proper bone growth in children.

Growing scientific evidence points to the relationship of eating foods containing beta-carotene, such as that in green, orange, and yellow vegetables and fruits to a reduced risk of some cancers—perhaps even the prevention of some types that arise in epithelial tissues. Mouth and throat cancers removed by surgery often are prevented from recurring with large doses of an artificial vitamin A drug developed for acne, according to recent studies.

Given their health benefits, we don't do as much with carrots as we could—or should. The ubiquitous carrots and peas of our childhood dinner plates, often overcooked and tasteless, probably turned a whole nation against both of these superb vegetables. Carrots can be cooked in many ways, including blanching, boiling, steaming, braising, sautéing, frying, deep-frying, glazing, baking, microwaving, and pressure-cooking.

They can be eaten raw or juiced. They can be made into desserts, cookies, and cakes—in fact they can contribute healthy, colorful, flavorful qualities to any course of a meal. They combine well with many other vegetables (to our tastes, least well with peas), such as potatoes, onions, celery, and parsley. They add sweetness and an aromatic quality to soups and stews. They contribute crunch and color to salads. They are sweet because they contain large amounts of sugar, yet they are low in calories; an average carrot has only 30 calories. They were once tried as a commercial source of sugar, like the sugar beet was in France. They failed. But who cares? They're so good at so many other things!

It is also interesting to note that if a dish is listed on a French menu as *Crecy*, it means that one of its main ingredients is carrots. Crecy is the region in France that grows the bulk of French carrots.

Varieties

Dozens of varieties of carrots are grown and marketed in this country. They may be different in size and shape, but they are quite similar in taste, color, and nutrition whether eaten raw or cooked. There are many differences in appearance, however: some are short and stubby, some are long and thin, some are straight, some are twisted, some are hairy-looking, some are smooth. They all come from pretty much the same strain of seed; it's the soil and climate that make for slight differences. Then there are the "baby" carrots that delight miniature-vegetable fanciers. The delight, if any, is only in their cute size. They're so young they can be almost tasteless, so immature their color seems bleached out. Only true dwarf carrots are sweet and flavorful. If they are the immature roots dug up in the thinning process during cultivation, forget them unless you just want them for decoration. Except for these bantams and bunched fresh carrots with their tops still on, carrot prices rarely fluctuate throughout the year. Ask your greengrocer where the carrots originated; the farther west the source, the sweeter and better the flavor will be. Carrots from California and Arizona are the best ones produced in this country. Then come those from Texas, Michigan, and last (and least), Florida. Northeastern and Canadian carrots, except those just pulled, can be woody and less sweet.

Availability

Carrots are available twelve months of the year. Older carrots, those that have been in storage, will have increased their beta-carotene content with age. Sometimes they will have almost twice as much as when they were fresh.

Storage

Carrots will keep in plastic bags in your refrigerator for several months. *Do not store carrots with their tops on.* The tops rob the roots of their freshness, their moisture, and many of their nutritional qualities. The tops are inedible and, if they're bright green and lively looking, are only left on to tell you how fresh the roots are. When your produce man offers to remove the tops, take him up on it. You'll probably be paying a premium price for these tops—often twice that of cut-top bagged carrots—but they're useless.

What to Look For

Bright, shiny, moist-looking carrots with smaller cores and wholesome, unblunted tips are best. Their crowns (where the feathery tops sprout and where you can often see the size of the core) can be slightly green, red, or purplish in color without affecting the flavor, but the carrot itself must be deep, fiery orange, and free from bruises, cuts, cracks (vertical cracks mean they were left in the ground too long, hori-

zontal cracks just mean poor handling), rot, and blackened skin. If the carrots are sold in cello bags, peer through and be sure all the carrots in the bag are of uniform quality and well shaped. Avoid the limp and wilted ones. (However, carrots that have become limp and rubbery during storage can be rejuvenated by putting them in ice water for an hour or two.) If they are old, they may be dry-looking as well and have tiny white root hairs growing from them. Steer clear of these. Always check the tips of the carrots because this is the first place decay appears. If the tops show signs of resprouting, they are beyond their prime and should be left in the store.

Basic Preparation and Cooking Methods

Because carrots retain a good deal of their nutrition in or just below the skin, it is best to clean them by washing well with a stiff vegetable brush or nonmetallic pot scrubber. If they are unsightly or you want a smooth, uniform look, use a swivel-bladed vegetable peeler to remove a hair's breadth thickness of skin. Trim off the crowns and tips. Carrots can be cooked whole, sliced into coins, cut diagonally, cut into julienne strips, cut into sticks (batons); they can be shredded, grated fine or coarse, quartered and cut into

1-inch or 2-inch pieces, or diced. When cooking sliced, diced, or julienned carrots in liquid just to cover, cooking time is about 4 to 8 minutes, depending on the size of the pieces. The thicker the pieces, the longer the cooking time.

Just be sure to test for doneness. Carrots should be tender but not mushy, firm but not crisp. Whole carrots will take at least twice as long as slices or batons, but that, of course, depends again on their size.

nutrition

In 100g of boiled and drained carrots, there are 45 calories, 1.09g protein, 10.48g carbohydrates, 1.47g fiber, 31mg calcium, .62mg iron, 13mg magnesium, 30mg phosphorus, 227mg potassium, 66mg sodium, .30mg zinc, .134mg copper, .752mg manganese, 2.3mg vitamin C, .034mg thiamine, .056mg riboflavin, .506mg niacin, .304mg pantothenic acid, .246mg vitamin B_6, 13.9mg folacin, and, hold on to your hat, 24,554IU vitamin A! They also have more than a trace of all amino acids, and no cholesterol.

SPICY CARROT BEIGNETS FLECKED WITH SCALLION AND JALAPEÑO

Makes about 3 dozen beignets

We always serve food with drinks before dinner. What's needed is something light enough not to dull appetites, yet tasty enough to compete with Bloody Marys and vodka and tonics. These beignets are so good that they sometimes compete with the conversation—or stop it while guests enthuse. This we don't like. A little praise at the end of a meal is fine, talking it to death while it is being eaten means we've either over-reached or invited the wrong people.

2 cups grated peeled carrots (about 3 medium)	1 teaspoon salt, or to taste
1 scallion, white and green parts, minced	½ teaspoon white pepper, or more to taste
2 large eggs, lightly beaten	1 small fresh jalapeño, seeded, de-veined, and minced
2 tablespoons all-purpose flour	Peanut oil or vegetable oil for deep-frying
1 teaspoon double-acting baking powder	

In a bowl, stir the carrot, scallion, eggs, flour, baking powder, salt, pepper, and jalapeño until well combined. In a deep skillet, sauté pan, or electric frying pan, bring 1 inch of oil to 400° F. Drop in the batter by teaspoonfuls without crowding, turning the beignets for about 1 minute, or until they are golden brown. Transfer the beignets to paper towels to drain. Be sure the oil has returned to 400° F. before you add the next batch.

Heap the beignets in a napkin-lined basket and serve them warm with drinks.

SKILLET-CHARRED PUREE OF CARROT SOUP

Serves 4

"If you burn it, toss it" is a kitchen maxim we tossed out when we tried this soup. Actually, it is the carrot's own sugar that burns, and burnt sugar is one of the great flavoring agents. We use a cast-iron skillet for this recipe because preheating our favorite stainless-steel sauté pans would discolor them. If you don't own a cast-iron skillet, use an enameled one. If you do use stainless steel, don't preheat, just bring the oil almost to smoking before adding the carrots.

1 tablespoon vegetable oil	½ cup heavy cream, yogurt, or milk
3 cups shredded peeled carrots (about 5 or 6 medium)	1 tablespoon red wine vinegar
	½ teaspoon salt, or to taste
2 shallots, coarsely chopped	½ teaspoon freshly ground black pepper
1 tablespoon chopped garlic	
½ teaspoon dried thyme	1 tablespoon unsalted butter, at room temperature
1 small Idaho potato, peeled and coarsely chopped	
	1 tablespoon chopped chives or scallion greens, or more, to taste
3½ cups homemade chicken stock or canned broth	

Preheat a 12-inch cast-iron skillet over high heat for 5 minutes, add the oil, and a few seconds later the carrots. Stir to coat the carrots evenly with the oil and cook, stirring frequently, until the carrots begin to char and blacken around the edges, about 15 to 20 minutes. Reduce the heat to moderately low and add the shallots, garlic, and thyme. Simmer for 2 or 3 minutes, or until the shallots are softened.

Add the potato and the stock and cook until the carrots and potato are quite soft, about 15 minutes. Puree the mixture in batches in a food processor, and return the puree to the skillet or a saucepan. Stir in the cream and, if you prefer a thinner consistency, additional stock. Add the vinegar, salt, and pepper and cook over low heat until heated through. Stir in the butter and serve in heated bowls, sprinkled with the chives.

VANILLA-SCENTED CARROT PUREE

Serves 6 generously

- - - - - - - - - - - - - - - -

Carrots and vanilla would seem at first glance to be an odd combination. But when you taste this unusual accompaniment for grilled meats, fish, or roasts, you'll wonder why the two aren't paired more often. So here is the recipe—something new to replace sweet potatoes on the Thanksgiving menu or to serve as an unusual vegetable at any meal. Any leftovers make an uncharacteristic but delicious omelette filling.

2 pounds carrots, peeled and cut into 1-inch pieces	1 tablespoon Dijon mustard
½ teaspoon vanilla extract	2 large eggs
½ cup crème fraîche or milk	½ teaspoon salt, or to taste
3 tablespoons unsalted butter	½ teaspoon freshly ground black pepper

Preheat the oven to 350° F.

Butter a 1-quart soufflé dish or ovenproof serving dish and set aside.

In a medium saucepan, cover the carrots with water and bring to a boil over high heat. Cook for 20 minutes, or until they are very tender, not crisp. Drain the carrots, transfer them to a food processor, and puree until smooth. Add the vanilla, crème fraîche, 2 tablespoons of the butter, the mustard, eggs, salt, and pepper and puree again until all the ingredients are well combined. Transfer the carrot puree to the prepared dish, dot the top with remaining 1 tablespoon butter, and bake in the center of the oven for 45 minutes.

NOTE: For a more distinct vanilla flavor, split a vanilla bean, scrape the seeds from one half of it, and add them in place of the vanilla extract.

SHERRY-GLAZED CARROTS WITH DILL

Serves 4

Sherry and the carrots' natural sugar help to caramelize the vegetable without any additional sugar. Sherry also adds a nutty flavor balanced nicely by the fresh dill. You can substitute parsley, if you like, or even a handful of chopped watercress or chives. In any case, these quick-to-prepare carrots make the perfect accompaniment to any fall or winter meal.

1½ tablespoons unsalted butter or margarine

1 pound carrots, peeled and sliced into ¼-inch rounds

2 tablespoons water or canned chicken broth

½ teaspoon salt

½ teaspoon white pepper

2 tablespoons creme sherry or Marsala wine

1½ tablespoons snipped fresh dill

In a small heavy saucepan, melt the butter over high heat. When the foam subsides, add the carrots and stir until evenly coated with the butter. Stir in the water, salt, and pepper, bring to a boil, cover, reduce heat to a simmer, and cook for about 8 minutes, shaking the pan every once in a while. Remove the cover, increase heat to moderately high, and boil 2 minutes, or until almost no liquid remains. Add the sherry, reduce heat to a simmer, and stir until the sherry has evaporated. Remove the pan from the heat, gently stir in the dill, and serve.

MOROCCAN MINTED CARROT SALAD

Serves 4 to 6

- - - - - - - - - - - - -

This simple recipe takes just 5 minutes of actual work time. It mingles several sweet and spicy tastes with the crunch of carrots. Some Moroccan cooks, perhaps disliking a noisy salad, boil the carrots to the crisp-tender stage (about 5 minutes), drain, and dress them just before serving.

1 pound carrots (about 5 to 6), peeled

¼ cup olive oil

3 tablespoons freshly squeezed lemon juice

1 tablespoon minced garlic

¼ teaspoon ground cumin, or more to taste

¼ teaspoon ground cinnamon

1 tablespoon chopped fresh mint leaves, or ½ teaspoon dried

½ teaspoon salt, or to taste

½ teaspoon freshly ground black pepper

½ teaspoon confectioners' sugar, or more to taste

¼ teaspoon cayenne pepper

1 2-inch strip orange zest, cut into fine julienne

Mint leaves for garnish

Using the julienne cutting attachment of a food processor, cut the carrots into fine julienne shreds, or cut by hand into very fine strips. Whisk the remaining ingredients together in a bowl, and pour the mixture over the carrots. Chill, if you like, and garnish the salad with a few mint leaves.

COLD CURRIED CARROT VICHYSSOISE

Serves 6 to 8

- - - - - - - - - - - - - -

Of course, traditional vichyssoise is a potato-and-leek soup that is served cold. But we don't hold with traditions, not where flavor is concerned. Carrots offer a new and welcome sweetness to this old favorite, as well as a sunny color that adds to the taste appeal. In using walnuts as a garnish we borrowed from the classic carrot cake, where the two flavors are truly simpático.

2 tablespoons unsalted butter	1 teaspoon salt, or to taste
1½ cups chopped leeks, including 1 inch of the green part, washed well and drained	2½ cups homemade chicken stock or canned broth
½ cup chopped red onion	2 cups water
1½ tablespoons *garam masala* or good-quality curry powder	1 cup milk
1½ pounds carrots, peeled and sliced into ¼-inch rounds (about 4 cups)	1 cup sour cream Freshly ground white pepper to taste
1 pound boiling potatoes, peeled and cut into ½-inch pieces	6 to 8 teaspoons finely chopped walnuts for garnish

In a large saucepan, melt the butter over moderate heat. When the foam subsides, add the chopped leeks and onion and cook, stirring, until the vegetables are soft and just beginning to color. Stir in the *garam masala* and cook the mixture, stirring, for 2 minutes.

Add the sliced carrots, potatoes, 1 teaspoon salt, the stock, and water and bring to a boil over high heat. Reduce the heat and simmer the mixture, covered, for 35 to 40 minutes, or until the vegetables are very soft. Puree the mixture in batches in a food processor. Transfer the puree to a bowl and whisk in the milk, sour cream, white pepper, and more salt, if desired.

Chill the soup, covered, for at least 3 hours or overnight. Stir the soup well before serving and garnish each bowl with 1 teaspoon chopped walnuts.

CRUSTY CARROT, TURNIP, AND SCALLION GRATIN

Serves 6

- - - - - - - -

Gratins are homey, yet elegant, ways of serving a great variety of vegetables and meats, even leftovers. The bubbling gratin dish is always welcome at the dinner table because people seem to love offerings that are crisp on the outside, moist and flavorful inside. Most gratins, like this one, can be made ahead, at least partially, and reheated or finished in the oven and brought straight to the table. You can even add up to a cup of leftover chicken or cooked meat, shredded or diced, and turn the gratin into a light one-dish meal.

¾ pound carrots, peeled and shredded	½ cup heavy cream, half-and-half, or additional milk
¾ pound turnips, peeled and shredded	1 large egg Salt and freshly ground black pepper to taste
½ cup thinly sliced scallion greens	½ cup grated Parmesan
2 tablespoons minced fresh parsley	1 tablespoon cold unsalted butter, cut into pieces.
4 tablespoons cornstarch	
2 cups milk	

Preheat the oven to 375° F.

Butter a 1½-quart shallow baking dish or a 10-inch round or oval gratin dish and set aside.

In a mixing bowl, toss together the carrots, turnips, scallion greens, parsley, and 3 tablespoons of the cornstarch. Spread the vegetable mixture in the prepared dish, pressing and smoothing the mixture into place. In a saucepan, dissolve the remaining 1 tablespoon cornstarch in ¼ cup of the milk; add the remaining 1¾ cups milk and the cream, and bring the mixture to a boil over moderately high heat, whisking constantly. Reduce the heat to moderately low.

In a medium bowl, beat the egg with a fork, season with salt and pepper, then add the milk mixture in a slow, thin stream, beating until combined. Pour this hot custard over the vegetables. Sprinkle the top evenly with the Parmesan, dot with butter pieces, and bake in the middle of the oven for 45 minutes, or until it is bubbling through its golden crust. Let the gratin stand for 10 minutes before serving to crisp the crust and allow the custard to set.

NOTE: If you want to add cooked diced or shredded chicken or meat to the gratin, spread it over the vegetables *before* pouring on the custard.

INTERNATIONAL INTOXICATED CARROTS

Serves 4

Silly name. We're to blame. It just means that carrots made in this manner can use almost any liquor you have on hand. For instance: Using Scotch will give the carrots the smokey flavor associated with that rocky landscape, Irish whiskey a touch of that lush country, Spanish brandy offers a memory of flamenco—and so it goes.

2 tablespoons unsalted butter	Salt to taste
1 pound carrots (about 5 or 6), peeled, cut into 2 x ¼ x ¼-inch batons	½ cup Scotch, Irish whiskey, Spanish brandy, French Cognac, Russian vodka, German schnapps, or Swedish aquavit (see Note)
2 teaspoons sugar	

In a heavy skillet or sauté pan, melt the butter over moderate heat. When the foam subsides, add the carrots, sugar, and salt to taste. Stir the mixture until the carrots are coated with the butter. Add the liquor of choice, bring to a boil over high heat, reduce heat to a simmer, and cook the carrots, stirring occasionally, for 4 or 5 minutes, or until they are tender and the liquid has evaporated. Serve warm.

NOTE: You can also use a flavored sweet liqueur like amaretto or Cointreau. Just reduce the sugar to 1 teaspoon.

BRISKET OF BEEF BAKED WITH CARROTS, FRUIT, AND SWEET POTATOES

Serves 6

- - - - - - - -

*T*zimmes is inching its way into the American vernacular as a word that means a crazy, mixed-up, overblown situation. Actually it is a Yiddish word that describes a spiced carrot and fruit pudding often served with the meat course. It also lends its name to a dish often made by boiling meat, carrots, and prunes first, and then baking them in the oven with white or sweet potatoes. We bake the meat and carrot pudding together to begin with, coming up with a crazy, mixed-up *tzimmes* that we think is tastier, more tender, and, if not the classic, quite classy.

2 tablespoons peanut, safflower, or canola oil

3 pounds brisket of beef, trimmed of excess fat
Salt and freshly ground black pepper to taste

2 cups finely chopped onions

2 tablespoons minced garlic

3 tablespoons all-purpose flour

2 cups canned beef broth

2 cups water

1 tablespoon tomato paste

1 bay leaf

½ teaspoon dried thyme

½ teaspoon ground cinnamon

6 cloves

3 strips orange rind (2½ x ½ inches each)

½ pound pitted prunes

½ cup freshly squeezed orange juice

2 tablespoons freshly squeezed lemon juice

2 pounds carrots, peeled and cut into ½-inch rounds

1 Granny Smith apple, peeled, cored, and finely chopped

1 tablespoon light brown sugar or maple syrup

1 pound sweet potatoes (about 2 large), peeled and sliced ½ inch thick

In a stainless-steel or enameled roasting pan or large casserole, bring the oil to rippling over moderately high heat. Sprinkle the brisket with salt and pepper to taste and sear it, turning with tongs until it is well browned on all sides. Transfer it with the tongs to a plate and set aside.

Preheat the oven to 350° F.

Pour off all but 2 tablespoons of fat from the pan, reduce heat to moderate, and cook the onions and garlic, stirring, for 5 minutes, or until the onions are transparent and begin to turn golden. Add the flour and cook the mixture, stirring, for 3 minutes. Add the broth, water, tomato paste, bay leaf, thyme, cinnamon, cloves, and the orange rind and stir to combine. Return the brisket to the pan with any juices that have accumulated on the plate and bring the mixture to a boil over high heat.

Cover the roasting pan and bake in the oven for 1 hour.

Meanwhile, soak the prunes in the combined orange and lemon juices for at least 30 minutes. Add the soaked prunes with the juice mixture, carrots, apple, and sugar to the roasting pan after the hour is up. Continue baking for 1 hour more. Add the sweet potatoes and bake the *tzimmes* for 30 minutes more, or until the sweet potatoes are tender and the carrots and prunes have practically melted together. Remove the roasting pan from the oven and let rest for 10 minutes. Slice the meat, arrange the slices on a warm platter, and surround them with the fruit and sweet potato pudding.

SAVORY SPICED CARROTS
WITH YOGURT AND CURRANTS

Serves 4

Carrots originally came from what is now Afghanistan. This recipe has an earthy flavor, sweet and aromatic, that borrows from Middle Eastern cooking.

½ cup currants

1½ pounds carrots, peeled and cut into 3 x ¼ x ¼-inch batons

2 tablespoons light olive oil

1½ tablespoons minced garlic

2 teaspoons firmly packed dark brown sugar

1 teaspoon ground cardamom

1 teaspoon ground cumin
Salt and freshly ground black pepper to taste

1 teaspoon minced fresh gingerroot

¼ cup plain yogurt (regular or low-fat)

In a small bowl, cover the currants with boiling water and allow to plump for 15 minutes. Drain and set aside.

Meanwhile, in a medium saucepan cover the carrots with boiling salted water and boil over high heat for 4 minutes. Drain in a strainer.

In the same saucepan, bring the oil to rippling over moderately high heat. Add the garlic and drained carrots, reduce heat to a simmer, and cook, covered, for 2 minutes. Add the drained currants, brown sugar, cardamom, cumin, ginger, and salt and pepper and continue cooking for 4 or 5 minutes, stirring occasionally, or until the carrots are just tender. Remove the pan from the heat and stir in the yogurt. Serve immediately.

Sweet Carrot and Pistachio Custard Dessert Pudding

Serves 4 to 6

O range and green is a pretty color combination—even when it's canned carrots and peas—but decorator colors are not all this creamy pudding has to offer. It has a smooth *and* chewy texture, it's sweet but not cloying, and, if you serve it to your guests after dinner, it might even help them see their way home in the dark (carrots are supposed to aid night vision). It will certainly help them find their way back to your table.

10 tablespoons (1¼ sticks) unsalted butter or margarine
1 cup light brown sugar
2 large eggs, lightly beaten
2 cups peeled and grated raw carrots (about ⅔ pound)
¾ cup crushed vanilla wafers

2 tablespoons grated orange rind
1 teaspoon grated lemon rind
½ teaspoon powdered ginger
½ teaspoon ground mace
½ teaspoon ground allspice
¾ cup shelled unsalted whole pistachios

Preheat the oven to 350° F.

Generously butter a 6-cup baking dish and set aside.

In the large bowl of an electric mixer set at medium speed, cream together the butter and sugar. When blended, add the beaten eggs and grated carrots and beat for about 2 minutes. Add the vanilla wafers, orange and lemon rinds, ginger, mace, and allspice and beat well, about 2 minutes more.

With a rubber spatula, fold in ½ cup of the pistachios. Pour the batter into the prepared baking dish and bake in the center of the oven for 1 hour.

Meanwhile, chop the remaining pistachios in a food processor, with a nut grinder, or by hand.

When the custard pudding is finished baking, remove it from the oven and sprinkle the top with the chopped pistachios. Serve from the baking dish either warm, at room temperature, or chilled.

ORANGE-GLAZED CARROT CAKE

Makes one 10-inch cake; serves 10 to 12

The classic carrot cake is spread with a cream cheese icing. We love carrot cake but find the ubiquitous white frosting a little boring. Carrots and oranges are the same gorgeous color; their flavors are complimentary. Why not, we thought, combine them? We did and we're glad. The glaze can be poured over the cooled cake, spooned over individual slices, or the cake can be sliced horizontally in thirds, the glaze spread over the layers, and the cake reassembled.

2 cups sugar

1¼ cups vegetable oil

1 cup sifted whole wheat flour

1 cup sifted all-purpose flour

2 tablespoons baking powder

1 teaspoon baking soda

1 teaspoon salt

2 tablespoons ground cinnamon

4 large eggs

3 cups peeled and grated raw carrots (about 1 pound)

1 cup finely chopped pecans

½ cup finely chopped dried apricots (optional)

orange glaze

----

1 cup sugar

¼ cup cornstarch

1 cup freshly squeezed orange juice

1 teaspoon freshly squeezed lemon juice

2 tablespoons unsalted butter

2 tablespoons grated orange rind

¼ teaspoon salt

Preheat the oven to 350° F.

Oil a 10-inch tube pan and set aside.

In the bowl of an electric mixer at medium speed, thoroughly combine 2 cups sugar and the vegetable oil.

Sift together the flours, baking powder, baking soda, salt, and cinnamon. Add half the dry ingredients to the sugar-oil mixture and mix together on medium speed for 2 to 3 minutes. Beat in the remaining dry ingredients, in four batches, alternating with the eggs added 1 at a time. Beat in the carrots, pecans, and apricots, if used, until just combined.

Pour the batter into the prepared tube pan and bake in the center of the oven for 1 hour and 10 minutes, or until a cake tester inserted in the center comes out clean. Remove the cake from the oven and let it cool in the pan in an upright position.

Meanwhile, in a small saucepan mix together 1 cup sugar and the cornstarch. Gradually stir in the orange and lemon juices. When the mixture is smooth, set the saucepan over low heat and add the butter, orange rind, and salt. Cook the mixture, stirring constantly, until it is thick and glossy, about 3 minutes. Let the glaze cool completely.

When both the cake and glaze have cooled, run a narrow metal spatula or thin knife between the cake and the edges of the pan. Place a cake platter over the cake, invert both, and remove the pan. Pour the orange glaze over the cake, spreading it with a spatula and allowing it to drip down the sides.

NOTE: After glazing, the cake may be decorated with pecan halves or dried apricot halves, the cut sides set flush with the outer edge of the cake about 1 inch apart.

TIP: Toss the pecans and the apricots with a dusting of flour, just enough to coat lightly, before mixing into the batter. This will keep these "heavy" ingredients evenly distributed and stop them from slipping to the bottom of the cake during baking. This is something to remember when adding similar ingredients to any cake batter. It will keep nuts, raisins, chocolate chips, and their like suspended.

CASSAVA

[*MANIHOT UTILISSIMA;*
MANIHOT DULCIS]

manioc

yucca

mandioca

aipim

Brazilian arrowroot

tapioca

There is a story, which may be apocryphal, that tells of a Spanish explorer hopelessly lost in the Amazon jungles of Brazil. Knowing from the Indians that the sap of the cassava is highly poisonous, the explorer decided that rather than die a slow death from fever and starvation, he would commit suicide by eating cassava. So he boiled up a few roots in water to make what he thought would be a deadly soup. The heat dispelled the deadly poisons. Of course, instead of dying, he was nourished—enough so that he was able to find his way out of the jungle and tell the world of the cassava's food value.

You may never have come across cassava cooked as a vegetable. You know it, most likely, only in its commercial form—as tapioca, the little pregelatinized pearls of starch used mostly in puddings and pie fillings. But in the world's warmer countries where potatoes are difficult to grow in the lowlands, cassava is served much as potatoes are in temperate climes and is an extremely important source of starch in the diets of millions and millions of people.

Cassava's original homeland was Brazil, where early Portuguese explorers saw its food potential and transported the handsome bushy plant to the Asiatic tropics in the seventeenth century. Even before the Portuguese, the Spanish brought it to Spain in the sixteenth century. From there it was taken to Africa, and from Africa to Asia where it had become popular by the nineteenth century. The two types of cassava, bitter and sweet, are now planted over 37 million acres worldwide—about 20 million acres in Africa alone. Aside from the roots, Africans and Indonesians also eat the young leaves and stem tops of the shrub. But the really important part of the plant, as far as we are concerned, is its root. The root is produced underground in bunches somewhat like "hands" of bananas. Cassava in our markets usually measure about 8 to 10 inches in length and up to 2 inches in diameter. The skin is generally a pink color shading to brown. The ones we see have a mostly brown, intricately flaky-looking skin.

Pared of its skin, the hard cassava flesh has a faintly bitter odor. This is from the glucoside (related to prussic acid) or hydrocyanic acid contained in the roots. Thorough cooking gets rid of all traces of this dangerous, sometimes fatally poisonous, substance because the volatile acid is driven off by heat. Consequently, the roots should *never* be sampled in their raw state, even though improved varieties with reduced toxins are usually available commercially. It is also prudent to wear gloves when working with the raw root.

The bitter and sweet cassava are species of the *manihot* (a native word that also gives us one of the other names cassava is known by, *manioc*), which has nearly 150 near relatives, some of which produce a variety of rubber. One rubber-producing cousin grows to over 65 feet tall in just ten years. Others in the family are powerful laxatives, so powerful in fact that just two seeds can kill a human being. These seeds were used by the Indonesians to poison the wells of enemies—undetectably and terribly, gruesomely effective (a secret killer Alfred Hitchcock never thought of).

Varieties

There are two major varieties of fresh cassava roots, bitter and sweet. The sweet cassava or *aipi* is quite safe to eat; it is the bitter cassava that contains the toxic glucoside. However, the bitter cassava is the more important of the two commercially—perhaps because it can grow bigger roots (some weigh in at 30 pounds)—and yields more starch. In looks and taste, both kinds are identical, other than size, so always be on the safe side—if you're not sure which one you are buying, cook the root.

Availability

You'll find fresh cassava in Hispanic grocery and produce markets and in many Oriental markets throughout the year. Tapioca granules are found on the dessert-mix shelves of supermar-

kets alongside the gelatin and pudding mixes, and in Chinese and Southeast Asian markets in 1-pound packages. In Oriental kitchens, it is seldom used alone but is added in small amounts to rice flour to give pastries a translucent sheen and chewy texture.

Storage

Cassava can be stored for long periods in a dry, airy place out of the sun. It can also be stored unwrapped in the refrigerator for weeks at a time. Once peeled, however, it should be used promptly to avoid any discoloration of the flesh.

What to Look For

Look for good size roots 8 to 10 inches long and about 1½ to 2 inches in diameter. They should be very firm with no soft, mushy spots and a pinkish to light brown skin with an overlay of brown flaky scales.

Basic Preparation and Cooking Methods

When cassava's skin is pared away, the flesh should be firm and white to cream-colored. Cut it in half length- wise, then into 2-inch pieces; immerse the pieces in salted water, leave uncov- ered, and bring to a boil. Reduce heat to moderate and cook for at least 1 hour, until tender and all traces of toxic substances are carried off in the steam. The sections may then be split apart or cut into wedges and baked, fried, or sautéed. The texture of cooked cassava is like that of a moist white potato. The flavor is bland and takes well to many seasonings—especially garlic.

nutrition

Cassava is a low-calorie carbohydrate. A 100g serving has only 60 calories, 6.9g protein, 145mg calcium, 2.8mg iron, 8.3mg vitamin A, and 2.8mg vitamin C.

CASSAVA ROULADE WITH CORNED BEEF, TOMATO, AND CHILE FILLING

Serves 6

This is a Caribbean version of the soufflé roll made with a leek and sausage filling on page 144. Unlike a classic roulade, however, the cassava dough and filling are baked together. It can take dozens of fillings, anything from spicy to sweet, depending on what the cook has in the larder.

2 pounds fresh cassava root, peeled and cut crosswise into ½-inch slices

5 tablespoons unsalted butter, at room temperature

3 large eggs

2 cups all-purpose flour

2 teaspoons salt, or to taste

2 tablespoons peanut, safflower, or canola oil

1 large onion, finely chopped

1 tablespoon minced garlic

2 cups chopped and drained canned Italian tomatoes

2 small jalapeño peppers, seeded, deveined, and minced

½ teaspoon freshly ground black pepper, or more to taste

1 pound lean cooked corned beef, trimmed of fat, and cut into thin slices, or sliced deli corned beef

In a large saucepan over moderately high heat, place the cassava slices with salted water to cover and bring to a boil. Reduce heat to moderate and cook, uncovered, for about 1 hour, or until tender but not falling apart. Drain well, return to the pan, and steam dry for 10 to 15 seconds. Force the cassava through the fine disk of a food mill or through a ricer into the bowl of an electric mixer. With the mixer set on medium speed, beat in 4 tablespoons of the butter. When well combined, beat in 2 eggs, 1 at a time, beating thoroughly after each addition. Add the flour, ½ cup at a time, and 1 teaspoon of the salt. Continue to beat until the dough is firm enough to hold its shape when lifted on a spoon. If the mixture is too loose, beat in more flour, a tablespoon at a time. Cover the bowl tightly with plastic wrap and set aside.

Preheat the oven to 350° F.

With a pastry brush, coat a large baking sheet or jelly-roll pan with the remaining 1 tablespoon of softened butter.

In a large sauté pan or skillet over moderate heat, bring the oil to rippling. Add the onion and garlic and, stirring frequently, cook for 3 to 5 minutes, or until soft and translucent. Stir in the tomatoes, jalapeño, remaining 1 teaspoon salt, and the pepper. Increase heat to moderately high and cook, stirring frequently, until almost all the liquid in the pan has evaporated and the mixture is thick enough to hold its shape on a spoon. Remove from the heat and stir in the corned beef. Taste and adjust the seasonings, adding more salt and pepper, if necessary. Set aside.

Pat the cassava dough into a ball, and on a lightly floured piece of wax paper, press it with your fingertips into a thick rectangle. Flour a rolling pin and roll the dough into a rectangle about 12 inches wide, 18 inches long, and ½ inch thick. Dust the dough from time to time to prevent it from sticking to the rolling pin.

With a spatula, spread the meat mixture evenly over the dough to within about 1 inch of the edges. Starting with the long side of the dough, lift the wax paper and, using it as support, roll the dough into a compact cylinder.

Using the wax paper as a sling, or with 2 large spatulas, transfer the roll to the prepared baking sheet, seam side down. Remove the wax paper. Beat the remaining egg with a fork, and brush it over the top and sides of the roll.

Bake the roll in the middle of the oven for 1 hour, or until golden brown. Transfer the roll to a heated platter, cut into 3-inch slices, and serve immediately.

Celeriac

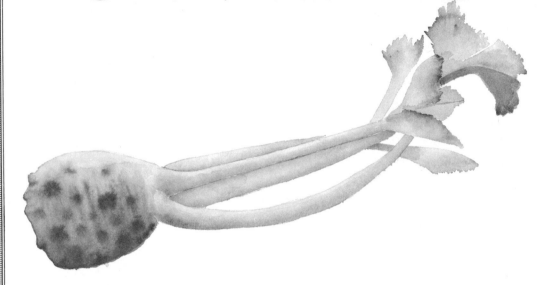

[*APIUM GRAVEOLENS* VAR. RAPACEUM]

celery root

knob celery

turnip-rooted celery

céleri or *céleri-rave* (Fr.)

You may call this peculiar-looking root knob celery, turnip-rooted celery, just plain celery root, celeriac, the French *céleri*, or by its botanical designation, *Apium graveolens*—but if you call it delicious, you'll be of like mind with us. Though not an acquired taste (it's akin to celery, only more intense), it is to some an acquired texture! Celery is crisp and crunchy; celery root is soggy-firm.

The two vegetables are members of the same family—the carrot family—but the aboveground stunted stalks of celeriac are too coarse and tough to be eaten, although they and their strong, aromatic leaves do make good soup greens. Celeriac is grown solely for its enlarged light-brown knobby root.

If you are not familiar with celeriac, it is definitely worth seeking out. Never tremendously popular here, it is well loved in Europe in spite of its unattractive appearance (of course, it is never served in its original state, but rather peeled, sliced, cubed, or julienned).

Cultivated first in the Mediterranean region and in northern Europe, it was introduced into England in the eighteenth century and found its way to our shores soon after. Like many of the root vegetables, celeriac is a temperate plant and is best during the colder months. A half-century ago, when lots of vegetables we now import all year round were not readily available during winter and early spring, celeriac was much more popular and inexpensive as well. It all but disappeared in the sixties and seventies and is only now making a comeback but—thanks to food writers and gourmands—as a status vegetable with prices to match. The high prices are a shame because celeriac is easy to grow and stores well. Perhaps as it becomes more popular and not just faddish, increased volume will lower prices.

Varieties

Although celery root has several names, it comes in only two varieties: long-leaved and short-leaved. Long-leaf celeriac is slow growing with a heavier root. The short-leaf variety has faster-growing roots that are usually smoother and rounder. In the early fall you'll see small knobs in produce markets usually sold three to the bunch, with some of the coarse green stalks attached. Later on, after the first frost, the roots come to market in much, much larger sizes with the greens trimmed away. They are then sold by the pound.

Availability

With the exception of June, July, and the first half of August, celeriac should be available year-round. The best roots are harvested in the late fall or early winter. The roots are often left in the ground and can survive a mild winter under a blanket of mulch before being pulled.

Storage

If stored in a cool, moist area like the refrigerator, or in a root cellar, celery root can keep for weeks, even months. Don't store roots with their green stalks attached. When storing for extended periods, individually wrap each knob well in plastic wrap.

What to Look For

Choose roots that are firm and heavy for their size. Large roots can have hollow centers, so heft them first. Small roots can have too much waste when peeled. Try to find mid-size knobs with as even a surface as possible. If there is dirt clinging to the root, brush it away to expose decay, if any.

Basic Preparation and Cooking Methods

Scrub the knobs well to remove any residual dirt and peel before cooking or using raw. Peeled celeriac tends to darken and discolor when exposed to air, so keep it in acidulated water (water to which a few drops of lemon juice or vinegar have been added) before and after you cube it, slice it, or cut it in julienne strips. If you find a soft, pithy, cottony-feeling center, cut it away and discard it. Some cooks like to cook the knobs first and peel them later, which preserves the color and makes them easier to peel. Cubes and slices become tender after 20 to 30 minutes of simmering or steaming. The root can be substituted for stalk celery in many recipes.

nutrition

Celeriac is one of the vegetables that weight-loss diets should embrace. It has only 154 calories to the pound. That's an awful lot of food volume for so little calorie intake. When you realize that it provides, ounce for ounce, almost as much protein as potatoes, you can see its enormous potential as diet food. Just think, you can eat all you want, take in little in the way of calories, and get a lot of nutrition in the bargain. Compared to the wonderful potato, celeriac has five times the fiber and five times the calcium. It contains twice the iron; three times the phosphorus; almost as much potassium; only a trifle less vitamin C; less than half the thiamine; but almost three times the riboflavin; half the niacin; half the vitamin B_6; and absolutely no cholesterol. For those on a low-salt diet, celeriac does have one drawback—it is high in natural sodium; about fifteen times the sodium found in potatoes.

Note: If you feel more secure with actual figures, turn to the nutrition section for potatoes and multiply, divide, add, and subtract at will.

HOT OR COLD CREAM OF CELERIAC SOUP

Serves 6

Soups that can be served either hot or cold are wonderful to have in your repertoire so that you don't have to give up those you really like with the change of season. Years ago we made this soup with an enrichment of heavy cream and egg yolk, but that was before cholesterol and calories became a concern. Now we use lowfat yogurt, no egg yolks, and margarine instead of butter. It's amazing how little the flavor of the soup is affected. The texture is slightly thinner but, then again, so are we.

2 tablespoons unsalted butter or margarine	2 all-purpose potatoes (about ½ pound), peeled and cut into ½-inch dice
1 pound celeriac (about 2 medium), peeled and cut into ½-inch dice	½ teaspoon salt, or to taste
	½ teaspoon white pepper, or more to taste
2 scallions, white and green parts, thinly sliced	½ cup plain lowfat yogurt
5 cups homemade chicken stock or canned broth	1 tablespoon minced fresh parsley

In a saucepan, melt the butter over moderately high heat. When the foam subsides, add the celeriac and scallion and sauté for 5 minutes, stirring occasionally. Add the chicken stock, potato, and ½ teaspoon salt and ½ teaspoon white pepper, and bring the liquid to a boil; reduce heat to moderate and cook the mixture, covered, for 25 minutes, or until the vegetables are soft.

Puree the mixture in a food processor in batches until it is smooth. Return the puree to the saucepan and bring it to a simmer; reduce heat to moderately low and add the yogurt, stirring to combine well. Cook until the soup is just heated through; do not let it boil. Taste and adjust the seasonings, adding more salt and white pepper, if necessary. Ladle the soup into heated soup bowls and sprinkle each serving with some of the parsley. Or, if you prefer, chill the soup after it has cooled to room temperature and serve it cold.

Pureed Celeriac, Potato, and Parsnip Soup

Serves 4 generously

If you like nice thick homey soups on a cold winter's night, try this one. It has a heartwarming herbal flavor, and is filling enough to stand on its own as a complete meal with an accompaniment of peasant bread and butter and a salad. If you like to garnish your soups, instead of the usual chopped parsley or herbs, try thin slices of broiled kielbasa or crumbled sautéed sausage meat, julienned ham, even a sprinkling of minced raw carrot—depending upon whether you want to garnish for color or heartiness.

2 tablespoons unsalted butter or margarine

2 medium onions, thinly sliced, or 1 large leek, including about 2 inches of the green part, cleaned well and sliced ¼-inch thick

2 large celeriac (a generous 2 pounds), peeled and cut into 1-inch dice

1 pound all-purpose potatoes, peeled and cut into 1-inch dice

2 parsnips (about ¾ pound), peeled and cut into 1-inch pieces

1½ teaspoons salt, or to taste

½ teaspoon dill seed

3 cups water

3 cups milk

½ teaspoon white pepper

In a large sauté pan, flameproof casserole, or kettle, melt the butter over moderately high heat. When the foam subsides, stir in the onions, reduce heat to moderately low, cover, and cook, stirring occasionally, about 10 minutes, or until just golden. Add the celeriac, potatoes, parsnips, 1½ teaspoons salt, the dill seed, water, milk, and pepper. Bring to a boil over high heat, then reduce to a simmer immediately, cover, and cook for about 30 minutes, or until the vegetables are very tender. Press the solids with a potato masher until the soup is partially pureed and partially lumpy. Taste and adjust seasoning, adding more salt and pepper if desired, and serve.

CELERIAC RÉMOULADE

Serves 6 as a side dish; 8 to 10 as an hors d'oeuvre

Often celeriac is cooked or blanched before being combined with a *rémoulade* sauce for this incomparable cold salad. But just as many cooks—as we do—julienne raw celeriac. Why go to the time and trouble of cooking it when it tastes as good, or better, raw? We think it's because celeriac is easier to peel after it's cooked. However, the difference in taste and texture are worth the extra effort—a minimum of extra effort at worst.

2 pounds celeriac (about 4 medium)

1½ cups homemade mayonnaise (page 107) or good-quality bottled mayonnaise

1 tablespoon Dijon mustard

2 tablespoons chopped sour gherkins

2 tablespoons tiny capers or chopped large capers

2 tablespoons minced fresh parsley

2 tablespoons chopped fresh chives

2 tablespoons chopped fresh tarragon

1 tablespoon anchovy paste, or more to taste

1 teaspoon freshly ground black pepper

Peel the celeriac with a sharp knife or swivel-bladed vegetable peeler. Cut the celeriac in half through the root and remove any spongy areas, if necessary. Using the knife, a food processor with the slicing blade, or a *mandoline*, cut into ⅛-inch slices. Stack several slices together at a time and cut into fine julienne.

In a small bowl, stir the remaining ingredients until well combined (if you like the sauce saltier, add more anchovy paste rather than salt). Pour at least 1 cup of the sauce over the julienned celeriac and toss to combine well. Add more sauce, if desired, until all the julienne strips are well coated.

Make the salad at least an hour in advance and serve chilled but not ice cold.

NOTE: Leftover celeriac *rémoulade* and the sauce itself keep well in the refrigerator, the sauce in a tightly sealed container and the salad in a plastic container with a tight-fitting lid.

As a main course for luncheon or supper combine the celeriac *rémoulade* with 1 or 2 pounds of mussels, steamed in white wine and herbs, cooled, and the shells discarded. Toss well and add more sauce, if necessary. Or use an equal quantity of cooked shrimp, or two 6.5-ounce cans of drained tuna.

NAKED MASHED CELERIAC AND POTATOES

Serves 4 to 6

No need to add cream or milk to this mixed mash. It allows the vegetables' full flavors to come through—and that's the very reason we're eating them, isn't it? The butter, added after cooking, is a flavor enhancer, not a disguiser, as is the nutmeg.

2 large celeriac (about 1 pound each), peeled and cut into 1-inch cubes

3 or 4 boiling potatoes (about 1 pound), peeled and cut into 1-inch cubes

6 large garlic cloves, peeled and quartered
   Salt and white pepper to taste

2 gratings of fresh nutmeg, or a scant ¼ teaspoon ground

2 tablespoons unsalted butter

Combine the vegetables, garlic, and salt to taste in a large saucepan with water to cover. Bring to a rolling boil over high heat, then cover, reduce heat to moderate, and boil gently for 20 to 25 minutes, or until quite tender. Drain the vegetables, reserving the liquid. Force the vegetables through a ricer or food mill or mash with a potato masher. Season with more salt, pepper, and the nutmeg. Add enough of the cooking liquid to soften the consistency and return the mixture to a pan over moderately low heat, stirring until heated through. Add the butter and stir to combine, then remove from the heat and serve immediately.

CELERIAC, PARSNIP, AND HORSERADISH PUREE

Serves 6

The success of any meal depends a good deal on the supporting cast, not just the star. These supporting players are so good and so unique that they might just steal the show.

1 pound celeriac (about 2 medium), peeled, cut in half, and shredded

1 pound parsnips (about 2 large), peeled and shredded

4 tablespoons (½ stick) unsalted butter

½ cup homemade chicken stock or canned broth

½ cup heavy cream

2 tablespoons freshly grated or drained bottled horseradish
Salt and white pepper to taste

1 tablespoon minced fresh parsley for garnish (optional)

In a large saucepan, combine the celeriac, parsnips, butter, and stock over moderately high heat. Bring to a boil, reduce heat to a simmer, and cook, uncovered, 10 to 15 minutes, or until the vegetables are tender and all the liquid has evaporated.

Meanwhile, in a small saucepan over moderately low heat, heat the cream and keep it warm.

Transfer the celeriac-parsnip mixture to a food processor and puree it with the heated cream, horseradish, and salt and white pepper to taste. Mound the puree in a heated serving dish and sprinkle with the parsley, if desired.

CELERIAC, TURNIP, AND GRUYÈRE PANCAKE

Serves 4 to 6

Because both celery root and turnips are underused vegetables, we've teamed them up for an elegant and hearty side dish that's easy and quick to prepare—especially if the blanching, grating, and combining are done the day before, and the mixture covered and refrigerated.

1 **pound celeriac, peeled**
   Juice of ½ lemon
1 **pound turnips, peeled**
1 **teaspoon salt, or to taste**
3 **ounces Gruyère, coarsely grated**
   (about 1¼ cups)

½ **teaspoon white pepper**
2 **tablespoons light Tuscan olive oil**
1 **scallion, white and green parts,**
   thinly sliced, for garnish

In a medium saucepan, combine the celeriac with the lemon juice and water to cover and boil for 15 minutes. Drain and refresh under cold running water.

In a medium saucepan, cover the turnips with water. Add the salt and boil for 15 minutes. Drain and refresh under cold running water.

With a hand grater or in a food processor fitted with the shredding disk, grate the cooked celeriac and turnips coarsely. In a medium bowl, toss the vegetables with the Gruyère and salt and pepper.

In an 8-inch skillet, preferably nonstick, bring the olive oil to rippling over moderately high heat. Add the pancake mixture, pressing it down firmly. Reduce heat to moderate and cook for 20 minutes, turning once. Transfer the pancake to a heated serving dish, cut it into 4 or 6 wedges, sprinkle with the sliced scallion, and serve.

CHIVES

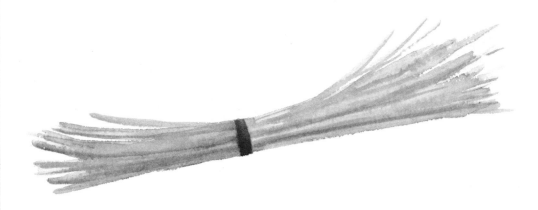

[*ALLIUM SCHOENOPRASUM*]

ciboulette or *civette* (Fr.)

schnittlauch (Ger.)

erba cipollina (It.)

cebolleta (Sp.)

*T*o include chives, which have virtually no bulb, in this compendium of underground vegetables is a bit of a stretch. But because they are a dwarfed onion relative, we thought we'd at least mention them.

Chives' seasoning power is as delicate as their hollow, grasslike stems. Their flavor is slightly peppery, slightly oniony. Yet subtle as they are, they can enliven many dishes: tarts, omelettes, crêpes, salads, soups, dressings, and sauces such as *rémoulade* and *ravigote*.

Native to the cooler climes of northern Europe, Britain, Canada, and the United States, chives are often found growing wild. Perhaps this is why they were not cultivated until the Middle Ages, although they have been used since antiquity.

Chives grow in clumps, and pots of them appear in the market beginning in late winter. Placed on a kitchen windowsill, they grow easily and recover rapidly from snipping of the foliage. If transplanted outside when the soil warms up in late April, the plant can live for years and multiply (if the clumps are divided from time to time). Use the lavender-colored blossoms they produce for a pretty garnish or in salads.

Clip chives with a scissors to within an inch of the bulb for best results. (We used to clip off tiny bits across the whole clump and then wondered why the plants withered and died. That was why.) Once you snip off several stems you can then cut them into ⅛-inch or ¼-inch lengths on a cutting board with a sharp knife or in hand with a pair of scissors.

Cut chives, bundled together and kept in a plastic bag in the refrigerator, will stay fresh for three or four days. Clippings can also be frozen. Flash-frozen chives are available, as are dried chives, in most supermarkets these days. Of course, they can't compare with fresh. Whether fresh, frozen, or dried, a tablespoon of chives has only 3 calories, its mineral content is negligible as far as nutrition is concerned, and the only significantly measurable vitamin is vitamin A, with 192IU.

Just remember, chives' destiny is not only to be mixed with sour cream and dolloped onto a baked potato. As good a use for them as that may be, they have other lives to lead, limited only by *your* imagination.

CHIVE-POTATO BRIOCHES

Makes 16 rolls; serves 8

These are not real brioches but they look like the real thing (partly because they're made in miniature brioche molds that are available at kitchenware shops and by mail order from kitchen catalog houses), and taste terrific. The chives give them the subtlest onion flavor and make them look pretty when they're split open—little flecks of green against the sunny yellow dough.

3½ pounds yellow-fleshed potatoes, such as Yukon Gold or Finnish, peeled and quartered

3 teaspoons salt

½ cup (1 stick) unsalted butter, cut into pieces and at room temperature

4 large egg yolks

½ cup snipped fresh chives

1 teaspoon white pepper, or more to taste

2 teaspoons milk

Generously butter 16 miniature brioche molds measuring 2½ inches across the top, and chill until ready to use.

In a large saucepan or kettle, cover the potatoes with cold water and bring to a boil. Add 2 teaspoons salt. Reduce heat to a simmer and cook the potatoes, covered, for 12 to 15 minutes, or until they are tender. Drain the potatoes and force them through a ricer or a food mill fitted with the fine disk into a bowl. Stir in the butter, 3 egg yolks, the remaining teaspoon of salt, the chives, and pepper and let the mixture cool for at least 30 minutes and up to 2 hours.

Preheat the oven to 425° F.

Transfer ¼ cup of the potato mixture to a lightly floured work surface. Lightly flour your hands and pinch off a marble-sized piece of the mixture: set aside. Lightly flour your hands again and roll the larger portion into a smooth ball and, without altering its shape, drop it into 1 of the chilled molds. Make a shallow indentation in the top of the ball, roll the marble-sized piece into a ball, and fit it into the indentation without pressing. Fill the other 15 brioche molds in the same manner.

In a small bowl lightly beat the remaining egg yolk with the milk.

Brush this egg wash over the brioches carefully so that it does not drip down into the molds (this could make them stick).

Bake the brioches on a baking sheet for 25 to 30 minutes, reversing the baking sheet after 15 minutes so that they brown evenly. When they are golden brown, remove them from the oven and let them cool on a rack in the molds for 20 minutes. Loosen the edges of the molds with a small thin knife, if necessary, invert the molds, and remove the brioches. Serve them warm, wrapped in a napkin.

CHIVE-MARINATED CHILLED SHRIMP

Serves 4

Who likes to stand over a hot stove when the weather is just as hot? Not us; a minute is about all we can take. And that's about as long as it takes to cook the shrimp for this recipe. This is one dish that takes longer to eat than to cook!

1 tablespoon Dijon mustard	Salt and freshly ground black
3 tablespoons freshly squeezed lime juice	pepper to taste
3 tablespoons snipped fresh chives	½ cup light olive oil
1 teaspoon Maggi seasoning	1 pound medium shrimp (28 to 30), shelled

In a bowl, whisk together the mustard, lime juice, chives, Maggi seasoning, and salt and pepper. Add the oil in a thin stream, whisking, until the dressing is combined and emulsified.

In a large saucepan, bring salted water to a boil over high heat and cook the shrimp for 30 seconds to 1 minute, or until they become opaque and are firm to the touch. Drain them well and while still warm add them to the dressing, tossing to coat well. Let the shrimp marinate, covered, in the refrigerator, stirring occasionally, for 2 hours or up to 24 hours.

DAIKON

[*RAPHANUS SATIVUS LONGIPINNATUS*]

Asian radish

Japanese radish

Chinese turnip

lo bok or *lo bak choi* (Ch.)

Korean turnip

white radish

*I*f you've ever ordered sushi or sashimi in a Japanese restaurant, you have eaten daikon, the little nest of long white shreds mounded at the top-center of the tray or sometimes placed in one corner. Daikon is a fundamental of Japanese cooking, and it is believed to help digestion, especially of oily foods, which is why a tempura dipping sauce always contains grated daikon. The Japanese even have a special tool for grating raw daikon, the *daikon-oroshi*, standard equipment in a Japanese kitchen. Our Western graters won't give you the same skinny strands, try as you may.

Daikon, sold at Japanese, Chinese, and Korean markets and at more and more American supermarkets, is a cylindrical radish, 12 to 20 inches long and about 2 inches in diameter (some can grow to 6 inches in diameter, 3 feet long and up to 50 pounds in weight) that the Japanese cook, pickle, and eat raw. They also press a juice from it that is used as a flavoring for bean curd and other dishes. The Japanese also use daikon expressively, cutting and carving it into intricate and decorative shapes for garnishes.

Japan probably uses more daikon than any other country in the world, although it is also a staple of Chinese cooking and is as integral to Korean cooking as to Japanese. The Chinese don't use daikon the same way as the Japanese and Koreans. First of all, their radish is oblong and smaller, no more than 4 inches in length and 2 inches wide. It is most often cut into chunks and simmered with meat and added to stewlike dishes. Cooked this way, daikon becomes tender and absorbs the juices and flavors of other ingredients, while remaining light and fresh-tasting.

Daikon's refreshing crunch and light flavor is welcome in Western dishes, too. Try adding diced daikon to tuna salad instead of the ubiquitous celery. Toss shreds or thin slices into hot or cold soups. Use chunks along with potatoes to surround a roast. Serve sliced daikon with a dipping sauce of powdered English mustard mixed with soy sauce and a little vinegar with cocktails.

The flavor of daikon, unlike most radishes, is not sharp or biting; it's refreshing and slightly sweet. It blends well with Western salads and many cooked dishes. You can peel daikon with a swivel-bladed vegetable peeler or simply wash it well under cold running water. It can be substituted in any of our radish recipes and is often used instead of turnips when a more subtle flavor is preferred.

Varieties

Despite its numerous nicknames, daikon comes in only one variety.

Availability

It's available year-round.

Storage

Daikon stored in the refrigerator will keep for several weeks. A cut piece should be wrapped in plastic wrap. If the cut end looks dry, puckered, and has tan spots, slice off a thin section before using. The remaining radish should be moist and sparkling-looking.

What to Look For

Daikon can vary in size from a hot dog to a long salami. It is sold by the pound either whole or, when the radish is un-usually large, by the piece. Look for creamy white skin that's unbroken and unblemished. The texture of daikon differs from Western radishes in that it is slightly more spongy. The flavor is very much the same but without the burning-mouth feel of its European and American relatives.

Basic Preparation and Cooking Methods

Daikon can be used the same way as white or red radishes. Pare away the skin or scrub well before using. It can also be sliced and used in place of crackers to hold a great variety of com-patible spreads from chopped chicken livers to vegetable pâtés to herb but-ters. Daikon is so versatile it can be served raw (on a crudité tray or com-bined with meats, fish, or other vege-tables in a salad), cooked (lightly sautéed, briefly boiled or steamed, or added to roasts and stews), or as a gar-nish (diced, julienned, or grated).

---

nutrition

See nutritional information for black, white, or red radishes. Daikon is more nutritionally important in the Oriental diet because, unlike Occidentals, they consume it in larger quantities.

PICKLED DAIKON-AND-CARROT BLANKET FOR FRIED FISH FILLETS

Serves 4 to 6

This is a dish to serve cold or at room temperature. Although it is made with daikon, it is not Oriental in origin or in design. It uses techniques and ideas borrowed from several cuisines and, well, just works.

1 cup finely julienned daikon

1 cup finely julienned carrots

3 garlic cloves, thinly sliced

1½ cups distilled white vinegar

¾ cup water

2 tablespoons sugar

1 teaspoon salt, or to taste

2 pounds fresh fillets of snapper, sole, or other firm-fleshed fish

Freshly ground black pepper to taste

Cornstarch for dredging the fish (about 1 cup)

⅔ cup peanut, canola, safflower, or light olive oil

Fresh coriander leaves for garnish

In a heatproof bowl, combine the daikon, carrots, and the garlic.

In a saucepan, combine the vinegar, water, sugar, and 1 teaspoon salt, and bring to a boil over high heat, stirring until the sugar has dissolved. Pour the hot mixture over the vegetables and allow them to come to room temperature before chilling, covered, overnight. (The pickled mixture may be kept, covered, in the refrigerator for up to 2 weeks.)

Rinse the fish fillets and pat dry with paper towels. Sprinkle with salt and pepper and dredge in the cornstarch, shaking off any excess. In a large skillet or sauté pan, heat the oil over moderately high heat until rippling. Add the fillets in one layer, in batches, and fry them for 1 or 2 minutes on each side, or until they are golden.

Transfer the fish with a slotted spoon to a serving platter (do not drain on paper towels), and arrange them decoratively. Allow the fillets to come to room temperature, then cover them with plastic wrap and chill for 1 hour or overnight (if chilling for longer than 1 hour, remove from the refrigerator at least 30 minutes before serving). Drain the pickled mixture and spread it evenly over the fillets. Sprinkle with coriander and serve.

DAIKON, SNOW PEA, AND BELL PEPPER SALAD WITH SESAME-GINGER DRESSING

Serves 6

Late in summer when bell peppers are in good supply we buy them by the dozen at our local farmers' market. We like the red and yellow peppers for salad because, to our tastes, the green is too assertive, too overpowering. Daikon blends well with red and yellow peppers and the snow peas—delicious, but very noisy with everything being so crispy. The sesame and ginger add just the right nuttiness and bite.

1 pound snow peas, trimmed and stringed

1 large red bell pepper, seeded, deveined, and cut into thin julienne strips

1 large yellow bell pepper, seeded, deveined, and cut into thin julienne strips

1¾ cups thinly julienned peeled daikon radish (about ¾ pound)

2 tablespoons freshly squeezed lime juice

2 teaspoons grated peeled fresh gingerroot

2 tablespoons Maggi seasoning Salt and freshly ground black pepper to taste

⅓ cup sesame oil

1 tablespoon toasted sesame seeds for garnish

In a large saucepan, bring salted water to a boil over high heat. Blanch the snow peas for 15 seconds, drain, and plunge them into a bowl of ice and cold water to stop the cooking. Drain again, pat dry with paper towels, and cut the snow peas diagonally into thin slices. In a bowl, toss the snow peas with the bell peppers and daikon.

In a small bowl, whisk together the lime juice, gingerroot, Maggi seasoning, and salt and pepper to taste. Add the oil in a thin stream, whisking until it is combined and emulsified. Pour the dressing over the vegetables and toss the salad well. Sprinkle with the sesame seeds and serve.

GARLIC

[*ALLIUM SATIVUM*]

ajo (Sp.)

ail (Fr.)

knoblauch (Ger.)

vitlok (Sw.)

aglio (It.)

chesnok (Rus.)

ninniku (Jap.)

suan (Ch.)

Did you know that Eleanor Roosevelt took three chocolate-coated garlic pills every morning on the advice of her physician to improve her memory? Or that Russians were advised in the 1960s to chew raw garlic cloves to protect themselves against the flu? Did you also know that researchers claim that the incidence of cancer in France is lowest where the consumption of garlic is highest? Or that Bulgarian garlic eaters do not get cancer at all? (We're just reporting what we have read.) And that a doctor in Victoria, British Columbia, claims to have treated certain malignancies successfully by having his patients eat quantities of garlic? Most people joke about garlic's curative powers by suggesting that it fights germs by warding off the people who carry them. Whether or not you believe all these claims, it has been proven that allicin, extracted from garlic, can act as a bactericidal and bacteriostatic agent with some organisms penicillin is ineffective against.

In some cuisines garlic is pervasive. In others it is merely persuasive. In one (Japan's) it is nonexistent. In our own, until comparatively recently, it was kept as far from the table as possible. As a matter of fact, those immigrants who used garlic with abandon in their cooking were mockingly pigeonholed by more established groups as "garlic eaters."

At last, Americans are finally realizing what they've been missing. More and more of us are becoming born-again garlic lovers. Thanks to food writers, the proliferation of ethnic restaurants from coast to coast, a sophisticated palate acquired by world travel and a more open attitude toward other cultures since World War II, formerly isolationist eaters are embracing the flavors of the Mediterranean, China, South and Central America, Eastern Europe, and India. (There is no substitute for garlic in these cuisines; they'd be radically different without it.) Roasted whole heads of garlic and pickled heads—a Mexican favorite of ours—are now considered haute cuisine.

It is garlic's lingering odor on the breath that distresses so many people. The antidote, books will tell you, is to chew a few leaves of parsley. Don't you believe it. The chlorophyll in the parsley will subdue some of the odor, but not enough to make you socially acceptable. The only solution to garlic breath is to have everyone you associate with, when eating garlic, eat garlic, too.

Throughout the ages, the fragrance of garlic symbolized to many the essence of a good meal, the promise of something delicious to come. But it could also mean more. Since ancient times it has held a peculiar fascination, esteemed by some, scorned by others. It has, at various times, been in favor with the ruling classes and at others deemed acceptable only for the peasantry.

The Greeks believed that anyone who ate garlic was not fit to enter the temple of the goddess Cybeline. Yet Hippocrates recognized its effectiveness in the treatment of a host of illnesses and infections. Dioscorides, a Greek physician who treated the ills of the Roman army in the first century B.C., prescribed it for intestinal woes and as a vermifuge. Physicians in those early years of civilization believed that garlic was a cure-all for numerous diseases. In particular, Galen, a Roman doctor of Arab origin in the second century A.D., swore by it and even used it as an antidote for certain poisons. Pliny the Elder, the Roman naturalist, advocated its use to cure toothaches, ulcers, asthma, and fifty-eight other ailments; even the prophet Mohammed recommended it for the bites of scorpions and snakes.

Early on the Chinese saw garlic as effective in the treatment of respiratory ailments and to reduce high blood pressure. Scientific studies today support this latter claim and also the old wives' tale that garlic can help cleanse arteries clogged with an accumulation of fatty deposits. In the 1970s an Indian doctor, Arun Bordia, along with his associates at the Tagore Medical College, proved that garlic helps break down a substance called fibrin, an essential component of blood clots, which, when they break away from artery walls, can travel to the heart and cause heart attacks. He and his colleagues also demonstrated that garlic helps reduce cholesterol—just like aspirin, beans, and the ubiquitous oat bran.

Recently, Chinese medical researchers claim to have proven garlic to be effective in blocking the formation of nitrosamine, a carcinogen. Garlic juice has also effectively inhibited the growth of the fungi that cause ringworm and athlete's foot. In the mid-nineteenth century, Louis Pasteur confirmed that another substance in garlic, allicin, has antibacterial properties, which came in handy during the First World War when, for lack of other medicinal supplies, garlic was administered to prevent gangrene. During the Black Plague, garlic was an important ingredient in the famous "Vinegar of the Four Thieves," used in Marseilles in 1722 as a preventative measure.

Garlic was used not only to prevent certain illnesses, but was also reputed to enhance sexuality. The Hebrews, wandering in the desert after being freed from slavery in Egypt, craved garlic, a staple of the Egyptian diet, which they believed capable of stimulating sexual desire as well as stimulating the palate (Numbers: 11.5). Ancient Romans thought so, too. Pliny the Elder extolled the virtues of love potions made by mixing garlic and other spices into wine (perhaps this explains the existence of Pliny the Younger). Aristophanes, the Greek playwright, was sure that garlic could restore masculine vigor. Henry IV, the French Henry, is reported to have consumed quantities of garlic before going forth on an amorous adventure. Because it is said to revitalize the whole body by the stimulation of gastric juices and various hormonal secretions, garlic is regarded still as an arousal agent in some Eastern cultures. We can neither confirm nor deny this.

In the ancient world, garlic was believed by some to possess not only sexual powers but magical powers as well. According to Homer, Odysseus used a species of wild garlic to protect himself against the sorcery and wiles of Circe. Hecate, the underworld goddess of magic and charms, received piles of garlic as offerings by the Greeks. Even today, Greek peasant women (Italian, too) ward off the evil eye and the caprices of the supernatural beings, Nereids, by hanging bunches of garlic at the entrances to their homes when a wedding or birth is imminent. In India, garlic is worn around the neck to protect against demons. Central and Eastern Europeans used garlic to ward off vampires, and bulbs of garlic were placed in the tombs and coffins of suspected vampires to keep them from rising from the dead. Garlic was found in King Tut's tomb to comfort him in the afterlife, no doubt.

Garlic, or *Allium sativum* as it is known botanically, is generally regarded as being indigenous to Central Asia, but its place of origin is a subject of controversy. Linnaeus, in his *Species Plantarum*, proposed Sicily as its home, but botanist Alphonse de Candolle claimed, in his 1883 *Origin of Cultivated Plants*, that garlic grew naturally only in the desert of the Kirghiz (presently part of the Soviet Union). *Structure and Composition of Foods* in 1935 placed garlic originally in temperate western Asia, and the U.S. Dpartment of Agriculture names Middle Asia. How then do botanists explain that American Indians used a wild variety long before any Europeans brought garlic to America? Medicine men of various tribes administered garlic to treat bronchitis and asthma, others are said to have prescribed a garlic-based syrup as a cure for headaches and garlic tea to rid the body of worms—just like Dioscorides. (Commercial dog foods use it as a vermifuge and because dogs like the taste!) The European variety, cultivated in the Mediterranean region since prehistory, is indigenous to Central Asia and was mentioned in the writings of the Sumerians as a staple food as early as 3000 B.C.

An infusion of garlic used as a spray is said to keep your garden free of pests, and growing garlic around and among other vegetable plants and flowers can also keep bugs from the vicinity.

But garlic isn't just good for you. It's good. You needn't take our word for it. Look at the facts: It is the most widely used herb flavoring-seasoning in the world. The production of garlic has soared over 1,000 percent in only the past couple of years. It may sound peculiar to those of us who were brought up on it and love it, but garlic has been discovered, even as a vegetable!

In Gilroy, California, the garlic capital of the United States, there is a garlic festival at harvest time late in the summer. If you are anywhere nearby, go. Six to 7 tons (12,000 to 14,000 pounds) of the bulbs are transformed into hundreds of different dishes. If you have the stamina and the appetite, you can taste them all. All that garlic sounds like a lot but not when you realize that they harvest about 200 million pounds a year and the production is growing. That's almost a pound for every man, woman, and child in America. And don't forget that we import a huge quantity from Mexico and Italy and some from France. Incidentally, the French garlic capital is Arleux, north of Paris around the Champagne district, where the harvest is probably as much as, or more than, Gilroy's, and the *foire*, on the first Sunday in September, is attended by at least 75,000 *fanatiques* who love their *ail*.

The word *garlic* derives from the old Anglo-Saxon for spear (*gar*) plus (*leac*) leek because as it grows it sends up a green spearlike stalk about 2 feet tall—similar to, but narrower than, the leek's stalk. Garlic had been brought to England along with onions by the Romans and was well known during Shakespeare's time. In *A Midsummer Night's Dream*, Act IV, Scene II, Bottom says, ". . . And, most dear actors, eat no onions nor garlick, for we are to utter sweet breath . . ." Later Mrs. Beeton wrote in her famous 1861 *Book of Household Management* that ". . . the smell of this plant is generally considered offensive, and it is the most acrimonious in its taste of the whole alliaceous tribe." As for the French, garlic did not find its way into haute cuisine until the early nineteenth century, though it was always an important ingredient in the *cuisine bourgeois* in the south of France. The noon meal on winter Fridays there in both homes and restaurants is known as *aïoli* after the garlic mayonnaise of the region that invariably is featured. The wise *provençals* consider garlic not only good for the heart, the liver, and the circulatory system, but the general well-being of the soul as well.

- - - - - - - - - - -
Varieties
- - - - - - - - - - -

Numerous varieties of garlic are grown in many parts of the world. Although the skin color ranges from white to striated dark purple, and the clove shape varies from long and thin to short and fat, the flavor varies only in intensity. The most subtle in flavor and aroma is the well-named elephant garlic, a bulb of which can weigh in at more than half a pound. Elephant garlic is not great for cooking unless you really want to keep the flavor at bay, but minced, it can be sprinkled raw over salads, grilled meats, vegetables, and, if you're like us, even eaten, salted, out of hand.

The two most ubiquitous varieties of garlic are aptly named California Early White and Late White. Late White is preferred by vendors because of its long shelf life; it can be stored for more than six months. Early White is more perishable, with a storage life of only about four months. One way to tell the difference between the two varieties is that the Late White has cloves with skin that varies from pale pink to red, while the Early White is sheathed in a pearly white skin. Garlic with lavender outer skin is usually imported from Italy or Mexico and is worth searching out; the cloves are plumper, usually more aromatic, and the flavor more pungent. Braided strings of garlic are quite decorative hung in a kitchen, and will keep for a month or more if kept out of the sun and in an airy part of the room. If you use a lot of garlic, by all means buy a braid. Just inspect it carefully for sprouts, soft spots, mold, and discoloration. One last caveat: Pass up those miniature bulbs packed two to the plastic-windowed carton. The cloves are tiny and a pain to peel and they've often been stored too long.

Part of the tremendous growth in garlic's popularity is the universal availability in this country of dehydrated garlic. If you must use it, seek out the minced, chopped, or sliced kinds. Garlic salt (powdered dehydrated garlic mixed with table salt) usually imparts a chemical taste to foods; it is unacceptable as a seasoning and unnecessary. Peeled and sliced fresh garlic packed in oil can be useful when large quantities are needed. But fresh garlic is available all year long so there is really no reason to use anything else.

Availability

Late summer and early fall are harvest times, and offer the best, freshest selection. Garlic stores well for months in warehouses, but if American-grown varieties are in short supply, there are always plump heads imported from Italy, France, Spain, or Mexico. The Mexican purple-skin garlic has small cloves that are tedious to peel but are worth the effort because they are loaded with garlic oil, which prevents them from burning quickly when sautéing or frying. Italian garlic is usually very white, with firm broad cloves. It comes loose or braided. Late in winter you will sometimes find garlic from Chile or Argentina.

Storage

Garlic stores well in a dim, airy place. Sunlight and moisture are its enemies. Most experts tell you not to store garlic in the refrigerator or to wrap it in plastic. We've done both for one or two weeks with no harm done. Wherever it's stored, garlic with high oil content will keep longer than other varieties. If you're not using it up right away, look for the Italian, Mexican, and South American imports, which stay fresh-tasting for weeks. Don't freeze fresh garlic; it becomes mushy and loses its flavor.

What to Look For

Look for firm, hard heads with crisp, papery shells. Discard dented or bruised bulbs, sprouted cloves, or bulbs with white or greenish spots. It is not necessary to buy the biggest heads to get the fattest cloves. Often small bulbs have inordinately large cloves and conversely, large heads can have clusters of tiny cloves. Buy heads with large cloves that look like they're bursting out of their tight, silky skins. These will be easiest to peel and will probably be the freshest.

Basic Preparation and Cooking Methods

The end use determines how to treat garlic for a particular recipe. How you prepare it can rule how much flavor and aroma it adds to a dish. Even raw garlic varies in pungency depending on whether it is sliced, minced, chopped, or crushed because each method releases a different amount of oil or enzyme. Cutting or crushing breaks the cell membranes, releasing certain amino acids that react with a specific enzyme to create the flavor- and aroma-controlling substance allicin. Because the more you crush or cut garlic the stronger its flavor becomes, crushed garlic has the strongest garlic flavor and aroma, minced a little less, chopped still less, and sliced the least. A clove of garlic squeezed through a garlic press is ten times as powerful as a clove minced fine.

Peeling garlic is simple. To peel a few cloves, put the flat of a knife over them level with the work surface and rap your fist on the blade. Don't be shy, but don't crush the cloves either. The skin should crack and slip off easily. Or simply snip off the ends of the clove and strip off the skin with the point of a paring knife. To peel many cloves quickly, drop them all into a saucepan of boiling water for 30 seconds, drain and rinse under cold water, drain and peel the skins easily.

When you cook garlic remember that the longer it is heated the more subtle its flavor becomes. Heating it in liquid also makes the flavor gentler. Heat de-

stroys the allicin, which, as we said, is responsible for garlic's intense flavor and aroma. Try not to allow sautéed garlic to become dark brown or to burn. It will taste bitter and destroy the taste of the dish.

The later in a recipe you add fresh garlic, the heartier the garlic flavor will be. Add minced garlic to steamed or sautéed vegetables a few minutes before they finish cooking and they're more garlicky than if you had added the garlic at the start. Garnishing grilled or roasted meats, fish, or birds with raw garlic, sometimes minced with parsley or fresh basil leaves, delivers a very Mediterranean zing. A little oil or melted butter added to the mixture and tossed with *al dente* steamed vegetables or spooned onto or mixed into mashed potatoes is a winner. In soups, roasts, and stews where it will cook for longer periods, use it with abandon.

nutrition

The labels on all kinds of garlic concoctions sold in health-food stores in the form of tablets, pills, oils, extracts, and capsules contain the statement: "The need for garlic in human nutrition has not been established." Well, aside from thousands of years of alluded to curative substances, garlic is not considered nutritionally very powerful. It does contain extraordinary amounts of vegetable protein and phosphorus. A single medium clove contains only 4 calories.

DOUBLE GARLIC SOUP

Serves 6

Garlic soup is simple and basic. Ours uses a whole head of garlic, an amount we wouldn't have thought of even suggesting in a cookbook only a decade ago. We've seen garlic soup recipes in old cookbooks that tell the cook to spear a half a clove on a toothpick, leave it in the simmering broth for only 10 minutes, then remove and discard it. Happily, tastes have changed and garlic soup can really taste of garlic in this country without apologies.

- 2 tablespoons olive oil
- 1 large head of garlic (about 3 ounces), separated into cloves and peeled
- 6 slices French bread, ¼ inch thick
- 6 cups strong homemade chicken stock or canned broth with 1 teaspoon powdered chicken bouillon added
- ¼ teaspoon dried thyme
- ¼ teaspoon white pepper
- ¼ teaspoon ground cumin
- 2 tablespoons dry (*fino*) sherry
  Salt to taste
- 2 large eggs, at room temperature
- 1 tablespoon minced fresh parsley, for garnish

In a large sauté pan or casserole, bring the oil to rippling over moderately high heat. Add the garlic cloves, reduce heat to moderately low, and cook the garlic slowly, stirring frequently, until it is golden on all sides. Remove with a slotted spoon and reserve.

Raise heat to moderate and fry the bread slices in the remaining oil until golden on both sides. Remove and reserve.

Reduce heat to moderately low and add the stock, thyme, pepper, cumin, and sherry. Crush the garlic cloves with a fork and stir them into the soup. Add salt to taste.

Bring the soup to a simmer and cook for 20 minutes. In a small bowl, beat the eggs lightly, then pour them into the soup and stir quickly with a fork to make strands of cooked egg. Serve with a slice of fried bread sprinkled with parsley floating in each soup bowl.

PROVENÇAL GARLIC
MAYONNAISE CALLED AÏOLI

Makes about 2 cups

This is the very rich, very thick, very garlicky mayonnaise that is combined with the fish stew known in the south of France as *bourride*. Actually *aïoli* is not only whisked together with the stewing liquid, but also accompanies the tureen to the table to be added to each serving by the diner, thereby perfuming and enlivening the stew even more. You don't have to make *bourride*, however, to enjoy *aïoli*. Serve it with any boiled or cold poached fish; whisk it into a fish soup; sauce a bowl of hot green beans with it; top boiled or baked potatoes with it; mix it into chicken, potato, or egg salad; or serve with *crudités*.

⅓ cup bread crumbs, or ½ cup mashed potatoes

2 tablespoons wine vinegar or freshly squeezed lemon juice

6 to 8 garlic cloves put through a garlic press

½ teaspoon salt, or to taste

¼ teaspoon white or cayenne pepper, or more to taste

3 large egg yolks, at room temperature

1½ cups olive oil

In a mortar or a metal bowl, moisten the bread crumbs or mashed potatoes with the wine vinegar. Pound in the garlic with a pestle or heavy flat-bottomed glass tumbler, pounding and grinding the mixture until it is absolutely smooth. Add the salt and egg yolks and pound and stir until the mixture is very thick. Add the oil by drops and continue pounding and stirring until about 2 tablespoons of the oil have been incorporated. Transfer the mixture to the bowl of an electric mixer and beat at high speed for 5 minutes. With the beaters on, add the remaining oil in a thin, steady stream until it is all incorporated. The sauce should hold its shape in a spoon. It if is too thick, add a few more drops of vinegar or lemon juice. Taste and adjust the seasonings, adding more salt and pepper, if needed.

SAVORY GARLIC AND RED ONION APPLESAUCE

Makes 3 cups

This is one of those recipes that sounds strange at first glance but wait—don't get turned off yet. Think about it. Just because you know applesauce as a sweet dish doesn't mean it can't be just as good savory. How many times have you combined foods in your mouth that you'd never think of putting on the same plate? Have you ever washed down bites of a ham sandwich with hot chocolate? But ham with Hershey's syrup—never! Try this sauce with poultry, roasts, or grilled meats. It's not traditional, but it works, especially with lamb instead of mint jelly. Mint jelly?

6 large garlic cloves, peeled

6 McIntosh apples, peeled, cored, and cut into eighths

½ cup homemade chicken stock or canned broth

2 tablespoons balsamic or white wine vinegar

2 tablespoons unsalted butter

1 large red onion, chopped

½ teaspoon freshly ground black pepper, or more to taste

Salt to taste

In a large saucepan, combine the garlic, apples, broth, and vinegar and bring to a boil over high heat. Reduce heat and simmer the mixture, covered, stirring occasionally, for 15 to 18 minutes, or until the apples are just tender.

Meanwhile, melt the butter in a skillet over moderate heat. When the foam subsides, add the onion and pepper. Reduce heat to moderately low and cook, stirring frequently, until the onion is soft. Transfer the onion to a large bowl and add the cooked apple mixture, combining well. Force the mixture, including the garlic cloves, through a food mill fitted with the fine disk, into a bowl. Add salt to taste. Serve at room temperature or slightly chilled.

Pasta with Garlic, Oil, and Capers

Serves 4

As far as we are concerned, this is the simplest and quickest of pasta recipes and for garlic lovers one of the best. A can of drained flat anchovies can be added to the sauce with the garlic and cooked, stirring, until the anchovies dissolve. Perfect with or without. But no cheese, please.

1 pound thin linguini (No. 18)

8 large garlic cloves, or more, coarsely chopped or sliced

½ cup light Tuscan olive oil

½ cup chopped fresh flat-leaf Italian parsley

½ teaspoon dried red pepper flakes, or more to taste

1 tablespoon drained capers

Salt and freshly ground black pepper to taste

In a large steamer pot fitted with its deep perforated insert, bring 4 to 6 quarts of salted water to a rolling boil over high heat. Add the linguini and cook for 7 to 8 minutes, stirring often, or until it is *al dente*. Remove the insert with the linguini and drain, reserving the cooking liquid in the pot and keeping it hot over moderately low heat.

While the linguini is cooking, bring the oil to rippling in a small, heavy skillet or saucepan over moderate heat. Add the garlic and sauté, stirring, until the garlic is just golden. Add the parsley and the red pepper flakes and cook for 30 seconds more. Add the capers and remove from the heat.

Transfer the linguini to a heated serving bowl and pour ¾ cup of the reserved hot cooking liquid over it. Top with the garlic-caper mixture and toss to combine well. Serve on heated serving plates.

SOCCA WITH GARLIC AND CUMIN

Serves 4 as a snack or hors d'oeuvre

What is *socca*? Around the Mediterranean, especially in Nice and in southern Italy, it's a street snack made with chick-pea flour and oil; a crisp pancake made in a pizza pan. The only thing difficult about it is finding the chick-pea flour. But if you have access to a good Italian or Indian market or even some health-food stores, you can lay in a supply. Actually, if you serve *socca* to friends and family once, you'll need a good supply. *Socca* could replace pizza.

1⅓ cups cold water
1¼ cups chick-pea flour
 1 teaspoon salt
 ½ teaspoon freshly ground black
   pepper

¾ teaspoon ground cumin
 1 tablespoon minced garlic
 ¼ cup light olive oil

Preheat the oven to 450° F.

Into a bowl containing 1⅓ cups cold water sift the chick-pea flour a little at a time, whisking constantly. Skim off the froth that rises to the top. Whisk in the salt, pepper, and the cumin and let the batter stand at room temperature for 4 hours.

Pour the oil into a 12-inch pizza pan (preferably nonstick) and tilt the pan until the bottom is evenly coated. Stir the garlic into the batter and pour the mixture into the pan. There should be enough to cover the bottom by ¼ inch. With a wooden spoon or rubber spatula, gently blend the batter with the oil. Bake the mixture in the upper third of the oven for 30 to 35 minutes, or until it is golden brown and crisp. Transfer the *socca* to a heated platter, cut it into wedges or rectangles, and serve warm with paper napkins.

GARLIC-PICKLED SQUID WITH ROOT VEGETABLES

Serves 4 to 6

Squid are like shrimp; they're sociable with dozens of other ingredients and flavorings. They have a tender, chewy texture and a mauve-white color that can look handsome combined with vegetables and greens as we've done here, in a salad that's both cooling and piquant. Serve it as a main dish, or in smaller portions as a first course.

4 cups water

⅔ cup rice vinegar

1 3-inch piece fresh gingerroot, peeled and thinly sliced

1 bunch scallions, white and green parts, trimmed and cut into 2-inch lengths

1 small head garlic, cloves peeled and coarsely chopped

4 teaspoons salt, or to taste

½ teaspoon hot dried red pepper flakes

½ teaspoon freshly ground black pepper

1 pound all-purpose potatoes, peeled and cut into ½-inch dice

1 large carrot, peeled and sliced into ¼-inch rounds

1 medium onion, thinly sliced

1 pound cleaned squid, cut into ½-inch rings

1 medium kohlrabi or turnip, peeled and cut into ½-inch dice

1 4-inch piece daikon, cut in half lengthwise and sliced into ¼-inch semicircles

1 bunch watercress, washed and dried, for garnish

In a large saucepan, combine the water, vinegar, gingerroot, scallions, garlic, salt, and red and black peppers. Bring to a boil over high heat, then reduce heat to moderate and boil gently, uncovered, for 10 minutes. Add the potatoes, reduce heat to a simmer, and cook, uncovered, for 5 minutes.

Add the carrot and onion and cook 5 minutes more, uncovered. Stir in the squid and simmer 2 minutes more, until the squid turns opaque.

Add the kohlrabi and daikon and simmer until just crisp-tender, about 2 to 3 minutes more. Remove the pan from the heat and let cool to room temperature.

With a slotted spoon, transfer all solids to a 2-quart jar or plastic container with a lid. Pour cooking liquid into the jar to fill. Cover tightly and refrigerate for 1 to 2 days.

To serve, arrange watercress around the edge of a serving platter, drain liquid from container, and pour or spoon squid salad into the center. Serve slightly chilled.

NOTE: If you like, you can reserve some of the cooking liquid drained from the jar to moisten room-temperature cooked rice. Mound a portion of moistened rice on each plate and spoon the squid salad over it. Decorate with watercress.

BROWN-AND-WHITE GARLIC CROUTONS

Makes about 1 cup

These two-toned croutons look prettier floating in a soup than the monochrome variety. The contrast of color is no sleight of hand; it's done with white and pumpernickel breads. Of course, you can use just one or the other, but if you have both on hand it takes no extra effort and looks like you've given the smallest detail a lot of extra thought.

2 tablespoons unsalted butter
2 large garlic cloves, minced
½ cup ½-inch cubes pumpernickel bread

½ cup ½-inch cubes homemade white bread
Salt to taste

In a small skillet, melt the butter over moderately high heat. When the foam subsides, reduce heat to moderately low and add the garlic, stirring for 1 or 2 minutes, or until it just begins to color. Add the pumpernickel and white bread cubes and cook them, tossing and stirring, until they are toasted lightly. Sprinkle the croutons with salt to taste, and transfer to paper towels to drain.

CHILLED FRIED SARDINES WITH GARLIC, VINEGAR, RAISINS, AND PIGNOLI

Serves 4 to 6

This is our variation on an old Venetian theme, *Sardelle in Saor*. It's an unusual appetizer or main dish with the kind of melting-pot flavorings that distinguish many Venetian dishes. Venetians traveled everywhere and returned with not only exotic merchandise, but with exotic food ideas that often combined techniques and ingredients borrowed from the Arabs, the Spanish, the Turks, the North Africans, the French, and the Jews—but with an Italian touch. This dish is sweet and sour and spicy.

2 pounds fresh sardines, cleaned and rinsed, with heads removed Salt and freshly ground black pepper All-purpose flour for dredging the fish (about 1 cup)	1 red chile pepper, about 4 inches long, seeded, deveined, and minced
⅔ cup olive oil	1½ tablespoons ground cumin
6 large garlic cloves, thinly sliced	3 tablespoons red wine vinegar
2 tablespoons sweet paprika	3 tablespoons raisins plumped in warm water for 15 minutes
	3 tablespoons pignoli (pine nuts)

Pat the fish dry with paper towels, sprinkle with salt and pepper, and dredge them in the flour, shaking off any excess. In a large skillet or sauté pan, heat the olive oil over moderately high heat until rippling. Add the sardines in batches and fry for 1 to 2 minutes on each side, or until they are golden.

With a slotted spatula, transfer the fish to a serving platter (do not drain on paper towels). Add to the oil remaining in the skillet the sliced garlic, paprika, chile pepper, cumin, and salt and pepper to taste; reduce heat to moderately low and cook, stirring, for 2 minutes. Add the red wine vinegar, raisins, and pignoli. Cook just until heated through, and pour the mixture over the sardines. Allow the mixture to cool and chill it, covered with plastic wrap, in the refrigerator overnight. Remove from refrigerator at least 30 minutes before serving.

NOTE: In lieu of sardines, you can substitute 2 pounds sole or flounder fillets cut into 2 x 4-inch pieces. Another splendid way of preparing this dish is to sauté 4 medium onions, thinly sliced, in the oil remaining in the pan after the fish are removed. The onions should be done past the golden stage to almost brown, adding a little more oil, if necessary. Continue with the recipe adding the garlic, chile pepper, paprika, cumin, and salt and pepper, cooking for 2 minutes, then stirring in the vinegar, raisins, and pignoli. Pour the marinade over the sardines, cool, cover, and chill as above, but remove from refrigerator at least an hour before serving so that everything is only a touch cooler than room temperature. As a warm-weather main dish, we often accompany this with rice or buttered orzo.

CARAMELIZED GARLIC

Makes 1½ cups

We serve these soft, tender cloves with roasts, grilled chicken, or fish — or as a spread for buttered rounds of French bread to accompany a thick vegetable soup, a hearty stew, or a green salad.

1½ cups (about 3 heads) garlic cloves, peeled

3 tablespoons olive oil

1¼ cups balsamic or white wine vinegar

Salt to taste

Combine all the ingredients in a sauté pan or heavy saucepan that accommodates the garlic in one layer. Over moderately high heat, bring the liquid to a boil, reduce heat to a simmer, and cook gently until garlic is soft and the vinegar has become thick and syrupy, about 30 to 40 minutes. Set aside to cool. Serve warm or at room temperature.

GINGER

[*ZINGIBER OFFICINALE*]

ginger root

gingerroot

gingembre (Fr.)

ingwer (Ger.)

zenzero (It.)

jengibre (Sp.)

imbir' (Rus.)

shoga (Jap.)

chiang (Ch.)

Ginger is one of the best known and most widely used of all the spices. The part we use is a fat creeping rhizome known as a "hand" because it does look something like a swollen hand with stumpy little fingers. The plant itself reaches about 3 feet in height, has a slight resemblance to bamboo (a neighbor in ginger's original habitat, Southeast Asia), has thin, saber-shaped leaves, and flowers that are mainly yellow touched with purple at the lip. As the rhizome creeps along under the earth it sprouts new stalks, which is how it propagates itself; ginger is not grown from seeds. Its wild ancestors probably produced seeds, but the variety we use today has been in cultivation for thousands of years and has forgotten how. It is grown from pieces of the harvested rhizomes.

Finding fresh ginger at even the most commercial of supermarkets is no longer the problem it used to be. Air cargo shipments arrive almost daily from Hawaii, the Fiji Islands, Taiwan, the Philippines, Nicaragua, Costa Rica, Brazil, and Ecuador. One comparatively new area of cultivation, Australia, is coming up fast. India and China harvest the bulk of the world's ginger, but it hardly ever reaches our shores because their own demand is so high. We do get some of their dried ginger, however.

Asian food from Japan to India would not be the same without ginger. Every cuisine in that part of the world uses it. It is as ubiquitous as salt, more common than pepper, and works in great synergy with fish, seafood, pork, beef, chicken, and other seasonings as well, especially garlic.

For thousands of years it has been valued for its perceived medicinal qualities—in early Hindu and Chinese medicine to aid digestion; restore the appetite; regulate menstruation; cure the common cold; curb flatulence; alleviate nausea, liver complaints, anemia, rheumatism, piles, and jaundice; combat tetanus and leprosy; and stimulate sexuality. It was thought of as both a preventative and a cure, and the Chinese, whose theories of health concerned a balance between heat and cold, felt ginger was able to preserve that balance or correct an imbalance.

Apparently, from its first introduction into Europe, ginger became an important medicine as well as a food. Hippocrates and Galen endorsed its use as a medicine. And by the time the Arabs introduced dried ginger to the ancient Greeks, the Persians had already refined its use in their cuisine. The Assyrians and Babylonians were next, then the Egyptians. The Phoenicians at the behest of King Solomon got into the trade and plied routes up and down the Red Sea and, perhaps, beyond. It is said that outriggers brought fresh ginger to East Africa and Ethiopia, where it is still grown, from as far away as Java.

But it was the Arabs who really controlled the spice trade from the very beginning and were consummate sales-promotion men besides. They kept its origins secret.

While the Greeks used ginger because they thought it was good for them, the hedonistic Romans consumed it voraciously just because they loved it. The Roman government earned considerable revenue from a luxury tax on a list of spices, ginger included, imported to Alexandria from the Red Sea. Though more plentiful than black pepper, ginger was in such demand that it cost fifteen times as much. It was mostly ginger's hotness for which the Roman citizen paid dearly. It was hotter than pepper, which most people thought came from the same plant. Pliny the Elder put them wise, however, writing, "Many have taken ginger for the root of that [pepper] tree; but it is not so." Confusion or great cost may explain why the first cookbook of the Roman Empire by Apicius lists only a dozen or so recipes calling for ginger, but nearly all the rest calling for pepper.

Ginger was well known in England before the Norman conquest of 1066. By the fourteenth century, it was the most coveted spice after pepper. A pound of ginger shipped to England through Venice cost the same price as a sheep — 1 shilling, 7 pence. In spite of its price, ginger became as common on the dining tables of the time as pepper and salt are now.

It was the exorbitant price middlemen extracted from European nations that finally convinced their merchant-explorers to search for the spice lands. Ginger was at that time delivered from the Far East in the form of living rhizomes, so it was not surprising that it was the first Oriental spice to be planted when the New World was discovered. As early as the sixteenth century, transplanted rhizomes of ginger were thriving in the West Indies. By 1547 Jamaica was already exporting sizable shiploads back to Spain. Other West Indian islands soon followed suit.

Slaves from West Africa who worked the Spanish ginger plantations soon concocted new dishes from a sympathetic combination of African, New World, and Old World foods such as tomatoes, peanuts, and chile peppers along with ginger. The Portuguese at the same time began growing ginger in West Africa and Brazil also using slave labor. Soon some of the slaves' unique food marriages were making their way back to Africa and into South America. Today fresh ginger is part of the cuisines of these and every other inhabited continent.

During the American Revolution ginger, which was consumed with passion in the colonies, was even listed as part of the rations provided to American soldiers. Gingersnaps, gingerbread, and ginger ale are all part of our culinary heritage handed down by the first English settlers.

Varieties

Fresh Ginger Hawaii produces the best fresh ginger we get in the States, and even its lesser grades are better than most other ginger. Hawaiian ginger is at its peak during January and February but is great through late spring. Some of these "hands," if unbroken, can weigh in at over 5 pounds. The flesh is golden in color, has little fiber, and its heat is in the medium range. Baby Hawaiian ginger, appearing in June almost exclusively at Asian markets, has a wonderful creamy texture and practically no heat. It is used mostly for pickling, but is also preserved in syrup and candied. Young or baby ginger is really too mild for flavoring and seasoning but can be added to dishes and cooked like any other root vegetable.

When Hawaiian ginger is out of season, Fijian ginger is the next best thing. Fijian ginger arrives in late summer and stays until early winter. Unlike Hawaiian ginger, Fijian has rough rather than smooth skin. It has a good, strong flavor, a minimum of fiber, and is quite hot. When markets can't get ginger from these two main sources, or won't pay the price, they get supplies from the countries mentioned above.

Powdered Ginger Powdered ginger has a completely different flavor from the fresh rhizome and the two should never ever be substituted for each other, although sometimes recipes will call for both. In Middle Eastern cooking, powdered ginger is always used in preference to fresh. Of course, dried ginger, like other spices, is best when ground as needed. Powders in bottles and cans lose strength and freshness if left on the shelf too long. Spice stores and Indian, Asian, and Middle Eastern markets often carry hands of dried ginger that you can grind into powder at home in a spice grinder or an electric coffee mill.

Candied Ginger In the West, any sweetened ginger product would be listed under the generic name *candied ginger*, but there are several specific products in this category. *Crystallized ginger* is ginger slices or cubes cooked in sugar syrup and then coated with granulated sugar or sugar syrup. The best is made from fiberless young rhizomes. We feel that the crystallized ginger made from fiber-free baby ginger is too mild, without the flavor, the heat, or the resistance to the tooth that slightly more mature ginger offers. Sugar syrup gives the slices a smooth crust, whereas the kind with a granulated-sugar coating is crunchy. *Preserved ginger* is what the Chinese label any ginger cooked in sweet syrup with spices like licorice added along with salt. We don't particularly love it, but it will do when other forms of sweet ginger are not available. *Stem ginger in syrup* is the mild, young rhizome jarred in sugar syrup. Without the syrup and in plastic bags it is called *sweetened stem ginger. Ginger marmalade* can be found at most supermarkets and is a wonderful change from fruit jams and jellies. Try it over dark chocolate ice cream—to our taste there is nothing better for dessert. In fact, chocolate-covered ginger is addictive and many chocolatiers and confectioners offer this inspired combination.

Availability

See above under "Fresh Ginger."

Storage

Because fresh ginger is so easily obtained, storing it is no longer a prob-

lem. If you have some knobs left over, peel them, cut into sections, store in a clean jar with vodka or dry sherry to cover, seal well, and keep for months in the refrigerator. Otherwise, just leave ginger out on your kitchen counter. It will stay fresh (if it was fresh to begin with) for a week. To store longer, wrap loosely in paper towels to absorb any moisture, place in a plastic bag, and keep in your refrigerator's vegetable crisper for two to three weeks. Ginger does not freeze well. It becomes mushy and should only be used when a recipe calls for grated, juiced, or smashed ginger. If you buy powdered ginger, keep it well sealed and in a dark place. It will lose its pungency and some of its flavor if it is kept too long, so buy it in small quantities. Crystallized ginger keeps well, but if you are like us it won't last long. If you want to have some on hand, keep it in a tightly sealed container and try to forget it's there.

What to Look For

Press a hand of ginger for firmness; the harder it is the better. Heft it. If it feels heavy for its size, terrific. Smooth or rough skin is not an indication of freshness, but wrinkled skin is; it means dryness and shows age. Maturity, however, is different from age and not necessarily bad. Mature rhizomes are more fibrous than young ginger, which may have no fibers at all, and will have more flavor and bite. They will also be more difficult to slice. The size of a hand only tells you where it might have been grown. If the hands are big and fat they are probably Hawaiian. If ginger has mold on it, usually over the broken portion, don't buy it. If it is all you can get and it is hard and weighty, take it and scrape or cut off the moldy portion before using.

Basic Preparation and Cooking Methods

Ginger is generally peeled—but only for aesthetic reasons—if the skin is scaly or unsightly. A sharp paring knife will do the trick, as will a swivel-bladed peeler. If the ginger is young or has a smooth skin, washing is all that is necessary. To slice ginger, use a sharp knife and cut across the fibers as thinly as possible. Stack the thin slices for julienne strips or mincing and cut them with a sharp knife. We don't recommend using a food processor except for grating. To make ginger juice, chop or grate ginger and press small quantities through a clean garlic press, or wrap the tiny pieces in cheesecloth and twist and squeeze. The Japanese also use a special ginger grater, available in Japanese cookware stores, that has a reservoir for catching the ginger juice. You can pound fresh ginger with other herbs and spices in a mortar and pestle—adding a little liquid or oil to make a paste. (This can also be done in a blender.)

nutrition

Raw fresh ginger has only 69 calories in 100g. This amount of the rhizome will also provide 1.74g protein, 15.9g carbohydrates, 1.03g fiber, 18mg calcium, .50mg iron, 43mg magnesium, 27mg phosphorus, 415mg potassium, 13mg sodium, 5mg vitamin C, .023mg thiamine, .029mg riboflavin, .7mg niacin, .203mg pantothenic acid, .16mg vitamin B_6, all the amino acids and no cholesterol.

GINGER AND VODKA SHRIMP OVER SNOW PEAS

Serves 4

Ginger and seafood go well together. The Chinese combine the two in dozens of dishes. This recipe borrows methods and ingredients from various cuisines, shuffles them, and deals out a whole new game.

½ cup thin julienne strips of peeled fresh gingerroot (about 1½-inch piece)

¾ cup water

2 tablespoons unsalted butter

2 tablespoons minced shallots

1½ pounds medium shrimp, peeled

¼ teaspoon dried rosemary, crumbled

¼ teaspoon dried thyme, crumbled

¼ teaspoon dried marjoram, crumbled

¼ teaspoon dried basil, crumbled

2 tablespoons vodka

1 tablespoon orange-flavored liqueur, such as Grand Marnier

½ cup homemade fish stock or bottled clam juice

½ cup heavy cream

1 tablespoon vegetable oil

¾ pound snow peas, trimmed, stringed, and cut in half crosswise

Salt and freshly ground black pepper to taste

In a small saucepan over high heat, combine the ginger with the water and bring to a boil. Reduce heat to a simmer and cook the mixture, uncovered, for 10 minutes. Drain the ginger, reserving it and 3 tablespoons of the cooking liquid separately.

Melt the butter in a heavy sauté pan over moderately low heat. When the foam subsides, cook the shallots, stirring occasionally, about 4 minutes, or until golden. Raise the heat to moderately high and add the shrimp, rosemary, thyme, marjoram, and basil. Sauté the mixture, stirring, for 2 minutes, or until the shrimp are just opaque. With a slotted spoon, transfer the shrimp to a bowl and reserve.

Add the vodka and orange liqueur to the sauté pan and deglaze, scraping up any brown bits. Add the reserved ginger cooking liquid and the stock and boil the liquid until there is just enough left to coat the bottom of the pan. Add the cream and boil the mixture until it is reduced by half.

Meanwhile, in a small skillet heat the oil until rippling; reduce heat to moderately low and cook the snow peas with salt and pepper to taste, stirring, for 1 minute.

Add the reserved shrimp, any juices accumulated in the bowl, and the reserved gingerroot to the reduced cream mixture. Reduce heat to moderately low and cook the mixture, stirring, until it is just heated through. Arrange the snow peas on 4 plates, and top each with the shrimp and sauce. Serve immediately.

GINGERED RAW SCALLOPS WITH SHREDDED ROOT VEGETABLES

Serves 4

Quick and easy—there's no cooking—this dish is perfect for lunch on a warm summer day. It's sort of an oriental variation of Mexican seviche. Try it with tuna or with mako shark, swordfish, or other firm fleshed, mild fish. But use only the very freshest fish.

1 tablespoon distilled white vinegar	¾ pound bay scallops
1 tablespoon sugar	1 cup grated carrot
½ teaspoon salt, or to taste	1 cup grated daikon radish
3 tablespoons minced, peeled fresh gingerroot	1 cup finely chopped red onion
	¼ cup peanut or oriental sesame oil
¼ cup fresh lime juice	½ cup dry roasted peanuts or ¼ cup toasted sesame seeds

In a mixing bowl stir the vinegar and sugar together until the sugar dissolves. Add the salt, gingerroot, lime juice, scallops, carrot, daikon, onion, and oil. Toss to combine well and marinate for 1 hour in the refrigerator. Half an hour before serving, transfer to a serving platter, sprinkle with the peanuts and let stand at room temperature.

GINGER ANGEL FOOD CAKE WITH BITTERSWEET CHOCOLATE-GINGER ICING

Makes one 10-inch cake

If you have cholesterol problems, and let's face it, most of us could do with a little lowering of the numbers, old-fashioned angel food cake is the answer to what to have for dessert. It contains no egg yolks, no butter — nothing to elevate the cholesterol. This version does contain ginger, which is said to lower cholesterol. Serve it without frosting if you are watching your fat intake — with the frosting if you can afford to cheat a little.

4 ounces fresh gingerroot (about a 4-inch piece), peeled and coarsely chopped
1½ cups sugar
1 cup cake flour

10 large egg whites
1½ teaspoons cream of tartar
½ teaspoon salt
Bittersweet Chocolate–Ginger Icing (recipe follows)

Preheat the oven to 350° F.

In a food processor, combine the gingerroot and ¼ cup of the sugar and process, pulsing, until blended into a thick paste. Set aside. In a medium bowl, sift the cake flour and ¾ cup sugar together 3 times. In the large bowl of an electric mixer, beat the egg whites on high speed until foamy, about 1 minute; add the cream of tartar and salt, and beat in the remaining ½ cup sugar, a little at a time, beating constantly, until soft peaks form and hold their shape, about 5 to 7 minutes longer. Sift the flour over the whites and, at low speed, gently blend it in, about 5 seconds. Still on low speed, add the reserved ginger paste and blend in; do not overmix. Remove the bowl from the mixer and, with a rubber spatula, fold a few times to ensure incorporation. Transfer batter to an ungreased 10-inch tube pan, running a spatula through the center of the batter to eliminate air pockets. Bake for 35 to 45 minutes, or until a toothpick inserted in the center comes out clean. Invert the pan on a rack and let cool completely before running a knife around the sides of the cake and freeing it from the pan. Frost the cake with Bittersweet Chocolate–Ginger Icing.

NOTE: Of course, this cake can be served unfrosted. You might like it simply dusted with confectioners' sugar, or each serving spooned with fresh or stewed fruits in syrup, or sprinkled liberally with Stone's Ginger Wine (available in most liquor stores).

BITTERSWEET CHOCOLATE–GINGER ICING

Makes 2¼ cups

- - - - - - - - - - - - - - - -

1 cup semisweet chocolate bits
1 tablespoon unsalted butter
⅓ cup strong coffee

1 cup confectioners' sugar
2 tablespoons finely minced crystallized ginger

Melt the chocolate bits, butter, and coffee together in a small saucepan over the lowest possible heat. Cool to lukewarm, and stir in the sugar and crystallized ginger. Beat until thick enough to spread. Using a metal spatula, smooth the icing over the top and sides of the cake. This makes enough frosting to cover the cake completely and generously.

BUTTERY GINGER-PEAR POUND CAKE

About 10 to 12 servings

This is a loaf cake with a zingy flavor. It needs no icing, but does have a ginger-wine glaze that moistens and heightens the piquant taste. It goes wonderfully with tea—or with a scoop of vanilla ice cream.

8 tablespoons (1 stick) unsalted butter, at room temperature

1 large firm Bosc pear, unpeeled, cored, and cut into ½-inch dice

3 tablespoons minced crystallized ginger

1⅓ cups all-purpose flour

1 teaspoon baking powder

1¼ cups sugar

1 large egg

1 teaspoon vanilla extract

½ cup milk

½ cup Stone's Ginger Wine (available at most liquor stores)

Preheat the oven to 350° F.

Butter a 9 x 5-inch loaf pan, line the bottom with parchment or wax paper, and dust the sides with flour. Set aside.

In a small skillet, melt 2 tablespoons of the butter over moderate heat. Add the diced pear and cook, stirring occasionally, for 4 minutes. Stir in the crystallized ginger and cook 1 or 2 minutes more, or until the pear is just tender. Set aside to cool.

Sift together the flour and baking powder three times. In the bowl of an electric mixer, beat together the remaining 6 tablespoons of butter with 1 cup of the sugar at high speed until light and fluffy, about 3 minutes. Reduce speed to medium, add the egg and vanilla, and beat until smooth, about 1 minute. Add the milk and the flour mixture alternately in four batches, continuing to beat at medium speed after each addition. Continue to beat until the batter is smooth and light in color, about 1 minute more. Remove the bowl from the mixer and add the pear-ginger mixture by hand, using a wooden spoon or spatula to blend evenly. Turn the batter into the prepared loaf pan and smooth the surface with a rubber spatula.

Bake in the middle of the oven for 1 hour, or until the top is golden brown and a toothpick inserted in the center comes out clean. Set the pan on a wire rack to cool for 10 minutes.

While the cake is cooling, cook the ginger wine with the remaining ¼ cup sugar in a small stainless-steel or enameled saucepan over moderate heat, stirring occasionally, until thickened and syrupy and reduced to ¼ cup, about 3 to 5 minutes.

Prick the cake all over with a toothpick and pour the hot wine glaze over the top. Let stand in the pan until the wine has soaked into the cake. Turn the cake out of the pan and let cool completely on a rack before serving.

NOTE: Try this with other fruits like apples, apricots, or Italian plums. Use with peaches and call it Ginger-Peachy Pound Cake.

GINGER BUNDT CAKE

Makes a 9- to 10-inch Bundt cake

Y̶ou've probably guessed by now that ginger is one of our most favored baking ingredients. It's so versatile — and such a surprising flavor to most people. This cake has even more surprises. It looks innocent enough, but packs a wallop and has a crunchy crust that is a welcome counterpoint to the moist cake it surrounds.

2 sticks (1 cup) unsalted butter, at room temperature	½ teaspoon baking soda
2 cups sugar	½ teaspoon salt
4 large eggs, at room temperature	½ cup buttermilk
2½ cups all-purpose flour	2 tablespoons grated peeled fresh gingerroot
1 teaspoon baking powder	1 cup chopped crystallized ginger

Preheat the oven to 350° F.

Butter a 3-quart Bundt pan or other decorative tube pan with the same capacity, dust it with flour, and set aside.

In the large bowl of an electric mixer, cream the butter at medium speed. Add the sugar, a little at a time, and continue beating until the mixture is light and fluffy. Add the eggs, 1 at a time, beating to combine well after each addition.

Sift together the flour, baking powder, baking soda, and salt. Add the flour mixture to the butter mixture alternately with the buttermilk in three batches, beginning and ending with the flour mixture. Beat the batter after each addition to combine. Reduce speed to low and fold in the grated gingerroot and candied ginger, combining well.

Spoon the batter into the prepared pan and bake in the center of the oven for 1 hour and 20 minutes, or until a cake tester inserted in the center comes out clean. Let the cake cool on a rack for 10 minutes; invert onto the rack, remove the pan, and cool completely before serving.

NOTE: This cake can be made up to a week in advance. Wrap it tightly and keep in a cool, dry place or in a cake tin with a tight-fitting lid. It can be kept for up to 2 months securely wrapped and frozen.

GIGANTIC GINGER–CHOCOLATE CHUNK COOKIES

Makes about thirty 5-inch cookies

"Betcha can't eat just one" was an advertising slogan that sold lots of potato chips years ago. It wouldn't work for these enormous cookies. As incredible-tasting as they are, they're just too filling to eat more than one—at a time. Luckily, they keep well in a cookie tin or cookie jar with a tight-fitting lid, so you can go back for another—and another—and another—but *not* at one sitting.

1½ cups (3 sticks) unsalted butter, at room temperature	3½ cups all-purpose flour
1¼ cups firmly packed light brown sugar	1½ teaspoons baking soda
	1½ teaspoons salt
1¼ cups granulated sugar	12 ounces good-quality semisweet or bittersweet chocolate, coarsely chopped (about 2 cups)
2 teaspoons vanilla extract	
3 large eggs	2 cups chopped crystallized ginger

Preheat the oven to 350° F.

In the large bowl of an electric mixer, cream the butter on medium speed. With the mixer on, add the brown sugar and granulated sugar and beat the mixture until light and fluffy, about 3 minutes. Add the vanilla and continue beating until it is combined. Still beating, add the eggs, 1 at a time, beating well after each addition.

In another bowl sift together the flour, baking soda, and salt. Add the dry ingredients to the butter mixture and beat on medium speed until well combined. On low speed, add the chocolate and crystallized ginger.

Drop level ¼ cupsful of the batter 3 inches apart on lightly greased cookie sheets. With wet hands, flatten the cookies into ½-inch-thick rounds. Bake in the middle of the oven for 12 to 15 minutes, or until golden. Transfer the cookies to racks and let cool.

FROZEN GINGER AND BITTERSWEET CHOCOLATE TERRINE WITH GINGERED CUSTARD SAUCE

Serves 20 to 24

The liaison between ginger and bittersweet chocolate, to our tastes, is one of the best in all food-dom. But heed this *caution*: Do not even think of serving this dessert to any one with cholesterol problems unless you wish them ill. We remember an Alfred Hitchcock mystery on TV in which the murderess bludgeoned her victim to death with a frozen leg of lamb, then roasted it and served it to the detectives investigating the case, who ate the murder weapon. This terrine could be the basis of another plot where the murder weapon is consumed by the victim. But what a way to go!

15 ounces very best quality bittersweet chocolate, chopped

1½ sticks (¾ cup) unsalted butter, cut into pieces

10 large egg yolks

¼ cup plus 1 tablespoon sugar

¾ cup heavy cream, well chilled

1 cup chopped crystallized ginger

2 large egg whites, at room temperature

2 ounces very best quality bittersweet chocolate, chopped

glaze

4 ounces very best quality bittersweet chocolate, chopped

3 tablespoons unsalted butter

¼ cup plus 1 tablespoon heavy cream

gingered custard sauce

6 large egg yolks

3 tablespoons sugar

2 cups half-and-half, scalded

1 teaspoon fresh ginger juice (page 89)

Line an oiled 2-quart 12 x 4½-inch loaf pan with plastic wrap, allowing the excess wrap to hang over the sides.

In a bowl set over a saucepan of barely simmering water, melt 13 ounces chocolate and ¾ cup butter, stirring until the mixture is smooth; remove the bowl from the pan.

In the large bowl of an electric mixer, beat 10 egg yolks with ¼ cup sugar until the mixture is very thick and pale and forms a ribbon when the beaters are lifted. Beat in the chocolate mixture, beating until it is well combined.

In a chilled large bowl of an electric mixer beat the cream until it holds soft peaks. With the mixer on low fold in the chocolate mixture along with the crystallized ginger.

In another bowl of an electric mixer with cleaned beaters (or another bowl with a wire whisk), beat the egg whites until they hold soft peaks. Add remaining tablespoon of sugar and beat until egg whites are stiff but not dry. Fold the whites into the chocolate mixture carefully, and pour it into the prepared pan. Fold the excess plastic wrap over the terrine and refrigerate for 4 hours.

In a bowl set over a saucepan of barely simmering water, melt 2 ounces chocolate.

Unwrap the terrine and spread the melted chocolate in a thin layer on top of the chilled terrine. Refrigerate until the chocolate base sets, about 30 minutes, then re-cover with the excess plastic wrap and freeze for 2 hours.

In a bowl set over a pan of barely simmering water, melt 4 ounces chocolate with ¼ cup plus 1 tablespoon cream and 3 tablespoons butter, stirring until the mixture is smooth; remove the bowl from the pan.

Place a platter over the unwrapped frozen terrine and invert. Remove the pan and carefully peel off the plastic wrap.

Pour the warm glaze over the terrine, spreading it smoothly on the top and sides with a metal spatula. Chill the terrine for 30 minutes or, covered well, up to 2 days.

In a bowl, whisk together 6 egg yolks and 3 tablespoons sugar. Add the scalded half-and-half in a stream, stirring constantly until well combined.

Cook the custard in a heavy saucepan over moderately low heat, stirring with a wooden spoon, until it thickens. Do not let it boil. Remove the pan from the heat and stir in the ginger juice.

Pour the custard (straining, if you like, through a fine sieve) into a metal bowl set in a larger bowl of ice, to cool, stirring occasionally. Chill, covered, until ready to serve.

To serve, cut the terrine into ½-inch slices with a thin knife dipped in hot water. Spoon the Gingered Custard Sauce onto flat dessert plates, and center each slice in the pool of sauce.

FOUR-GINGER CHEESECAKE

Serves 12 to 14

We don't think there is a dessert more gingery than this one. Oddly enough, even some gingerphobes among our acquaintances seem to go gaga over it. Maybe it's the cool, smooth cheese that gentles the heat. All we know is that it's one of the desserts our friends ask us to make most often. It uses gingersnaps, fresh gingerroot, crystallized ginger, and ginger preserves. If this is too overwhelming to contemplate, substitute chocolate wafers for half or all the gingersnaps—or mix ⅓ cup mini bittersweet chocolate bits into the crushed gingersnap crust.

1 cup crushed gingersnaps	2 tablespoons grated peeled fresh gingerroot
⅓ cup unsalted butter, melted	
2 pounds cream cheese, at room temperature	1 cup finely chopped crystallized ginger
½ cup heavy cream	2 tablespoons ginger preserves
4 large eggs, at room temperature	(available at many supermarkets
1½ cups sugar	and specialty food stores)
1 teaspoon vanilla extract	

Preheat the oven to 300° F.

Butter the inside of a metal cheesecake pan 8 inches across and 3 inches deep, or a round 8 x 3-inch cake pan. (Do not use a springform pan, as it will leak when surrounded by water during baking.) Combine the crushed gingersnaps and melted butter and press the crumb mixture into the bottom of the pan and halfway up the sides.

In the large bowl of an electric mixer, beat the cream cheese, heavy cream, eggs, sugar, vanilla, and the grated gingerroot until thoroughly combined and very smooth. With the mixer on low speed, blend in the chopped crystallized ginger.

Pour the batter into the prepared pan and shake gently or tap the pan on the work surface to level the mixture. Set the pan into another slightly larger pan (or use a large roasting pan) and pour boiling water into the larger pan to a depth of 2 inches. Do not allow the edges of the pans to touch.

Bake in the center of the oven for 1 hour and 40 minutes. Turn off the oven and let the cake rest in the oven 1 hour longer.

Lift the cake pan out of the water and place it on a rack to cool at least 2 hours before unmolding. To unmold, run a sharp knife around the edges of the cake, invert a flat round cake plate over the pan, and carefully turn both upside down. Place a serving plate over the bottom of the cake and invert the cake right side up onto the serving plate.

With a metal spatula, spread the top of the cake with the ginger preserves. Keep the cake refrigerated until 1 hour before serving.

HOMEMADE CRYSTALLIZED GINGER

Makes about 1 pound

Why make your own crystallized ginger when it is so readily available in candy shops? And in boxes at the supermarket? Mainly because it is not the most popular confection in the world and in some stores it stays on the shelf for months and months—often drying out and becoming tough. Then again, some crystallized ginger is made from older roots and can be very fibrous. So try making your own, but make it from the fattest, largest young gingerroot you can find. Fresh young gingerroot is a specialty of Oriental markets in January, February, July, and August.

1½ **pounds of fresh young ginger-** 3½ **cups sugar**
  root

Trim the small knobs from the gingerroot and reserve for another use. Cut the larger segments into 1-inch pieces, peel, and slice lengthwise ⅛ inch thick.

In a large heavy saucepan, cover the gingerroot with 8 cups cold water and bring to a boil over high heat. Reduce heat to moderately low and barely simmer for 1 hour.

In another large heavy saucepan, combine 3 cups sugar with 1½ cups water and cook the mixture over moderately low heat, stirring, until the sugar is dissolved, about 3 minutes.

Drain the gingerroot and add it to the sugar syrup. Bring to a boil, then reduce heat to moderately low, and barely simmer the mixture for 2 hours, or until the gingerroot is translucent.

With a slotted spoon, transfer the gingerroot to a piece of foil, saving the syrup for another use (see Note). Let the gingerroot cool until it can be handled and roll it in the remaining ½ cup sugar, coating it well. The sugar coating will prevent the ginger pieces from sticking together. Keep the crystallized ginger in an airtight container.

NOTE: The ginger syrup is delicious in tea or as the basis of a refreshing sorbet.

HORSE-RADISH

[*COCHLEARIA ARMORACIA*]

rabano picante (Sp.)

raifort (Fr.)

pepparrot (Sw.)

rafano (It.)

khren (Rus.)

seiyo wasabi (Jap.)

*M*any diners think that the little mound of damp, green fire served with many foods in Japanese restaurants is mustard, but it's *wasabi*, made from the dehydrated and ground root of Japanese horseradish reconstituted with a bit of water.

How and when horseradish arrived in Japan and became the popular condiment it is today is anybody's guess. Horseradish is indigenous to temperate Eastern Europe from the region around the Caspian Sea, up through the Soviet Union into Poland and Finland. A hardy perennial plant of the mustard family, it produces thick, elongated, cylindrical roots with white flesh. When these are scraped, bruised, or cut they emit a highly pungent, penetrating odor and a volatile oil invisible to the eyes that, seen or not, will instantly let the eyes know it's there—the sting is worse than onions and will undoubtedly cause tears to flow and sinuses to be unblocked immediately. Unbroken roots have no odor. The sharp smell and sting is caused by the glycoside sinigrin, which, by enzymatic action, frees the acrid, volatile oil containing sulfur (similar in taste and other properties to the oil released by mustard).

The English named this radish "*horse*radish" to distinguish its coarse, strong nature from other edible radishes. It is the ugly duckling of the family, gnarled and fibrous—hard as a rock, sometimes too hard to be cut with an ordinary kitchen knife so that it must be grated or scraped.

Horseradish is a relatively recent addition to the list of condimental herbs. Although there has been vague evidence of its use found in the tombs of the Egyptian pharaohs as far back as the Twelfth Dynasty, and authorities claim the Greeks used it a thousand years before Christ and that it was in England before the Romans arrived, De Candolle (1806–1893), in his *L'Origine des Plantes Cultivées,* says that horseradish is among the species probably cultivated for less than two thousand years.

About the thirteenth century, horseradish was being grown in Western Europe. In the Middle Ages, both the roots and the leaves were eaten in Germany, the leaves as a vegetable much like mustard greens (both greens are wonderful as a salad addition).

By the middle of the sixteenth century it became naturalized in England, where John Gerard listed it in his *Herbal* (1597) as a condiment consumed by the Germans with fish and meat dishes. Early colonists brought it to America, and it was mentioned by McMahon in his 1806 list of edible American garden plants. Once established, its deep roots are difficult to eradicate. It is thought of as a noxious weed in parts of England (they prefer mustard and serve horseradish only with roast beef) and North America where it is frequently found growing wild, having escaped agricultural captivity. Oddly enough it is little known in southern Europe, and in Italy it is used only from Turin to Venice—very, very rarely farther south.

Since medieval times horseradish has been used medicinally especially in Europe. It was used for hundreds of years to prevent scurvy—even though vitamin C (which prevents scurvy) wasn't discovered until the twentieth century. In England, horseradish mixed with honey is still prescribed as an expectorant and to treat coughs and hoarseness.

But by far the most important use of horseradish is as a condiment. The grated root is mixed with a little vinegar and bottled to be used at the table with fish, raw oysters, roast beef, and smoked tongue; mixed with mayonnaise, mustard, or ketchup; used to make sauces whose origins are Scandinavian, British, German, and French; as an ingredient in Bloody Marys and dips for crudités and potato chips.

If horseradish is cooked at high heat or for long periods, as in a soup or stew, it rapidly loses its pungency—heat drives off the volatile oils and consequently its unique flavor. If you wish to season a hot dish with horseradish, it should be added toward the end of the cooking time and at very low heat, like mustard.

Varieties

There are two varieties of horseradish known in the United States: the "common" type, which produces the highest quality roots, and the "Bohemian," which has roots of inferior quality. The kind you usually find at the greengrocers is the "common" horseradish. This is the root to buy and grate yourself. It is far superior to the bottled product.

Availability

Look for fresh horseradish from early spring through late fall. The packaged condiment is available in the dairy case at supermarkets or grocery stores all year round, but try to find a store in a German, Russian, Polish, Scandinavian, or Jewish neighborhood where there is constant turnover; otherwise it may have lost its distinctive sting.

Storage

Uncut and ungrated, the fresh root can languish in your refrigerator for several weeks, or even longer if it comes fresh from the farm and hasn't been sitting in a warehouse or supermarket bin for weeks before you get it home. It will keep its pungency and bite as long as it stays firm and hard.

What to Look For

Look for husky, well-formed roots about 8 to 12 inches long and as hard to the touch as possible. Don't buy any roots that give in to finger pressure. Most horseradish in the store will have been washed so that the skin is a yellowish tan with lateral brown pinstripes here and there along its length. At a farmers' market where the root appears freshly dug, it might have the color of rich, dark earth.

Basic Preparation and Cooking Methods

To grate your own horseradish, brush, wash, and pare the root. Cut it into about 1-inch chunks and drop them into your food processor. Stand back and pulse until it is the consistency you like. Don't puree it; leave some tooth. A hand grater can be used, but be aware that your nose and eyes will sting, you'll shed lots of tears, your eyes will turn bloodshot, and your nose will run. It'll happen even with the food processor. Turn away when you first remove the work bowl cover in order to miss the worst of the pungent oils.

You can also use a blender, but cut smaller chunks and don't leave the machine on for too long or the result will have little or no texture. Add a little sugar and vinegar, if you like, before blending.

---

nutrition

Either as a condiment or as a seasoning, horseradish is used so sparingly that its nutritional value is insignificant. It does have a high concentration of vitamin C, however, and lots of potassium. A teaspoon of the prepared grated condiment has only 2 calories.

HORSERADISH-YOGURT MAYONNAISE WITH CAPERS

Makes about 1½ cups

This tasty, assertive concoction can be served with grilled meats, roasts, smoked fish, or beef tartare. If you make your own mayonnaise, you've started on the right foot. If not, use a high-quality bottled brand.

1 cup homemade or good-quality bottled mayonnaise

½ cup plain yogurt

½ teaspoon Tabasco sauce, or to taste

1 tablespoon minced capers

2 tablespoons drained bottled horseradish, or 1½ tablespoons peeled grated fresh horseradish

Salt to taste

In a small bowl, mix together the mayonnaise, yogurt, Tabasco, capers, horseradish, and salt to taste, stirring until the mixture is well combined. Refrigerate until ready to serve.

QUICK METHOD MAYONNAISE

Makes about 1 cup

Here's a recipe for a quick food processor or blender mayonnaise.

1 large egg, at room temperature

5 teaspoons freshly squeezed lemon juice

1 heaping teaspoon Dijon mustard

¼ teaspoon salt, or to taste

¼ teaspoon white pepper, or to taste

1 cup olive oil, vegetable oil, or a combination of both

In a food processor or blender set on high, process all the ingredients except the oil for a few seconds, then add the oil in a slow stream and turn the motor off. If the mayonnaise is too thick, thin it with a little water.

CREAMED
HORSERADISH-BREAD CRUMB
SAUCE

Makes 1½ cups

Here's another horseradish sauce—warm this time—to serve instead of gravy over sliced turkey breast, poached or grilled chicken or fish, or any bland food that needs a little perking up. Try it on steamed vegetables: Brussels sprouts, zucchini, kohlrabi, peas. It can make the simple into something special.

1 cup homemade chicken stock or canned broth

½ cup heavy cream

⅓ cup grated peeled fresh horse-radish, or ½ cup drained bottled horseradish

¾ cup milk

¼ cup fresh bread crumbs or white bread torn into pieces

½ cup (1 stick) unsalted butter, at room temperature

Salt and freshly ground black pepper to taste

Combine the stock and the cream in a small saucepan and bring them to a boil over moderately high heat. Immediately reduce heat to a simmer and cook the mixture until it is reduced to about ½ cup. Reduce heat to low and keep mixture warm.

In a blender or food processor, combine the horseradish, milk, and bread crumbs until the mixture is very smooth. Whisk this mixture into the reduced cream mixture. Stir in the butter, and whisk the sauce until it is well combined. Season with salt and pepper to taste and serve warm.

HORSERADISH-MUSTARD-ORANGE SAUCE

Makes about 1½ cups

When you make tempura or any batter-fried fish or vegetable, try this sauce instead of the usual soy sauce combination. Or serve it as well as the traditional accompaniment, giving your guests or family a choice. It's just a mixture of things you often have on hand, so it's quick and easy. It also keeps well for several weeks in a tightly closed jar in the refrigerator. If it loses its bite from storing too long, perk it up by adding a teaspoon each of powdered mustard and drained bottled horseradish.

1 cup orange marmalade
3 tablespoons Dijon mustard
½ teaspoon powdered mustard
1 teaspoon Maggi seasoning

3 tablespoons drained bottled horseradish or 2½ tablespoons grated peeled fresh horseradish

In a bowl combine the marmalade, Dijon mustard, powdered mustard, Maggi seasoning, and horseradish until well mixed. When blended completely, transfer the sauce to a decorative bowl or gravy boat and serve as a dipping sauce for batter-fried shrimp, fish, or vegetables.

BATTER-FRIED VEGETABLES WITH WASABI MAYONNAISE DIP

Serves 6 to 8

Ground Japanese horseradish, called *wasabi*, is packaged in little round tins and comes in handy when you want to whip up a quick dip for raw or batter-fried vegetables. Try it with batter-fried cherry tomatoes or cauliflower or use it as the dressing for tuna salad or, thinned with oil or water, as a sauce for carpaccio. *Wasabi* is available at Oriental markets and some supermarkets.

dipping sauce

2 tablespoons *wasabi*

1½ tablespoons water

1½ tablespoons soy sauce

1 cup homemade mayonnaise (page 107) or good-quality bottled mayonnaise

batter-fried vegetables

2 pints cherry tomatoes; or 1 medium head cauliflower, broken into florets; or 3 large turnips (about 1 pound), cut into bite-size pieces

1 cup all-purpose flour

1 cup cornstarch

3 teaspoons baking powder

½ cup mustard oil (available at Indian and Oriental food specialty stores), mayonnaise, or peanut, canola, or safflower oil

1 to 1¼ cups cold water

Peanut oil for deep-frying

In a small bowl, stir together the *wasabi*, water, and soy sauce until a paste is formed. Let the mixture stand for 5 minutes to develop flavor (to reactivate the enzymes). Whisk the mayonnaise into the wasabi mixture. Refrigerate while preparing the vegetables.

Rinse the tomatoes and dry thoroughly with paper towels. Set aside.

Combine the flour, cornstarch, and baking powder in a medium bowl. Gradually whisk in the mustard oil. The batter will be quite thick. Whisk in the water, ¼ cup at a time, until the mixture thins to the consistency of pancake batter.

In a deep fryer or medium saucepan, heat the peanut oil to 375° F. on a deep-fry thermometer. Dip the tomatoes into the batter to coat, and add 1 at a time to the hot oil. Fry in batches of 3 or 4 (do not overcrowd) for 2 or 3 minutes, turning with tongs to puff up and brown on all sides. Drain on paper towels. Serve with the Wasabi Mayonnaise Dip.

NOTE: This batter may be used for almost any vegetable and for shrimp, scallops, and other shellfish. Wasabi Mayonnaise Dip can be kept for weeks in a tightly closed jar in the refrigerator, but it will lose some of its potency. Whisk in a little more *wasabi* paste before serving.

Tuna Sauvage with Horseradish

Makes about 20 hors d'oeuvres

We know beef is out of style, but every once and a while we get a craving for a steak or a thick slice of rare roast beef. To still this craving we often have a seared tuna steak *au poivre* or sushi. We used to serve steak tartare often. Now we serve tuna in the same manner, call it Tuna Sauvage, and our guests enjoy it equally well and are also grateful that we are not tempting them to add to their cholesterol intake. By the way, serving this on daikon radish rounds, rather than on cocktail bread or crackers, saves on calories, too.

¾ pound tuna fillet, trimmed of any membranes

1 teaspoon Dijon mustard

1 teaspoon freshly squeezed lemon juice

2 teaspoons Worcestershire sauce

2 teaspoons peanut, safflower, or canola oil

1 tablespoon grated peeled fresh horseradish or drained bottled horseradish, or more to taste

1 tablespoon chopped drained capers

2 tablespoons minced onion

2 tablespoons minced scallion greens

Salt and freshly ground black pepper to taste

1 daikon radish piece (about 5 or 6 inches long), sliced into ¼-inch rounds (about 20)

Cut the tuna into large chunks and place them in a food processor. Pulse until the fish is finely chopped but still retains some texture.

In a bowl, whisk together the mustard, lemon juice, Worcestershire sauce, oil, and horseradish. When combined well, add the tuna, capers, onion, scallion, and salt and pepper to taste. Combine the mixture well, mound it on a serving plate, and surround it with the sliced daikon arranged decoratively.

Or, as an alternative, mound the Tuna Sauvage by the teaspoon on each of the daikon slices, arrange the hors d'oeuvres on a platter, and serve.

SOUR CREAM–HORSERADISH SALAD DRESSING

Makes 2 cups

Every once in a while we change our salad dressing from a vinaigrette to an inspiration of the moment. This is one of those inspirations. It works well on greens, potatoes, seafood, meat, or cold vegetable salads.

¼ cup grated fresh peeled horse-radish or ⅓ cup drained bottled horseradish

1 cup homemade mayonnaise (page 107) or good-quality bottled mayonnaise

½ cup sour cream or plain yogurt

1 tablespoon freshly squeezed lemon juice

1 tablespoon Dijon mustard

1 tablespoon Maggi seasoning

¼ teaspoon freshly ground black pepper
Salt to taste

2 dashes Tabasco sauce

1½ teaspoons toasted sesame seeds

2 tablespoons water

In a bowl, whisk together the horseradish, mayonnaise, and sour cream until well combined. Whisk in the lemon juice, mustard, Maggi seasoning, pepper, salt to taste, Tabasco, sesame seeds, and water. Pour the dressing into a jar with a tight-fitting lid and chill for at least 24 hours before serving. The dressing keeps, chilled in a tightly closed jar, for about 10 days.

JERUSALEM ARTICHOKES

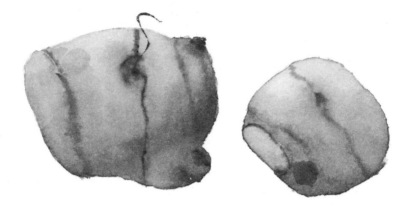

[*HELIANTHUS TUBEROSUS*]

sunchoke (renamed by Western growers)

topinambour (Fr.)

The Jerusalem artichoke is native to the Americas. The plant was popular with the early settlers who found the Indians cultivating it and sent it back to Europe in 1616. When Lewis and Clark journeyed across our continent for two and a half years, between 1804 and 1806, they and their forty-man party (with little money or trading goods) had no choice but to survive on wild plants and roots. The Jerusalem artichoke was one of these.

First called the Canadian potato, Jerusalem artichokes are widely grown and well loved in England, and especially on the continent—unlike in its homeland, where it is practically unknown (now it is making a very quiet and slow comeback) and definitely underused.

Jerusalem artichokes have nothing to do with Jerusalem. Nor are they related to the French globe artichoke. They don't even taste like artichokes, so how they came to be called after that member of the thistle family is anybody's guess. Jerusalem is another matter. The tuber is a member of the sunflower family, a close relation. The Spanish word for sunflower is *gerasol*, the Italian is *girasole*. Both mean "turn to the sun," which the sunflower does. The English corrupted *gerasol* and *girasole* easily into Jerusalem—but artichoke? Samuel de Champlain, the early seventeenth-century explorer whose name graces the large and lovely New York lake, is probably to blame because he was the first to describe the flavor of the tuber as being like that of an artichoke.

Jerusalem artichokes are available almost year-round. They look something like knobby new potatoes crossed with gingerroot. The flavor, however, is mild and sweet, nutty. We were first introduced to them by a good friend, Sam Wiener, an artist from Shreveport, Louisiana, who was using part of our apartment as a studio. His mother sent him jars of a delicious raw pickle she put up that was made from homegrown tubers. We devoured the crunchy delicacy and have been trying to duplicate them ever since. We finally succeed on page 120.

Besides pickling them, you can serve Jerusalem artichokes raw, sliced, or chunked into salads, adding a nice almost spicy (but not hot or biting), clean, crisp taste and texture; steamed with butter or a cream sauce; mashed alone or with potatoes; made into soup with potatoes, onions, celery, and herbs; fried in batter, like tempura; sautéed with garlic; and eaten out of hand with a sprinkling of salt.

Cold weather changes the chemical structure of the sugars in the tubers—they are often left in the ground over the winter to be harvested in the spring—making them sweeter and more digestible. They are recommended for diabetics as a "safe" vegetable, because they have a low glucose content and their fructose allows them to be digested without insulin.

Varieties

Although they come in many shapes and sizes, there are basically only two kinds in the market: the pale beige, plump, roundish western sunchoke; and the longer, knobbier, red midwestern or northeastern type. Inside they are both the same in taste, color, and texture.

Availability

Although they are available all year long, Jerusalem artichokes are freshest in the late fall through winter. The midwestern and northeastern variety is often left in the ground over the winter and harvested in early spring. These are sweeter and come just in time for the salad season.

Storage

Kept in the refrigerator, the tubers should stay fresh for a week or two.

What to Look For

Tubers should be very firm and be free of skin wrinkles (would that we were, too), and bright-looking. Don't worry if there are many convolutions and knobs, unless you are planning to peel them. Western sunchokes come in cello bags and should be pressed to be sure they are firm and fresh.

Basic Preparation and Cooking Methods

All they require is a good scrubbing with a brush to get them grit-free. The skin is edible. (Some cooks peel them, but only for aesthetic reasons.) If you are peeling or even just slicing them, drop them into acidulated water or the cut sides might discolor. Use raw slices and chunks for salads or alone, dressed with oil, vinegar, and a little garlic; boil, steam, sauté, blanch, mash, grate, deep-fry in batter, stir-fry, combine with other vegetables like carrots or potatoes, or add toward the end of cooking time to soups. Cooked Jerusalem artichokes should be served *al dente*, that is with a little crunch and crispness preserved. They take only 10 or 15 minutes to cook to the right tenderness, and it's better to undercook them than to overcook them to mushiness. You can use them as a substitute for water chestnuts in Oriental dishes, but be sure to add them just before serving to retain crispness.

nutrition

Jerusalem artichokes are an easily digested source of vegetable protein, are very low in calories (only 35 per 100g), and have no cholesterol. Their calcium content is high (14mg per 100g), along with good quantities of vitamin A (20IU), vitamin C (4.0mg), thiamine (02.mg), riboflavin (.06mg), and niacin (1.3mg). They contain the minerals iron (3.4mg), magnesium (17mg), and phosphorus (78mg).

JERUSALEM ARTICHOKE AND CHICKEN SALAD IN MUSTARD MAYONNAISE

Serves 4 to 6

Jerusalem artichokes are wonderfully crisp and crunchy raw—so they are especially good as the basis of a cool salad. Like potatoes, however, when peeled and cut they tend to darken quickly and should be held by submerging them in cold acidulated water. If you can choose, pick the smoothest Jerusalem artichokes. They're easier to wash clean if you're leaving the skin on, and easier to peel if they are to be denuded.

½ cup dry vermouth or dry white wine

¼ cup canned chicken broth or water

3 sprigs fresh parsley

1 bay leaf

4 large garlic cloves, peeled and lightly crushed
    Salt and freshly ground black pepper

2 whole chicken breasts (about 2 pounds), split

1 cup homemade mayonnaise (page 107) or good-quality bottled mayonnaise

1 tablespoon Dijon mustard

1 pound Jerusalem artichokes, peeled and cut into julienne strips, reserved in a bowl of cold acidulated water

1 medium onion, finely chopped

¼ cup coarsely grated parsnip

1 tablespoon minced chives for garnish

In a sauté pan over high heat, combine the vermouth, chicken broth, parsley, bay leaf, garlic, and salt and pepper to taste. Add the chicken breasts in one layer, bone sides down, and bring the liquid to a boil. Reduce heat to moderately low, cover, and simmer gently for 10 minutes. Turn the breasts skin sides down, re-cover, and continue cooking for 10 minutes more. Transfer the breasts and garlic to a cutting board or work surface to cool, reserving the poaching liquid. Mash the garlic cloves to a paste; reserve.

Raise the heat under the liquid remaining in the pan to high and boil until it is reduced to about 3 tablespoons. Strain the liquid through a sieve into a large mixing bowl and let the liquid cool.

Meanwhile, remove the chicken meat from the bones and discard both the skin and bones. Cut the chicken into ½-inch dice. Reserve.

When the cooking liquid is lukewarm, whisk in the mayonnaise, mustard, and reserved garlic paste. Combine well, then add the chicken, Jerusalem artichokes, drained and patted dry, the onion, parsnip, ½ teaspoon salt, and ½ teaspoon pepper and toss well. Taste and add more salt and/or pepper, if needed. Transfer the salad to a serving bowl and sprinkle with the chives. Serve chilled or at room temperature. (The salad may be made a day in advance and kept, covered tightly, in the refrigerator.)

SAUTE OF JERUSALEM ARTICHOKES, CUCUMBERS, AND PEPPERS

Serves 6

Here is a quick and pretty accompaniment to grilled meat, fish, or chicken.

1 **pound Jerusalem artichokes, scrubbed well or peeled and cut into ¼-inch rounds**

2 **medium cucumbers, scrubbed, ends trimmed, cut in half lengthwise, seeded, and cut into ¼-inch slices**

1 **tablespoon unsalted butter**

1 **tablespoon olive oil**

1 **red bell pepper, seeded, deveined, and cut into ¼-inch slices**

1 **yellow bell pepper, seeded, deveined, and cut into ¼-inch slices**

1 **teaspoon dried thyme, crumbled**

½ **teaspoon salt, or to taste**

½ **teaspoon freshly ground black pepper**

In a medium saucepan over moderately high heat, bring salted water to a boil. Add the Jerusalem artichoke and cook about 1 minute. Add the cucumbers to the same boiling water and cook until just tender, about 1 minute. Drain both vegetables in a colander and pat dry with paper towels.

Melt the butter with the oil in a large sauté pan or skillet over moderately high heat. When the foam subsides, add the bell peppers and cook, stirring frequently, until heated through but still crisp, about 2 minutes. Add the Jerusalem artichokes and cucumbers and cook, stirring, until just heated through, about 3 minutes. Stir in thyme, salt, and pepper and serve.

MARION WIENER'S LOUISIANA JERUSALEM ARTICHOKE PICKLES

Makes 4 pints

- - - - - - - - - - - - -

About thirty-five years ago one of our favorite artists and sculptors, Sam Wiener, brought over a bottle of his mother's southern-style Jerusalem artichoke pickles. They were unforgettable. Crisp and spicy, with the lively taste of Shreveport (and Mrs. Wiener's hometown, Little Rock) in every bite. Needless to say, the bites didn't last very long in our kitchen—but the memory lingers. Here, to the best of our ability, is a recipe that tries in every way to duplicate Marion Wiener's delectable Louisiana nuggets.

3 pounds Jerusalem artichokes, peeled

½ cup plus 2 tablespoons coarse (kosher) salt

1 medium yellow onion, thinly sliced

4 garlic cloves, slightly bruised

½ teaspoon dried red pepper flakes, or more to taste

1 tablespoon white, black, or mixed mustard seeds, bruised

2 bay leaves, broken in half

1 teaspoon celery seeds, bruised

4 allspice berries, bruised

4 cloves

12 peppercorns, bruised

2 cups cider vinegar	½ cup light-brown sugar, or more
1 cup water	to taste
1 cup distilled white vinegar	

Cut the Jerusalem artichokes into ½-inch pieces or leave whole, if small. Pour 2 quarts water into a glass or ceramic bowl and add ½ cup coarse salt, stirring well to dissolve. Add the Jerusalem artichoke pieces, being sure the chokes are submerged. Cover with plastic wrap and let stand at room temperature for 24 to 36 hours.

Drain and rinse the chokes in a colander. Divide the pieces evenly among 4 pint-size sterilized, dry canning jars, adding one-quarter of the onion rings and 1 garlic clove to each jar.

In a stainless-steel or enameled saucepan (do not use aluminum), combine the remaining 2 tablespoons coarse salt and the rest of the ingredients. Bring to a boil and cook for 5 minutes. Pour the hot pickling liquid into the jars, dividing the spices as best you can, so each jar has a share. The liquid should come to within ¼ inch of the jar rims.

Wipe off the jar rims and screw on the two-piece jar lids that have been sterilized for 5 minutes, or according to the manufacturer's instructions. Place the jars on a rack in a deep soup pot or steamer filled halfway with boiling water. Add more boiling water to cover the jars by at least 2 inches. Bring to a boil, cover, and boil over high heat for 15 minutes.

With tongs, remove the jars from the water and let stand overnight. Press down on the center of the lids to be sure they are depressed. (If they are not, they have not been sealed properly. Store these in the refrigerator and serve them first.) Store the other jars in a cool place. Refrigerate for a few hours to chill before serving.

NOTE: You can vary the pickling spices to your taste, adding chunks of fresh gingerroot, pieces of cinnamon stick, fennel seeds, or whatever strikes your fancy. But don't stray too far. Mrs. Wiener's taste buds were quite refined, as was everything else about her.

JERUSALEM ARTICHOKE AND PORK STEW WITH OLIVES AND GINGER

Serves 4

Stews are made in one pot, bear little watching, are virtually complete meals in themselves, and use few plates at the table and consequently need little clean up after they're eaten. The seasonings give this one a Middle Eastern feeling, although no real Arab or Jewish dish would feature pork.

2 tablespoons peanut, safflower, or corn oil

2 pounds lean boneless pork shoulder, cut into 1-inch pieces

1 large onion, finely chopped

1 tablespoon minced garlic

1 tablespoon minced peeled fresh gingerroot

4 tablespoons minced fresh coriander (cilantro)

½ teaspoon salt, or to taste

½ teaspoon freshly ground black pepper, or more to taste

1 35-ounce can Italian tomatoes, drained and chopped, juice reserved

3 saffron threads, crumbled

2 pounds Jerusalem artichokes, scrubbed well or peeled, cut into 1-inch pieces, and reserved under cold water

½ cup Kalamata or other brine-cured black olives

2 tablespoons minced fresh parsley

2 tablespoons chopped walnuts for garnish (optional)

In a large sauté pan or saucepan, bring the oil to rippling over high heat. Brown the pork pieces in batches, transferring them with a slotted spoon to a plate when they are browned.

Reduce heat to moderately low and, in the oil remaining in the pan, cook the onion, stirring, for 2 or 3 minutes, or until it has softened. Return the pork to the pan, reserving the juices that have accumulated on the plate, and add the garlic, ginger, 2 tablespoons minced coriander, ½ teaspoon salt, and ½ teaspoon pepper. Cook the mixture, stirring, for 3 minutes.

Stir in the reserved juices from the pork, the tomatoes and their reserved juices, and the saffron. Bring the liquid to a boil, stir, then reduce heat to a simmer and cook, covered, stirring occasionally, for 1 hour and 10 minutes, or until the pork is tender when pierced with a fork.

Remove the lid and skim off any fat from the liquid. Add the Jerusalem artichokes, drained and rinsed, and simmer the stew, covered, for 20 minutes more, or until the artichokes are just tender.

With a slotted spoon, transfer the solids to a bowl. Raise heat to moderately high and bring the liquid remaining in the pan to a boil. Continue to boil until the liquid is reduced to about 1⅓ cups. Return the pork and vegetables to the pan, stir in the olives, reduce heat to moderately low, and cook the stew for 2 minutes.

Remove the pan from the heat and stir in the parsley and the remaining minced coriander. Taste and add more salt and pepper, if necessary. Sprinkle with the chopped walnuts, if desired, and serve.

JICAMA

[*PACHYRHIZUS EROSUS*]

yam bean (Eng.)

sha got (Ch.)

*M*exico and the American tropics are home to jicama (pronounced hee-*kah*-ma), the yellow turnip look-alike that has become available recently in more and more American supermarkets, on Southeast Asian vegetable stands, wherever Vietnamese have settled, and, of course, at Hispanic markets.

As Mexican cooking has become more popular, so has this starchy tuberous root vegetable, which is delicious raw (sliced and sprinkled with lime juice and a little chili powder), in salads, diced and combined with other vegetables and chiles for salsa, cooked like white potatoes or sweet potatoes, or served with guacamole. Raw, it has a decidedly crunchy texture reminiscent of the water chestnut (for which it often substitutes) but is not as dense. The flavor is pleasantly bland with just a hint of sweetness.

The Spanish introduced jicama, a large, woody vine of the morning glory family, to Asia through the Philippines. Chinese farmers in the island nation grew it and in turn introduced it to Malaysia. It is grown in China but is rarely served as a vegetable there, where the crop is almost exclusively processed into starch and used like cornstarch.

The vine is also called *bejuco blanco* or "white vine" in Mexico because of the masses of showy white flowers it produces. Consequently, it is also used ornamentally as a garden plant.

Varieties

There is only one jicama, whether it is grown in its native land, in Florida, California, or the islands.

Availability

Throughout the year jicama can be found in supermarkets, at food specialty shops, and at Oriental and Hispanic produce stands.

Storage

Jicama can be kept for long periods in a cool, dark, airy place—a month or more. It is a good idea, however, to refrigerate it after purchase. Do not wrap it in plastic.

What to Look For

Choose large round or oval roots from 4 to 6 inches in diameter and 2 to 3 inches deep, with a thin deep-tan skin. Because the white-fleshed centers can often be pithy or empty, especially if the jicama has been stored for a long time, heft the root to see if its weight is appropriate to its size.

Basic Preparation and Cooking Methods

Peel the thin skin with a swivel-bladed vegetable peeler, and slice into rounds or semicircles to eat raw with lime juice. Cut jicama into sticks to serve with a dip, or dice it for salsa. Jicama- may be boiled, mashed, fried, sautéed, or baked, just as you would prepare white or sweet potatoes—with the timing pretty much the same. Remember, though, that even after it is cooked, jicama retains much of its crunchy, crisp texture.

Some of our favorite for jicama uses are in salads, dressed with a simple vinaigrette; diced or julienned raw as a lovely garnish for clear soups; or coarsely chopped and added to fish soups and chowders as a crunchy replacement for potatoes.

nutrition

Jicama is low in calories, only 41 per 100g. In a 100g serving, you can also expect 1.40g protein, 8.75g carbohydrates, .70g fiber, 175mg potassium, 15mg calcium, 16mg magnesium, 18mg phosphorus, 6mg sodium, 20mg vitamin C, and no cholesterol.

JICAMA, CELERIAC, AND UNPEELED APPLE SLAW WITH YOGURT DRESSING

Serves 4

You might, at first glance, turn up your nose at this combination of flavors. Don't. It's a salad dish worth trying and the flavors blend surprisingly well. Jicama is the bond. It is a very social root, which, raw or cooked, is almost as affable as the potato.

⅓ cup plain lowfat yogurt
¼ cup lowfat sour cream
2 scallions, white and green parts, minced
4 teaspoons freshly squeezed lime or lemon juice
2 teaspoons minced fresh coriander (cilantro)

1 teaspoon grated lime or lemon peel
½ teaspoon salt, or to taste
¼ teaspoon cayenne pepper, or to taste
1 large red apple
1 cup grated peeled celeriac
1 cup grated peeled jicama

In a medium bowl, mix together the yogurt, sour cream, scallions, lime juice, coriander, lime peel, salt, and cayenne. Core the apple but do not peel. Grate the apple directly into the yogurt mixture to prevent it from browning (any apple skin that does not go through the grater should be minced and stirred into the mixture). Add the celeriac and jicama and blend. Let the salad stand at room temperature for 1 hour to meld the flavors. Cover and refrigerate until 1 hour before serving, then allow it to return to just below room temperature.

NOTE: This is a low-calorie slaw due to the use of lowfat yogurt and lowfat sour cream. Using regular yogurt and sour cream does not improve the flavor, so why take in more calories and fat than necessary?

JICAMA HASH BROWNS

Serves 4

This is a quick version of hash brown potatoes. Jicama cooks in less time and has fewer calories—just over half—than potatoes. We don't like to fool our guests, but done in this manner even potato fanatics can hardly tell the difference.

2 tablespoons canola, safflower, or peanut oil

1 tablespoon minced garlic

1 pound jicama, peeled, sliced ¼ inch thick, and slices cut into 2-inch julienne strips

3 tablespoons diced red bell pepper (¼-inch dice)

¼ teaspoon paprika

¼ teaspoon salt, or to taste

¼ teaspoon cayenne pepper, or to taste

In a large skillet or sauté pan over moderately high heat, bring the oil to rippling and add the garlic, jicama, and bell pepper. Stir for a few seconds, and add the paprika, salt, and cayenne. Cook the mixture, stirring constantly, for 5 minutes. Serve immediately.

NOTE: You can add 1 chopped medium onion to the hot oil and cook it until it is just transparent before adding the rest of the ingredients—but this will add another 5 minutes to the cooking time.

KOHLRABI

[*BRASSICA OLERACEA*]

chou rave (Fr.)

col rabano (Sp.)

cavolo rapa (It.)

kohlrabee (Rus.)

kaalrabi (Dan.)

couve rabano (Port.)

agrio lahano (Gr.)

kohlrabi (Ger.)

Kohlrabi barely makes it into the underground category. The part most often eaten, its bulbous growth, is really a swollen stem, half submerged beneath the earth. But we like it so much and it is so underused that we wanted to remind you of it and urge you to try it if you never have.

The flavor of kohlrabi is somewhat like cabbage and somewhat like turnip (without any of the bite or sharpness of either) but different from both—sweeter. Raw, it is delightfully crisp and crunchy and, when sliced, makes a wonderful addition to a tray of raw vegetables; cooked, it is soft and smooth with a tender, nonfibrous texture that lends itself easily to ricing or mashing. The leaves are also edible—most often they are steamed or sautéed or used in salads.

Kohlrabi is most popular in Central Europe, where its cultivation first began. The name means "cabbage turnip" in German, but some early herbals called it "wild head cabbage." It found its way from Europe to China via the Silk Road in the seventh century A.D., during the T'ang Dynasty, but some historians claim that Attila the Hun introduced the vegetable to Europe during one of his forays in the fourth century.

Charlemagne would not feed kohlrabi to his soldiers because his court physicians told him that the "wintry root" would turn them stupid and indifferent. By the sixteenth century, kohlrabi's reputation had turned around and doctors recommended it to cure dropsy, flatulence, and temporary deafness. It was also prescribed to repair gums, teeth, and bone, at which it was probably helpful because it does contain significant amounts of calcium, phosphorus, and iron—all bone builders.

Although kohlrabi has few fans in the United States, it does find its way into the kitchens of southern cooks, who use it, greens and all. It is easily grown in the garden, in almost every part of the country.

Varieties

Along with the more common pale green version, there is also one that is purple in color. Even some of the green varieties are tinged with purple above the ground level.

Availability

The peak season is from late spring to early fall but, because kohlrabi is grown during the winter in Florida, Texas, and California, it is available twelve months of the year.

Storage

You can store kohlrabi for up to two weeks if you first cut off the stems and leaves. Store it in a plastic bag in your refrigerator's vegetable crisper. The leaves, when packed separately, will last for a few days, if the tops were green and fresh when you bought them. When it is past its prime, kohlrabi becomes dull-looking and its skin begins to wrinkle.

What to Look For

Select those that are relatively small—about 2 inches in diameter—rounded rather than flat, pale green (sometimes flushed with purple), with bright green, crisp-looking leaves (if the whole vegetable is sold intact). Large globes tend to be woody. Also avoid buying any that are cracked, bruised, or split. It will have white flesh tinted the palest green when peeled. Kohlrabi is usually sold in bunches of three or four with stems and leaves—without its stems and leaves it is sold by the pound.

Basic Preparation and Cooking Methods

Cut off the stems as close to the skin as possible, then pare with a swivel-bladed peeler. Cut it into cubes, dice, slices, or julienne strips. To serve raw or toss in a salad, we like to cut kohlrabi into slices, but it is also good cut into thin wedges. To serve cooked, boil, steam, or blanch it in salted water to cover. Kohlrabi takes only 15 minutes to become tender; don't overcook it or the texture becomes mushy and too soft. The vegetable can be cubed and added to stews and soups toward the end of the cooking time.

nutrition

Per 100g kohlrabi has only 27 calories, 1.7g protein, 6.2g carbohydrates, 1g fiber, 24mg calcium, .40mg iron, 19mg magnesium, 46mg phosphorus, 350mg potassium, 20mg sodium, 62mg vitamin C, .05mg thiamine, .02mg riboflavin, .40mg niacin, .165mg pantothenic acid, .15mg vitamin B_6, 36IU vitamin A. And zero cholesterol.

RAW KOHLRABI WITH HOT ANCHOVY AND GARLIC SAUCE

Serves 4 to 6

This also works with turnips, daikon, Jerusalem artichokes, and jicama. All these vegetables are wonderful just plain raw—but, surprisingly, they benefit from a scalding of sauce. Of course, they could be blanched first, but that would remove some of their crispness and that's part of kohlrabi's—and the others'—charm. We like to serve this dish with thick slices of dense Italian peasant bread or a crusty French loaf to sop up any remaining sauce. Serve it as a side dish, a first course, or instead of a salad.

8 medium kohlrabi (about 2 to 2½ inches in diameter; about 3 to 4 pounds with leaves), tops trimmed, bulbs well pared
¼ cup light olive oil
1 small fresh jalapeño pepper, seeded, deveined, and minced
1 tablespoon minced garlic

½ teaspoon dried oregano
½ teaspoon dried basil
1 tablespoon red wine vinegar
1 2-ounce can flat anchovies, drained and coarsely chopped
8 stuffed green olives, chopped
1 tablespoon minced fresh parsley

Cut each kohlrabi in half and slice thinly. Set aside in a serving bowl.

In a small saucepan, heat the olive oil over moderate heat until rippling. Add the jalapeño, garlic, oregano, and basil, and stir just until the garlic begins to color. Add the vinegar and anchovies and stir until anchovies dissolve. Add the olives and pour the hot mixture over the kohlrabi slices. Sprinkle with the parsley and toss to combine well. Let stand for 10 minutes or more, to let flavors blend, and serve warm or at room temperature.

NOTE: You can turn this dish into a pasta sauce. Increase the oil to ½ cup, cut the kohlrabi into small dice, boil them for 3 minutes in salted water, then add them to the sauce after the olives are stirred in. Cook for 2 minutes, stirring occasionally, and pour the sauce over linguini that has been cooked *al dente* and drained and tossed with a tablespoon of butter.

KOHLRABI AND CELERY GRATIN

Serves 4 to 6

Kohlrabi, though subtle, is not overwhelmed by the celery in this gratin. The two vegetables seem to meld into a new and delightful taste. That's what we like about most gratins—their flavor increases geometrically, it seems, not arithmetically, so a couple of vegetables seem to be a crowd. See if you don't agree.

6 large celery stalks	1 tablespoon minced garlic
4 medium kohlrabi (about 2 to 2½ inches in diameter; about 1½ to 2 pounds with leaves)	1 cup heavy cream
	⅓ cup homemade chicken stock or canned broth
Salt and white pepper to taste	1 cup freshly grated Parmesan

Preheat the oven to 350° F.

Discard the celery leaves and scrape away the ribs. Cut into ¼-inch-thick, diagonal slices (about 5 cups). Trim the tops of the kohlrabi, pare the bulbs, and slice them thin (about 3 cups).

Butter a 16 x 10 x 2½-inch oval gratin dish, and arrange one-third of the celery in the dish. Layer half of the kohlrabi on top, and sprinkle with salt and white pepper to taste and half the garlic. Make another layer with half the remaining celery and the remaining kohlrabi. Sprinkle the kohlrabi with more salt and white pepper, the remaining garlic, and top with the remaining celery.

In a bowl, stir together the cream and stock, pour this mixture over the vegetables, and sprinkle with the Parmesan.

Bake the gratin in the middle of the oven for 50 minutes to 1 hour, or until the top is golden. Serve at the table from the gratin dish.

KOHLRABI-LEEK SOUP WITH POTATO AND PARSLEY

Serves 4 to 6

This is another of those peasant soups (we're the peasants) that can be tarted up, as the English say, to serve company. All you do is coat a thin slice of lemon with some of the minced parsley from the recipe and float it in the center of each serving. It's impressive and adds a nice, concentrated bit of bright color to a pastel soup. This soup also can be served cold, which is especially welcome because some of the best and tenderest kohlrabi are in the market during the summer.

2 tablespoons unsalted butter

6 large leeks, white and tender green parts, washed well and sliced (about 4 cups)

1 large boiling potato, halved and thinly sliced

8 medium kohlrabi (each about 2 inches in diameter), trimmed, peeled, and quartered

6 cups homemade chicken stock or canned broth

1 teaspoon dried marjoram, crumbled

Salt and freshly ground black pepper to taste

2 cups milk

1 cup minced fresh parsley

Melt the butter in a heavy soup kettle or large sauté pan over low heat. Add the leeks and let them sweat, covered with a round of buttered wax paper and the lid, for 30 minutes. Add the potato, kohlrabi, stock, marjoram, and salt and pepper to taste and bring the liquid to a boil. Reduce heat to a simmer and cook, covered, for 20 minutes, or until the potato almost falls apart. With a potato masher, mash some of the vegetables until the texture of the soup is both smooth and coarse and it thickens (or cool the mixture for 15 minutes and puree half of it in a blender or food processor, returning it to the remaining mixture in the kettle). Stir in the milk and parsley, return the soup to a simmer, and cook for 5 minutes more. Taste and adjust seasoning, if necessary. Serve hot, or bring to room temperature and refrigerate for an hour or more before serving.

LEEKS

[*ALLIUM POORUM*]

poireau (Fr.)

porro (It.)

puerro (Sp.)

breitlauch, porree (Ger.)

ity the poor leek. In this country it is primarily relegated to the soup pot. Even its one claim to fame, the cold potato and leek soup called vichyssoise, is rarely served in this age of cholesterol watching. But the leek seems to have survived despite the demise of our Francophile hot-weather refresher.

Just a decade or so ago it was almost impossible to find bundles of leeks at your local vegetable market. You had to frequent a "gourmet" shop or have them special-ordered. If you could find them, they were undoubtedly imported and horrendously expensive. Luckily, whether you like it or not, *nouvelle* and *nouveau* cuisines have spiked a new interest in leeks, they are now regular visitors to supermarket vegetable bins.

Leeks look like goofy, giant scallions. The best of them are usually 1½ to 2 inches in diameter; larger ones and those with bulbous root ends tend to be woody, pulpy, or dry—or all three. Generally only the white part of the leek is used, the flat green upper leaves being too coarse for most culinary purposes. But don't discard them; they can lend their wonderful flavor to soups and stocks.

Leeks may not grace every kitchen larder in the United States, but they are a staple in French households, where they're so common that they are called "the asparagus of the poor" (both leeks and asparagus are in the lily family, though they have few other similarities). Common or not, the French do extraordinary things to leeks: they braise them like celery, use them in tarts and terrines, sauté them, deep-fry them into crackling curls, make them into superb soups, and, in short, *treat them like a vegetable*, not just a flavoring.

Scots, too, have a signature soup made with leeks called cock-a-leekie. This is a simple recipe consisting of nothing more than a soup chicken (an old fowl, the *cock* in the name), lots of leeks, perhaps a handful of barley, maybe some carrots and potatoes or celery, some water, a bay leaf, salt, and pepper. This is simmered for hours until the chicken falls from the bone and the vegetables are almost completely disintegrated. Some traditionalists add chopped prunes toward the end of the cooking time, but we have never tasted it this way and have resisted the temptation to even test the idea. Perhaps it is our loss.

As for the Welsh, you may or may not know that leeks are their national emblem, and appear on their coat of arms. This came about from the habit of early Welsh warriors to adorn their helmets or hat bands with leeks to distinguish themselves from the enemy in the confusion of battle. Now all good Welshmen wear leeks in their buttonholes like a flower on St. David's Day, March 1, to commemorate the victory of the last Briton, King Cadwallader over the Saxons in A.D. 640. Every Welshman serves leek broth (*cawl cennin*) and a sort of solid version of the Scots' cock-a-leekie soup, a chicken-and-leek pie.

The cultivated leek was no doubt derived from the wild leek, which grows from Persia to the Mediterranean, throughout Europe to the coasts of Cornwall and South Wales. But the leek is such an old vegetable that no one can be quite sure of its true place of origin. There is certain proof that it was grown in Egypt at the time of the Pharaohs, was used by the Greeks as a "love medicine" they called "Philtron," and later by the Romans who, some say, introduced it to Great Britain (as well as the rest of Europe), where it stayed long after the Romans departed. As a matter of fact, there are leek competitions in England today that produce stalks of such prodigious size that they make the *Guiness Book of World Records*. On the continent, cultivation takes the opposite road, one that favors miniaturized versions, stressing delicate taste and tenderness rather than gigantism.

Leeks are tremendously hardy. They will take a lot of rough treatment but grow best in soil rich with phosphates. What is produced is a handsome plant, 2 or 3 feet tall and quite sturdy. Unlike onions, leeks do not grow bulbs. The stalks, thick and white, are the same diameter from leaf down to the root hairs. The broad, flat, ribbonlike leaves are arranged in a fascinating chevron pattern and are usually a brilliant green. As the plant matures, earth is piled around it so that the stalk is blanched and remains pearly white. Unfortunately this is also why leeks have a reputation for being dirty and hard to clean—the piled-up dirt gets down into the layers of leaves and the cook has to get the dirt out. It's not difficult, but tedious.

Leeks are probably the mildest of the onion family, with a delicate taste nowhere near as assertive as scallions—sweeter, subtler, they're the aristocrats, the nobility, the rich aunts and uncles of the family, refined yet sociable, mingling amiably with many other foods.

Some cooks think that you can substitute one member of the onion family for another, but there are distinct flavor differences. Onions can sometimes dominate the flavor of a dish; leeks will not. Their flavor is much more elusive. Young, fresh leeks may even be eaten raw like scallions, *but they don't affect your breath*. How's that for mild!

Varieties

It's not so much that there are different varieties of leeks as that there are different sizes—and the sizes affect flavor and cooking qualities. The slender stalks of spring, not much bigger than scallions, are the mildest and can be eaten raw out of hand or in salads. Varieties of 1 to 1½ inches are our favorites for serving simply braised or cooked tender and dressed with a vinaigrette or cream sauce or just plain butter. The later larger leeks, up to 3 inches in diameter, have a coarser flavor and texture and are best kept for soups and stews.

Availability

Leeks are best in fall, winter, and spring, but better stores will carry them all year long.

Storage

Untrimmed, unwashed leeks can be stored in a perforated plastic bag or wrapped loosely in plastic in your refrigerator's crisper for up to two weeks. After that they're best relegated to the stockpot. Raw leeks do not freeze well, but if you are saving just the green leaves for soups or stews they can be frozen. Just be aware that they will become sort of mushy when thawed.

What to Look For

Usually leeks are sold in bunches of 3 to 6, depending on size, weighing together about 1 pound. It is the white part that we eat, so look first for smooth, unblemished stalks about 6 to 8 inches long, and then for fresh-looking, bright green leaves. The stalks should be small to medium in diameter, tightly rolled, flexible, and fresh-looking. If the stalk isn't flexible it will, in all likelihood, be woody. Avoid those with flaring, bulbous root ends. These tend to be tough-textured. Also pass up greens that are limp and discolored with brown or yellow areas.

Basic Preparation and Cooking Methods

Leeks should be thoroughly washed before cooking to remove any dirt and sand wedged between the layers. First trim away the roots and cut off the green tops to within 1 or 2 inches of the white part. Strip off the outer layer if it is at all unsightly. Split the stalk lengthwise to open up the part where the mud may be lurking (sometimes this can be down to within a half inch of the roots). Wash carefully under running tap water, holding the stalk, root down, and rubbing with your fingers. If the leaves separate too much use toothpicks to hold them together or tie with string before cooking. Mature leeks become tender after 15 to 20 minutes of boiling, steaming, or braising. Of course, cut the time if the stalks are thin and increase it if they are more than 1½ inches across. A pound serves three, four in a pinch.

nutrition

Leeks have a good deal of potassium and calcium and vegetable protein superior to many popular vegetables like celery, string beans, peppers, and cabbage. In 100g of cooked leeks there are: 31 calories, .81g protein, 7.62g carbohydrates, .82g fiber, 30mg calcium, 1.10mg iron, 14mg magnesium, 87mg potassium, 17mg phosphorus, 10mg sodium, 4.7mg vitamin C, .026mg thiamine, .02mg riboflavin, .2mg niacin, 24.3mg folacin, 46IU vitamin A, and all the amino acids.

CRACKLING DEEP-FRIED SHOESTRING LEEKS

Makes enough to garnish 4 to 8 servings

Coppery colored strands of crisply fried leeks make a flavorful and beautiful garnish. Try them sprinkled liberally over a creamy pasta dish like fettuccine Alfredo, as topping for steamed green beans, mounded on a fillet of fish, with calves liver or breast of chicken, or as flavorful decoration on a vegetable terrine, mousse, or omelette. They can also stand on their own as a tasty side dish. Any leftovers can be frozen and quickly reconstituted right from the freezer by crisping them for a few seconds in a skillet just coated with oil and set over moderate heat.

2 **large leeks, trimmed, leaving ½**　　　　**Salt to taste**
inch green part
Vegetable oil for deep-frying,
preferably canola or peanut

Preheat the oven to 200° F.

Make a lengthwise slit through the leeks from top to root end. Cut the halves in half crosswise. With a very sharp, pointed knife slice the leek quarters lengthwise in narrow strips no more than ⅛ inch wide. Separate the sliced leeks, wash them well by rinsing them in a large sieve, and let them soak in a bowl of ice and water for 10 minutes. Drain the leeks and pat dry with paper towels.

In a saucepan, bring 1 inch of oil to 360° F. over moderately high heat. Fry the leeks, a tablespoon at a time, until browned lightly. (Be forewarned that the oil will splatter considerably unless the leeks are very well dried.) Transfer each browned batch with a slotted spoon to paper towels to drain. Make sure the oil returns to 360° F. before adding the next batch. Continue until all the leeks have been browned. Sprinkle the fried leeks with salt and keep them warm in the preheated oven until serving time, or freeze for up to 2 months.

LEEK AND BAKED POTATO VICHYSSOISE WITH RED CAVIAR AND CHIVES

Makes about 8 cups; serves 6 to 8

You can make vichyssoise with potatoes simmered with the leeks in the traditional way or do it our way, which allows more leek flavor and more potato flavor as well. The garnish of red caviar is a conceit that *works*, adding yet another flavor note and an attractive color accent.

4 large baking potatoes (about 2 pounds)

6 cups homemade chicken stock or canned broth

6 large leeks (about 2½ to 3 pounds), white parts only, cut in half lengthwise, washed thoroughly, and coarsely chopped

½ teaspoon white pepper
   Salt to taste

1 cup heavy cream or plain yogurt

¼ cup (4 ounces) red salmon roe caviar

¼ cup snipped fresh chives

Preheat oven to 400° F.

Bake the potatoes on the floor of the oven, turning once, for 1 hour, or until they are soft when pressed. Cut the cooked potatoes in half and scoop out the flesh (reserve the skins for another use; see Note below).

In a large saucepan, bring the broth to a boil over moderately high heat. Add the chopped leeks and white pepper, reduce heat, and simmer the leeks, covered, for 30 minutes, or until they are very tender.

Add the potato flesh to the leeks and puree the mixture, in batches, in a food processor until quite smooth. Transfer the puree to a mixing bowl, add salt, if desired, and chill, covered, for at least 2 hours or up to 24 hours. Whisk in the cream and chill again for 30 minutes, if necessary.

Ladle the soup into bowls, top each serving with 1½ to 2 teaspoons of the red caviar, and sprinkle with the chives. Serve very cold.

HEARTWARMING CREAM OF LEEK AND ROOTS SOUP

Serves 8 to 10

There is nothing better on a cold winter's evening than a hot, robust soup to warm the heart, soul, and extremities. We sauté the vegetables first before adding the liquid, which intensifies the flavors, creating a more satisfying soup. And remember, soups freeze well, so if there is more than can be consumed in a day or two, freeze the remainder and serve it again within about 2 months.

¼ cup (½ stick) unsalted butter or margarine

3 large leeks, white part and some pale green, cut in half lengthwise, washed well, and julienned (about 2 cups)

1 tablespoon minced garlic

1 teaspoon salt, or to taste

1 teaspoon freshly ground black pepper, or more to taste

2 small turnips, peeled and cut into ½-inch dice

1 large celeriac (celery root) (about 2 pounds), peeled, cut into 1-inch pieces, and reserved in a bowl of acidulated water

2 boiling potatoes (about 4 ounces each), peeled, cut into 1-inch pieces, and reserved in a bowl of cold water

2 large carrots, peeled and cut into ½-inch slices

2 small parsnips, peeled and cut into ½-inch dice

8 cups homemade chicken stock or canned broth

½ cup heavy cream

2 scallions, white and green parts, thinly sliced

2 medium beets, cooked, peeled, and cut into julienne strips

In a large soup pot or casserole, melt the butter over moderate heat. When the foam subsides, stir in the leeks and cook for 5 minutes, stirring occasionally, or until just beginning to color. Add the garlic, 1 teaspoon salt, and 1 teaspoon pepper and cook, stirring, for 1 minute. Add the turnips, drained celeriac and potatoes, carrots, and parsnips. Cook the vegetable mixture, stirring frequently, for 5 minutes. Add 7 cups stock, bring to a boil over high heat, then reduce heat and simmer the mixture for 20 to 30 minutes, or until the vegetables are very tender.

In a blender or food processor, puree the mixture in batches. Return the puree to the pot and stir in the cream, more salt and pepper to taste, and enough of the remaining 1 cup stock necessary to thin the soup to the desired consistency. Raise heat to moderate and return the soup to a simmer just long enough to heat through. Ladle the soup into heated bowls and garnish it with some of the scallions and beets. Or transfer the soup to a large tureen, ladle it out at the table, and garnish from small bowls of the scallions and the beets.

NOTE: Slivers of cooked chicken, beef, ham, fish, or shellfish can be added, if you like. But, of course, stir them in after the soup has been pureed and keep them in the pot just long enough to heat through. This is a way to use up leftovers and also offer the soup in a new guise.

SAVORY LEEK AND SAUSAGE SOUFFLÉ ROLL

Serves 4 to 8

*R*oulades are something like elegant giant omelettes. This spongy egg preparation, like a fallen soufflé, is baked, spread with a savory filling, and rolled like a jelly roll while still hot out of the oven and flexible. It's spectacular, and unexpected, when brought to a brunch table. It's economical, too, because it can be made from fresh or leftover ingredients, usually utilizes inexpensive vegetables in the filling, and can serve 4 for brunch, lunch, or a light supper—or 8 as a first course.

soufflé roll

- 4 tablespoons (½ stick) butter
- ½ cup all-purpose flour
- ½ teaspoon salt
- ⅛ teaspoon white pepper
- 2 cups milk, heated
- 5 large eggs, separated, at room temperature
- ½ cup freshly grated Parmesan (optional)

filling

- ½ pound sweet Italian sausage, removed from casing and crumbled
- 2 tablespoons unsalted butter
- 1¼ pounds leeks, trimmed, leaving 2 inches pale green part, cut in half lengthwise, washed well, and chopped
- ½ cup heavy cream
- ½ cup freshly grated Parmesan
- 1 teaspoon caraway seeds
- 2 tablespoons minced fresh parsley
- 1 tablespoon Dijon mustard
  Salt and freshly ground black pepper to taste

glaze (optional)

- 1 tablespoon unsalted butter, softened
- 1 tablespoon freshly grated Parmesan

Preheat the oven to 400° F.

Butter a 15½ x 10½-inch jelly-roll pan, line it with wax paper, butter the wax paper, and lightly sprinkle it with flour; set aside.

In a saucepan, melt 4 tablespoons butter over low heat and, when the foam subsides, blend in the flour and salt and white pepper. Cook the *roux*, stirring, for 2 minutes. Remove from heat and add the hot milk in a stream, whisking. Return to moderate heat and bring the mixture to a boil, stirring, and cook 1 minute. Beat the egg yolks lightly, and add a little of the hot milk mixture to them, whisking. Stir the egg mixture back into the remaining milk mixture in the pan and cook, whisking, 1 minute longer. Do not allow to boil. Fold in the ½ cup Parmesan, if you like, and set the mixture aside to cool to room temperature, stirring occasionally.

In a bowl, beat the egg whites with an electric mixer until they just hold stiff peaks. Stir one-third of the whites into the cooled egg mixture, then fold this mixture into the remaining whites gently but firmly.

Spread the soufflé batter evenly in the prepared jelly-roll pan and bake in the center of the oven for 25 to 30 minutes, or until well puffed and browned.

While the soufflé roll is baking, cook the sausage meat in a skillet over moderate heat, stirring and breaking it up, for about 3 minutes, or until it begins to brown. Transfer the sausage with a slotted spoon to paper towels to drain.

Pour off any fat left in the skillet and, over moderately low heat, melt 2 tablespoons butter in the skillet. When the foam subsides, cook the leeks, stirring, about 3 or 4 minutes, or until they are softened. Stir in the cream, bring to a boil over moderately high heat, then reduce heat to a simmer. Cook, stirring occasionally, until the mixture is thickened and the cream is absorbed. Remove the skillet from the heat and blend in ½ cup Parmesan, the caraway seeds, parsley, mustard, sausage meat, and salt and black pepper to taste.

When the soufflé roll has finished baking, remove the pan from the oven and invert it immediately onto a clean dish towel. Lift off the jelly-roll pan and carefully strip away the wax paper. Trim ¼ inch of crusty edge from the short sides, if you like.

In an even layer, spread the filling over the soufflé roll while it is still warm and flexible, leaving a 1-inch border all around. With the aid of the towel, roll the *roulade* jelly-roll fashion, beginning with a long side, and transfer it, seam side down, to an ovenproof serving dish.

To glaze the *roulade,* turn the oven down to 350° F.

Carefully and gently spread the soufflé roll with the softened butter, and sprinkle it with 1 tablespoon Parmesan. Return soufflé roll to the oven and bake for 10 minutes, or until it is heated through and the Parmesan is melted. Serve hot.

NOTE: The soufflé roll may be made a day ahead, spread with the glaze, and kept well wrapped in the refrigerator. To reheat, remove from the refrigerator at least 1 hour before baking. Preheat the oven to 350° F. and bake for 20 minutes, or until it is heated through and the Parmesan is melted.

SAVORY LEEK PIE

Serves 4 to 8 as a first course, side dish,
luncheon dish, or buffet offering

Most leek recipes, ours included, specify cutting away almost all the green part, the "leaves" of the leeks, and using only the white and some of the pale green. Should you discard the unused parts? Please don't. Use them to give flavor to soups, stocks, and to bed down roasts. They're usually a little fibrous, which is why they are cut away in the first place. But fiber does not diminish their flavor nor their nutritional value. Taste them for tenderness after cooking, and if they are not tender, then discard them.

two-crust pie shell

2 cups all-purpose flour	¼ teaspoon salt
½ cup (1 stick) unsalted butter or margarine	1 large egg yolk
	3 tablespoons ice water

1 tablespoon olive oil

2 tablespoons unsalted butter

3 pounds leeks (about 8 large),
   trimmed, leaving 2 inches of pale
   green part, cut in half lengthwise, washed well, and chopped

¼ cup whole milk or half-and-half

½ teaspoon salt, or to taste

½ teaspoon white pepper

glaze

2 tablespoons whole milk or half-
   and-half

1 large egg yolk

In a food processor or in a work bowl, blend the flour, ½ cup butter or margarine, and ¼ teaspoon salt until the mixture resembles coarse meal. Beat the egg yolk lightly with the ice water, and combine it with the flour mixture in a bowl until it can be formed into a ball. Divide the dough into 2 balls, 1 slightly larger than the other, dust the balls with flour, flatten them slightly, and wrap them in wax paper. Chill for at least 1 hour or up to 24 hours.

In a large sauté pan or skillet, heat the oil over moderate heat. Add the butter and, when the foam subsides, cook the leeks, stirring, for 10 minutes, or until they are softened. Add the milk, a little at a time, cooking and stirring the mixture for 2 minutes after each addition. Stir in ½ teaspoon salt and the white pepper and let the mixture cool for 10 minutes.

Preheat the oven to 425° F.

On a floured surface, roll the larger ball of dough into an 11-inch round and fit it into a 9-inch pie pan. Spoon the cooled leek mixture into the shell and moisten all around the edges of the dough with water. Roll the smaller piece of dough into a 9½-inch round and lay it over the filling. Crimp the edges together with a fork or your fingers. With a sharp knife, cut away any excess dough and make a small cross-shaped vent in the center of the pie.

Lightly beat 2 tablespoons milk with the egg yolk, and brush this glaze over the pie. Bake in the lower third of the oven for 40 to 45 minutes, or until the crust is golden brown. Let the pie cool on a rack for 15 minutes, cut into wedges, and serve warm or at room temperature.

CREAMY LEEKS WITH GRATED NUTMEG

Serves 4

This is a simple recipe but, because of the butter and the heavy cream, not to be chanced by those with high cholesterol unless you make some radical substitutions: margarine for the butter, nonfat yogurt for the heavy cream. The flavor will be affected, but only noticed by those who are used to the original recipe. It's just not as rich and not as subtle.

4 large leeks, white and 2 inches pale green part

2 tablespoons unsalted butter

½ cup heavy cream

⅓ cup homemade chicken stock or canned broth

Salt to taste

¼ teaspoon white pepper, or more to taste

Freshly grated nutmeg to taste

Cut the leeks crosswise into ½-inch slices, separate into rings, rinse well to clean, and drain. Melt the butter in a large sauté pan or heavy skillet over moderate heat, and when the foam subsides, add the leeks and stir to coat them thoroughly with the butter. Add the cream and broth, raise heat to moderately high, and bring the liquid to a boil. Reduce heat to a simmer and cook, stirring occasionally, for 10 to 15 minutes, or until thickened. Season the mixture with salt, white pepper, and several gratings of nutmeg. Stir well and serve.

LEEK RISOTTO

Serves 4 to 6

Risotto is not really worth making unless you use the right kind of rice. Italian-grown Arborio is the kind we use, but you can also use other imported brands such as Originario or Fino. Follow the directions and your risotto will be dense, creamy, and moist, the grains tender on the outside with a firm but thoroughly cooked center—in other words, *al dente*, like good pasta.

½ cup (1 stick) butter or margarine
1 garlic clove, minced
3 large leeks (about 1½ pounds), white and 2 inches of pale green part, washed thoroughly, and coarsely chopped
1 medium onion, finely chopped

2 cups Arborio rice
5 cups homemade chicken stock or canned broth
½ cup Marsala wine
2 tablespoons Dijon mustard
½ cup freshly grated imported Parmesan cheese (or Grana)

In a medium skillet over moderate heat, melt 2 tablespoons of the butter and when the foam subsides, add the garlic and sauté until just golden. Add the leeks and cook, stirring frequently, until golden, about 7 to 8 minutes. Set aside.

In a medium saucepan over moderate heat, melt 5 tablespoons of the butter and when the foam subsides add the onion and cook, stirring frequently, until transparent and lightly colored, about 5 minutes. Add the rice and stir until each grain is coated. Pour in the Marsala and simmer until all the liquid is absorbed. Reduce heat to moderately low.

Meanwhile, in another saucepan over moderately high heat, bring the stock to a boil, reduce the heat to simmer and keep hot. Add 1 cup of the stock to the rice mixture and stir until it is absorbed. Continue adding the hot stock, 1 cup at a time, stirring constantly, until all but 1 cup of stock has been absorbed. Fold in the reserved leeks and the mustard. Add the final cup of stock, continuing to stir, and when it too is absorbed, fold in the remaining butter and the Parmesan cheese. The texture should be moist and creamy and have a satin sheen. Serve at once.

Panfried Salmon Steaks with Leek and Fresh Coriander Sauce

Serves 4

We like our salmon steaks crusty brown on the outside and rare on the inside. The leek-dominated sauce that we suggest is a perfect and luxurious accompaniment.

2 tablespoons unsalted butter

1¼ pounds leeks (about 3 large), trimmed, leaving 2 inches pale green, cut in half lengthwise, washed well, and thinly sliced Salt and freshly ground black pepper

⅓ cup dry white wine

1 cup bottled clam juice or homemade fish stock

1 cup heavy cream

2 tablespoons minced fresh coriander (cilantro)

4 salmon steaks (each 1 inch thick), about 1½ to 2 pounds

2 tablespoons corn or vegetable oil

2 teaspoons freshly squeezed lemon juice

8 small fresh coriander sprigs for garnish (optional)

In a large skillet, melt the butter over moderately low heat. When the foam subsides, cook the leeks with salt and pepper to taste, covered, stirring occasionally, for 10 minutes, or until they are very tender. Raise heat to high, add the wine and clam juice, and bring the mixture to a boil. Add the cream and boil the mixture, uncovered, until it is thick enough to coat a spoon, about 2 to 3 minutes. Taste and adjust the seasoning, stir in the minced coriander, and keep the sauce warm over very low heat.

While the sauce is cooking, place the salmon steaks on a plate and drizzle them with the oil and the lemon juice. Turn to coat them on both sides and sprinkle with the salt and pepper. Heat a sauté pan large enough to hold all 4 steaks in one layer over moderate heat. Add the steaks and panfry for about 3 minutes on each side, or until browned on the outside and barely cooked through.

Divide the reserved sauce among 4 heated plates, arrange a salmon steak on each plate, and garnish with 2 coriander sprigs, if desired.

SAUTÉED LEEKS WITH SCALLOPS IN GINGER CREAM

Serves 6 as an appetizer; 4 as a main course

First courses that can double as main dishes when served over rice or pasta are nice to have in your repertoire. This one also has the virtues of being quick and easy—especially if you do some of the KP duty ahead of time, like sautéing the leeks and mincing the ginger and shallots.

4 tablespoons (½ stick) unsalted butter

3 large leeks, white part and some pale green, washed well and julienned (about 2 cups)

1 tablespoon minced shallot

1 tablespoon minced fresh gingerroot

½ cup dry vermouth

1 tablespoon freshly squeezed lime juice

1½ pounds sea scallops, rinsed, patted dry, and quartered, or an equal amount of bay scallops, rinsed and patted dry

1 cup heavy cream

½ teaspoon white pepper

½ teaspoon salt, or to taste

In a 10-inch sauté pan or skillet, melt 2 tablespoons butter over moderately low heat. When the foam subsides, sauté the leeks, stirring frequently, for 5 minutes. Transfer the leeks to a bowl and reserve.

In the same sauté pan, melt the remaining 2 tablespoons butter over moderately high heat and when the foam subsides, cook the shallot, stirring, for 30 seconds. Add the gingerroot, vermouth, lime juice, and scallops and cook the mixture, stirring constantly, for 1 to 2 minutes, or until the scallops turn white and are firm to the touch. Transfer the scallops with a slotted spoon to a plate and keep them warm.

Raise the heat to high and boil the cooking liquid until it is reduced by half, about 3 to 4 minutes. Add the cream, reduce heat to moderate, and cook the sauce, tipping and swirling the pan frequently, for 3 or 4 minutes, or until the sauce is thickened slightly. Add the white pepper and salt, return the scallops to the pan, and stir to coat them with the sauce. Divide the scallop mixture between 6 small plates or scallop shells and top each serving with some of the reserved leeks. Serve immediately.

LOTUS ROOT

[*NELUMBO NUCIFERA NELUMBO LUTEA*]

water lily

water chinquapin

water nut

duck acorn

nelumbo

lin-ngau or *lin-gow* (Ch.)

hasunone (Jap.)

The two kinds of lotus known to botanists and culinary experts are almost identical. Both have been prized since prehistoric times for their magnificent leaves, gigantic blossoms, and as an important food source, especially in Asia. Although they are called "roots" they are really rhizomes.

Sometimes called water lily, the oriental lotus is indigenous to Asia from the Caspian Sea eastward to Japan and south to northeastern Australia. Although the American lotus is native to the eastern United States, south to Florida, and westward through Texas, it is used only ornamentally, not for food. However, the Amerindians once ate all parts of the plant—from its young leaves, flower petals, and large seeds, to the thick, starchy sausage-shaped subaquatic rhizomes.

The Oriental lotus was introduced into Egypt about 700 B.C. where it was grown for its beauty. In China and Japan, Buddha is often shown in statuary or in paintings holding a lotus blossom. One can find it planted near temples, palaces, and other sacred places. In the Kashmir region of India, lakes are filled with lotus, their huge blossoms adding their own beauty to that of the spectacular countryside.

More than its Western relative, the Oriental or sacred lotus is an important part of Asian cuisine. The juvenile leaves are boiled, steamed, or stir-fried as a vegetable; the petals of the enormous flowers are often added to clear soups for garnish; the stamens of the flowers are used in Southeast Asia in teas and tisanes; the seeds are dried and roasted, sometimes pickled or ground into a starchy meal, or made into the lotus jam that fills pastries and desserts. The leaves are also sold dried for use as food wrappers, much like corn husks are used to enclose tamales.

But it is lotus root, the rhizome, which is the best-known edible portion of the plant both here and in the Orient. The rhizome can grow to upward of 4 feet in length and 3 inches in diameter, divided into segments resembling sausage links—they're even a reddish brown color like sausages. When cut through in cross section, each porous slice looks like the wheel of a modern car (at least to us) with large perforations alternating with small ones, divided by white to tan to pale orange fleshy "spokes." The shape and pattern is both surprising in a dish and disarmingly attractive. The flesh is fibrous and chewy and its slight astringency and flavor reminiscent of artichokes is for some an acquired taste.

The Chinese population in this country is supplied for the most part by lotus root harvested in Hawaii and shipped fresh to both coasts.

Varieties

Although there are two kinds of edible lotus, only the Oriental variety is commercially available.

Availability

Lotus root is in the market fresh from summer through fall. It is also available during other seasons sliced and canned, preserved in various ways (usually in a sweet sauce to which soy sauce and sometimes rice wine have been added).

Storage

If the "links" remain uncut, you may keep them in the refrigerator vegetable drawer for several weeks.

What to Look For

Examine the rhizome for bruises and choose those with smooth, unblemished skin.

Basic Preparation and Cooking Methods

Peel the lotus section and slice it quickly, dropping each slice immediately into acidulated water (water to which a few drops of vinegar or lemon juice have been added) because it tends to discolor rather quickly. The slices can be stir-fried or simmered with other foods, steamed, braised, used in soups, and, blanched and cooled, added to salads.

---

nutrition

In 100g of lotus root there are 56 calories, 2.60g protein, 17.24g carbohydrates, .80g fiber, 45mg calcium, 1.16mg iron, 23mg magnesium, 100mg phosphorus, 556mg potassium (more than the preferred American source, bananas, by in excess of 100mg), but, alas, 40mg sodium. It is a great source of vitamin C at 44mg, and has traces of thiamine, riboflavin, niacin, and no cholesterol.

LOTUS ROOT SALAD IN ORIENTAL-STYLE VINAIGRETTE

Serves 4

Because it tastes like artichoke hearts, but has a firmer, chewier texture, lotus root makes a delightfully filling salad or first course. The vinaigrette dressing we devised substitutes Oriental ingredients for the usual Western versions.

1 19-ounce can sliced lotus root in water, drained and patted dry
2 tablespoons rice wine vinegar
3 teaspoons soy sauce
1 tablespoon Maggi seasoning
½ teaspoon sugar
½ teaspoon freshly ground black pepper
¼ cup Oriental sesame oil
1 tablespoon toasted sesame seeds

Arrange the lotus root slices in a serving bowl.

In a small mixing bowl, whisk together the vinegar, soy sauce, Maggi seasoning, sugar, and pepper. Whisking constantly, add the sesame oil in a thin stream and whisk until combined and emulsified. Pour the dressing over the lotus root slices and let marinate at room temperature for 30 minutes. Chill or serve at room temperature, sprinkled with the sesame seeds.

Spicy Beef Stir-Fried with Lotus Root

Serves 4

When we eat out, we usually choose a restaurant that serves the kind of food we don't often make in our own kitchen. That's easy in New York, where we can sample Indian, Afghan, Japanese, or Thai food within a six- or seven-block area. A two-minute walk brings us to our favorite Chinese restaurant, Sung Chu Mei, where the food is so good we find there is no necessity to master the art of Chinese cooking over and above a dish as simple as this—and perfect boiled rice, of course.

¾ pound rump steak, placed in the freezer for 15 minutes

2 tablespoons light soy sauce

½ teaspoon salt, or to taste

1 tablespoon minced garlic

2 teaspoons minced fresh ginger-root

¼ teaspoon Chinese five-spice powder

¼ teaspoon cayenne pepper

2 tablespoons peanut oil

½ cup canned beef broth or water

1 tablespoon cornstarch

2 tablespoons cold water

1 19-ounce can sliced lotus root in water, drained and patted dry

2 scallions, white and green parts, thinly sliced

The meat should be semifrozen. With a very sharp knife, slice the meat paper-thin. Sprinkle the slices with the soy sauce, salt, garlic, ginger, five-spice powder, and cayenne. Mix well to season each slice. Let rest for 30 minutes.

In a wok or large sauté pan, heat the oil to rippling over moderately high heat. Add the beef, stirring and tossing, until it loses its red color. Add the broth. Mix the cornstarch and cold water quickly, and stir it into the beef mixture. Bring the liquid to a boil, stirring until the sauce becomes thick and clear. Stir in the lotus root slices and cook until just heated through. Transfer to a warm platter and sprinkle with the scallions. Serve with boiled white or brown rice.

ONIONS

[*ALLIUM CEPA*]

oignon (Fr.)

cebolla (Sp.)

zwiebel (Ger.)

cipolla (It.)

cebola (Port.)

luk (Rus.)

For thousands of years before it was ever cultivated, primitive man derived protection as well as sustenance from the onion by rubbing his body with its juices. It has been grown for food for over five thousand years and is the most common of all our seasonings—only salt is used more universally for flavoring. Probably a native of southwestern Asia, there are hundreds of species growing wild almost everywhere in Europe, Asia, and North America, though the wild ancestors of the species we use in our kitchens today have largely been lost to botanists, have become extinct due to changes in climate, or have vanished for other "civilized" reasons.

The Sanskrit language of the Sumerians was the first to record the use of onions as a staple in the diet of those ancient peoples, and the onion was a sacred symbol of the universe to the ancient Egyptians. Its nine layers of swollen leaf bases represented eternity; peel them away and you are left with two stem buds from which new growth begins—the beginnings of a new life. The name *onion* itself derives from the Latin *unio* or *unionem*, meaning a unity of a kind of large pearl—which makes sense because pearls are made up of many layers, just like onions.

Herodotus, the Greek historian in the fifth century B.C., recorded what was probably the first organized sitdown strike in history. Slaves building the Pyramid of Cheops refused to work until they were given and guaranteed their daily ration of onions and garlic. Several vegetables were sculpted in precious metals by Egyptian artisans and used as temple offerings to the gods by Egyptian priests, but only onions were ever crafted in gold.

The Greeks fed athletes on onions in order to "lighten the balance of the blood"—a good-sized onion to start the day and a smaller one to end it. The Romans, not to be outdone, fed their athletes a complete breakfast of onions before a competition. Romans introduced onions to Britain, not so much to feed the natives, but to keep themselves fit and their food well flavored. The Romans left eventually, but the onion stayed on in Britain to play an important role in the national cuisine and in folk medicine. *The Great Herbal* in 1596 claimed that onion juice rubbed on a bald head could grow hair (the Shakers agreed in the early nineteenth century, and used onion juice to stop hair from falling out), and onions were also said to clear up acne, relieve the pain of arthritis, and, of course, cleanse the blood. It even cured cowardice, according to Alexander the Great, who fed his armies on quantities of onions to give them courage.

Onions are believed to be one of the crops Columbus brought to the New World on his second voyage in 1494 and planted in the Dominican Republic. They were introduced rapidly thereafter into Mexico and Central America, into South America and into North America, where they were taken up by the American Indians who were used to the flavor of their own indigenous wild onion, the ramp (page 240). The Pilgrims brought onion seeds with them and planted them soon after they landed at Plymouth Rock, and they have been part of our food heritage ever since.

Over the millennia, onions have always been promoting good health—especially good blood. What was laughed at and previously thought of only as superstitions is today being substantiated: that onions and garlic contain compounds that inhibit blood clotting; that onions contain a chemical called Prostaglandin A-1, a potent agent to lower blood pressure; that raw onion chewed for five minutes is a powerful antibacterial agent, completely sterilizing the lining of the mouth and throat (the Russians came up with that one); that onions have a cholesterol-lowering effect and actually raise HDL (high-density lipoprotein, the so-called good cholesterol), which is believed to clear the arteries of platelets, fatty deposits that constrict the passage of blood; that sulphur-containing oils in onions and garlic, according to preliminary research, may prevent cancer in its initial stages.

In addition, onions are low in calories and strong on flavor, which means their inclusion in a diet can help dieters withstand ordinarily bland fare. They pack a nutritional wallop, too, with high fiber, good vitamin content, essential minerals and carbohydrates.

The cooks of most other countries treat the onion as a vegetable, while we tend to use it mainly for seasoning, minimizing its value in the kitchen. The onion has many faces; it can be transformed into a most intriguing side dish, a subtle sauce, a hearty soup. It can be grilled, deep-fried, sautéed, poached, braised, or baked. It can be stuffed, used as a garnish, or pickled and drowned in gin and vermouth to recast a martini as a Gibson. Depending on its sweetness, it can be eaten raw in salads and in sandwiches, or out of hand with a sprinkling of salt.

The most popular onion in the United States is the globe onion—either yellow or white—which accounts for at least 75 percent of our onion production and represents the archetypal onion. Globes are of moderate size, have a strong taste and aroma and a firm, crisp texture. Their growers say they are all-purpose, good for any dish, but in reality they are at their best in dishes that require long simmering, because it is the one onion that can survive hours of cooking with its flavor still intense and intact. Interestingly, when we make onion soup we use globes, but the French use the enormous and mild Spanish or Bermuda onions, perhaps because these varieties contain more sugar and the sugar caramelizes during the slow, preliminary sautéing or baking process, making the soup sweeter, darkening its color, and enriching its flavor.

Onion production in this country totals about 2 billion pounds or more a year, ranking it fourth among the vegetable crops. The two states that harvest the most are California and Texas, in that order. Onions that are allowed to cure in the sun after harvesting are called dry onions. The curing process develops the thin, papery dry skin that protects the bulb during storage and shipping, and prevents decay.

You can't always tell an onion by its covering, however. The skin color can be as deceiving as size. Sweetness, mildness, or strength is determined by the soil and especially the climate in which it is grown. The warmer the climate, the sweeter the onion. Color, shape, and size can tell you something—flat onions, like those we get from Texas in the spring, are sweet and mild. Red Italian onions are also sweet and mild—except those grown in our northern states, which can be quite pungent. Big onions, if they're Bermudas or Spanish, are also mild and sweet—but they can also be very strong if they are just overgrown globes. Colors can range from silvery white and palest green to yellow, rust, and dark brown to purple and red. Shapes can range from round to flat-round to oval. Sizes can range from the ½-inch pearl onion to the 5-inch-diameter Spanish onion.

The United States imports large quantities of onions, the most prominent being the sweet red Italian and the mild big Bermudas and Spanish. Mildness is the key word here, and if you like your onions mild try U.S.-grown Vidalias from Georgia, Walla Wallas from Washington, and the Maui from Hawaii. All have a high sugar content but look like regular globe onions, only bigger. Texas onions, on the other hand, smaller and flat with pale yellow, almost white, skins are also delicate and wonderful raw. We love a salad of onions, tomatoes, and basil. Unfortunately the best tomatoes don't appear until after the season for all the mild onions (late spring and early summer). We have learned to overbuy Texas, Vidalia, and Walla Walla onions and store a good number of them to enjoy during the tomato season. Finding these onions was once quite difficult, as they're perishable, making long-term storage and transport difficult. Now many supermarket chains and mail-order sources carry them. Because they lack the characteristic onion pungency, these onions are best eaten raw. Peel them, chop them, slice them without a tear! They won't irritate your eyes, or give you onion breath or heartburn.

Gardener's note: Have you wondered about those 4-foot-high stalks topped with large spheres made up of hundreds of tiny amethyst-colored flowers that you see at the florist? They are really giant onion plants (*Allium giganteum*). These spectacular flowers are ornamentals and are grown for display only. They can be cultivated in your garden, where they make a spectacular showing for about twenty days, or can be bought as a cut flower. When allowed to dry, the flowers turn a lovely topaz color and can last for years.

Varieties

You'll find most of the following dry onions at your local supermarket, greengrocer, or specialty food store:

Bermuda Mild and sweet, crisp-textured, and delicately flavored, Bermudas were once grown exclusively on the island but are now mimicked in parts of the United States. Island-grown Bermudas are still thought to be unique with their juicy, whitish flesh and a flattened round shape. Bermudas are harvested in the spring and should be used as soon as possible; they also arrive in markets in late summer and early fall. They are prone to ferment-ing and black mold, so storage life is short. Skin color can vary from white to tan with dark green or gray stripes running vertically from root end to stem. It is best to buy Bermudas when they are hard and as white as possible. Soft stem ends mean that the centers will be black and the onion inedible. They grow from 1½ to 4 inches in diameter, yielding 2 to 4 to the pound.

Globe or Yellow Onion Readily available everywhere, this is an all-purpose common kitchen onion, good for cooking, with a strong, pungent flavor and sharp bite. They are juicy and often irritating to the eyes. As the name implies, they are global in shape with a pointed stem end and yellow skin (but the skin can also be copper, white, or red). They are harvested when 1½ to 3 inches in size. Globes have a long shelf life and are available all year long. They usually number 3 to 6 to the pound.

Green Onion These are sometimes sold for and mistaken for scallions. But while the scallion is nonbulbing, the green onion is a true bulb. These very white, round, green-veined onions are the size of jumbo marbles and are usually sold in bunches with their long tubular green leaves attached. They're delicious braised, sauced, or grilled as they're often served in Mexico. These are the *real* spring onions that are confused with scallions and also go under the name Japanese onions. They appear in produce markets in May and June.

Pearl and Boiling Onions Pearl onions are tiny white onions about the size of marbles that are harvested before maturity. The slightly larger white boiling onion is the same, only larger. The little ones are a little milder, yet more flavorful, and are at their best from late summer through the holiday season. Buy those that are hard and have a white, papery skin and range in size from ½ inch (the pearls) to 1½ inches (white boiling onions). Peeling these peewees is a pain unless you first drop them into boiling water for 15 to 20 seconds, drain, cool, and cut off the root ends. The skins should then slip off easily and you can add them to a stew or casserole, or cook them until tender and serve them blanketed with sauce.

Maui Onion These are grown in volcanic soil in the state of Hawaii on the island of Maui. They have a distinctive flavor and sweetness, much like Vidalias and Walla Wallas. They are difficult to find east of the Rockies and very few stores carry them. There is no harm in asking, though.

Red Italian or Creole Onion The best are imported from Italy and get here during the midsummer. These round or oval Italians are often sold braided together by their long dried leaves. Slightly more pungent than Bermudas, Spanish, Texas Flats, Vidalia, Walla Walla, or Maui, they are nonetheless mild enough to eat raw, especially in a salad. The flesh is bright lavender-white rimmed in deep purplish red. They don't take well to cooking, becoming watery and colorless. Red Italians store fairly well and can be found in various stages of quality all year round. Flat California varieties arrive in the markets by late summer or early fall and continue to be shipped through December. In general, Italian reds are round, flat, or elongated in shape, depending on their source, with deep red to dark purple skins and are from 2 to 3 inches in size. Three or 4 make up a pound.

Spanish a.k.a. Valencias Not as sweet as Bermudas nor as mild, they still are wonderful raw (classically with a hamburger) or cooked. The flesh is pale yellowish white or milk-white, juicy, semisweet, crisp. It is large round or slightly oval in shape, with a light yellow to deep copper skin. These keep better than the Bermuda and are available out of storage most of the year, but are best bought before the spring. New crops appear in late spring from South America and Mexico. The best time to buy them is in the fall, at harvest time, and usually from local farms. These can be quite large, 3 to 5 inches across, and can weigh in at up to a pound each.

Texas Flats a.k.a. Sweeties Among other things Texas sends us are sweet, mild onions. They usually get to market in spring, with new shipments arriving until the end of June. To our tastes these are the most succulent of eating onions, with no bite, no sting, and yet a very definite onion flavor. They come prebagged or loose. We don't usually like to buy bagged onions, but these are so fresh, hard, and shiny that we have yet to find a bad onion in a bag. Texas Flats are just that, flat—about 1 inch thick from root to stem end and 1½ to 2½ inches in diameter. The skin is pale, pale copper, very thin, and fragile and shows much of the glossy outer layer of flesh. They don't take to cooking, they're too mild

for most dishes, and while they are in the stores globe onions are hard to find. But this is a minor complaint.

Walla Walla These big beauties come from the state of Washington, which has some of the best fresh produce to be found anywhere. In the past they were only available in limited quantities at specialty food stores, but now we have discovered them at our local supermarket. Sweet and juicy with thick layers of firm flesh, they're worth searching for. Walla Wallas are coppery-skinned, about 4 inches in diameter and 3 inches thick. They are available in mid-summer when Vidalias are gone. Eat them raw and in salads. Savor them because they aren't around for very long.

Availability

See above for different varieties.

Storage

Globe onions store well at home if kept in a dark, dry, well-ventilated area. If you buy bagged onions, be sure to go through them and discard any that smell or have soft stem ends, because they will affect the others. Keep them, if you can, at about 50°F. Don't refrigerate onions unless they are wrapped separately in paper towels, plastic wrap, or aluminum foil, or unless you intend to use them within a few days. Direct sunlight can stimulate the production of chlorophyll—remember, the onion layers are swollen *leaf* bases—which can turn the flesh green and the taste bitter. Braided onions can be hung from a hook in a cool, dry place. A wire egg basket is a good place to store onions; the air circulation is good and it can be hung up out of the way in a dark pantry or away from the light of a window.

What to Look For

The outside skins of properly cured (dried) onions become brittle and dry. They should be that way when you buy them. Moisture is death to onions—excepting those sold in bunches with the green leaf stems intact. These are uncured, freshly dug, and should be used quickly. Avoid cured onions that have sprouted or have soft bottoms or stem ends. Avoid brown outer flesh or any sign of black mold. Select onions with bright, dry, papery shells that give off a dull reflection. Be sure they are firm and hard, with thin, compact necks. If they feel at all spongy in body or neck, toss them aside. Decay, sometimes hidden by the skin, is indicated by this soft feeling and by smell. Properly cured onions have no onion smell whatsoever.

Basic Preparation and Cooking Methods

Onions are the only member of the *Allium* family that can bring tears to your eyes, because the cut surface of the onion releases into the air a volatile compound containing a kind of sulfuric acid. The spray irritates eye membranes, causing tears to flow. We usually cut and chop and let the tears fall where they may. But there are tried, if not true, methods to keep you dry-eyed. Here are a few, with our comments on their effectiveness:

- Refrigerating the onion before peeling and cutting is said to hold back the vaporization of the acid—do it if it makes you feel better to handle cold vegetables.
- Peeling under cold, running water is supposed to wash away the offending acids before they become airborne—too much trouble as far as we're concerned, and wasteful because you lose a lot of onion down the drain, not to mention precious water.
- Hold a slice of bread in your mouth while slicing—this should deflect the vapor, but it only makes a partial barrier and hides what you're doing so you could cut your finger.

- Keep your mouth firmly shut while peeling and slicing—this will help you cry silently.
- Keep the cut side of the onion face-down on the cutting board while slicing and chopping—this helps a little but only temporarily, putting off the tears until the first slice.
- Rinse your hands a lot while you're chopping and slicing—your hands will then be nice and clean when they wipe the tears away.

In other words, there is not much that will help, save the wearing of goggles. If you love onions enough, you'll be happy to cry over them.

Almost every cookbook that gives directions for sautéing onions is adamant about *not browning, scorching, or burning onions*. If you do, they say, throw them out and start over. We find that downright wasteful and silly. Browned onions are just well-caramelized; it's the sugar content that burns. Browned, even burnt onions can be delicious in omelettes, as a soup base, on hamburgers, or with steak, etc. They do not become bitter as other cookbooks say. They just aren't too subtle a flavoring.

To sauté onions to translucent or golden perfection: Heat the pan before adding fat or oil. Use a combination of butter and oil or oil alone (oil has a higher heating temperature than butter and there is less chance of its burning; combining butter and oil adds flavor you might want and prevents the butter from scorching). Once the fat is heated almost to smoking over high heat, reduce heat to moderate and add the onions. Stir constantly and keep the pan in motion, moving and turning the onions until they reach the desired degree of doneness.

As for dried, powdered, dehydrated onions, and onion salt: we've tried them, don't like them, never use them.

---

nutrition

Onions are an invaluable source of compounds to improve your health in many ways we've already discussed. Their vitamin and mineral content is not as spectacular as other vegetables, but is still quite respectable. In 1 cup (about 200g) of chopped onions there are: 65 calories, 3g protein, 15g carbohydrates, 46mg calcium, 61mg phosphorus, .9mg iron, 15mg sodium, 267mg potassium, .05mg thiamine, .07mg riboflavin, .3mg niacin, .05mg vitamin B, 1.0mg vitamin C, and no cholesterol.

PINK VELVET ONION SOUP

Serves 8

The Italian onion soup, *crèma di cipolle,* usually made with white onions, takes on a subtle blush when made with red onions. This recipe is from the Veneto area of northern Italy, which is why the onions are cooked in butter and a little cream is added. You may substitute croutons for the Gorgonzola-spread bread rounds, or serve the soup as is, if you'd like a lighter, but still savory, start to a meal.

8 tablespoons (1 stick) unsalted butter, at room temperature

5 large red onions (about 2½ pounds), thinly sliced

2 tablespoons Arborio (Italian short-grain) rice

¾ cup dry white wine

1 teaspoon salt, or to taste
Freshly ground white pepper to taste

10 cups water

2 ounces Gorgonzola cheese

8 ½-inch slices Italian bread, toasted

1 large egg yolk

1 tablespoon heavy cream

1 tablespoon all-purpose flour

Melt 7 tablespoons of butter in a large sauté pan or soup kettle over moderately low heat and, when the foam subsides, add the onions. Cook, stirring occasionally, for 20 to 25 minutes, or until the onions are softened. Add the rice and stir to coat each grain. Add the wine, 1 teaspoon salt, and the pepper and raise the heat to moderately high. Boil the mixture, stirring occasionally, until the liquid is almost evaporated. Add the water, return to a boil, then reduce the heat and simmer for 1½ hours.

About 10 minutes before the mixture has finished cooking, cream together the Gorgonzola with the remaining 1 tablespoon butter, and spread some of the mixture on each of the toasted bread slices; set aside.

In a small bowl, whisk together the egg yolk, cream, and flour. Whisk in 1 cup of the onion mixture, then incorporate the resulting mixture back into the onion soup. Simmer the soup, stirring, for 2 minutes. Taste and adjust the seasoning. Ladle the soup into heated bowls and float a bread slice on each. Serve immediately.

PARIS MARKET ONION SOUP

Serves 6

This is the famous one, the onion soup Americans in Paris ended their evenings with at a bistro in the former French food market, Les Halles. Les Halles may be gone but the onion soup recipe lingers on. It's really the method of cooking the onions in the oven that makes this soup different, meaning *better*.

1 pound mild onions (Vidalia, Walla Walla, Maui, Bermuda, or Spanish) (about 2 large), thinly sliced

2 tablespoons unsalted butter

2 cups dry white wine

3 13¾-ounce cans beef broth diluted with 1 cup water

6 slices French or Italian bread, cut ½ inch thick, stale or lightly toasted

2 cups grated imported Gruyère (about ½ pound)

Preheat the oven to 425° F.

In a medium baking dish or gratin dish, combine the onions, butter, and white wine. Place the dish in the center of the oven and cook, uncovered, for 1 hour, or until the onions are very soft and the liquid has almost evaporated, stirring a few times. Remove from the oven and set aside.

Preheat the broiler, setting the rack about 6 inches from the heat source.

In a large saucepan, bring the broth to a boil over high heat. Reduce heat to a simmer and cook gently while you arrange 6 deep ovenproof soup bowls on a baking sheet. Distribute the cooked onions evenly among the bowls and ladle the simmering broth over the onions. Sprinkle the cheese generously over each round of bread, and float a bread slice, cheese side up, in each bowl. Place the baking sheet with the bowls under the broiler and cook for 2 to 3 minutes, until the cheese is just melted and turning golden. Serve immediately.

FRIED ONION RINGS IN MUSTARD-BEER BATTER

Serves 4

········

We love onion rings, but good ones—not the kind that arrive in a tough batter that, when bitten into, reveals an empty tunnel where the onion should be. It's a mystery to us how these are made—and why! Good onion rings should have a tasty batter fried golden brown, enclosing a crisp-tender band of oniony-tasting onion. If that's your idea of onion rings, try these.

1 cup all-purpose flour
1 tablespoon powdered mustard
1 tablespoon salt
1 teaspoon finely ground white pepper
3 tablespoons Dijon mustard

1 cup beer
1 pound mild onions (about 2 large), cut into ⅜-inch slices
Peanut, safflower, or canola oil for deep-frying

In a bowl, whisk together the flour, powdered mustard, salt, pepper, Dijon mustard, and beer to make a smooth batter. Separate the onion slices into rings, and dip them into the batter, coating them well and letting the excess drip back into the bowl. Heat 3 inches of oil to 375° F. in a deep fryer. Fry the onion rings in batches, turning them, for 3 minutes, or until they are golden brown. As they are browned, transfer them with a slotted spoon to paper towels to drain. Sprinkle with salt, if desired, and serve hot.

Baked Sweet Onions with Rosemary Butter

Serves 4

Baked whole onions are easy to prepare and look lovely on a dinner plate. Perhaps it's the vertical dimension they add — or just the anticipation of cutting into them, and tasting that hot, celadon-colored globe — so fragrant, so inviting. We dust the shoulders of ours with Parmesan and add a little rosemary to evoke an Italian country flavor. Use only the sweetest onions available in the market — Vidalia, Maui, Walla Walla, Bermuda, or Spanish.

4 large sweet onions (about 2 pounds), peeled

4 tablespoons (½ stick) unsalted butter

2 teaspoons fresh rosemary leaves, or 1 teaspoon dried

Salt and freshly ground black pepper to taste

¼ cup freshly grated Parmesan

Preheat the oven to 400° F.

With a sharp paring knife, cut a cone-shaped depression ½ inch deep into the root end of each onion. Cut a thin slice off the stem ends, if necessary, to make them stand straight. Arrange the onions in a buttered stainless-steel or ovenproof baking pan just large enough to hold them in one layer.

Place 1 tablespoon butter into the cavity of each onion, sprinkle each with ½ teaspoon rosemary leaves, salt and pepper to taste, and 1 tablespoon Parmesan. Add to the pan ¼ inch water and bake the onions, covered with foil, for 55 minutes, or until they are tender when pierced with a fork or pointed knife. Transfer the onions with a slotted spoon to a serving dish.

Place the pan on a burner on top of the stove and reduce the cooking liquid to about ¼ cup over high heat. Spoon the sauce over the onions and serve.

DILLED GOLDEN CREAMED ONIONS

Serves 10

What would Thanksgiving dinner be without creamed onions? Not traditional, certainly. But these creamed onions are not exactly traditional, either. Our recipe serves 10, but if you'd rather serve only 4 or 6, freeze the remainder in a plastic container for another meal. To reheat, thaw the onions, place them in a small saucepan over moderately low heat, and cook, stirring, until hot.

3 pounds small white onions
2 tablespoons unsalted butter
1 teaspoon sugar
1 teaspoon salt, or to taste
⅔ cup heavy cream

1 tablespoon Dijon mustard
Freshly ground white pepper to taste
½ cup snipped fresh dill

Blanch the onions in boiling water for 2 minutes, drain, and peel. In a sauté pan large enough to hold the onions (there should be about 50) in one layer, combine the onions, butter, sugar, 1 teaspoon salt, and enough water to cover the onions by about ½ inch; bring the water to a boil over moderately high heat and boil the onions until the liquid has almost evaporated, about 10 to 12 minutes. Reduce the heat to moderate and continue cooking the onions, tipping and swirling the pan, until they turn golden and begin to brown, about 3 to 5 minutes more.

Add the cream, bring the liquid to a boil, and boil the mixture, stirring occasionally, until the sauce is thickened slightly. Turn off the heat and add the mustard, stirring, until well combined. Season the mixture with additional salt, if desired, and pepper to taste and stir in the dill. Serve hot in a warm covered dish.

NOTE: An elegant addition is ¼ pound mushrooms minced in a food processor and cooked in 1 tablespoon butter until their liquid is evaporated. Add them after the sauce has thickened, but while it is still boiling. Then turn off the heat and add the mustard, as above.

ONIONS AND GINGER WITH CURRIED CABBAGE

Serves 6

The flavor of curry is welcome in our house. Its fragrance invites guests to enjoy themselves, because greater enjoyment awaits them at the table.

3 tablespoons light olive oil

1 tablespoon white or black mustard seeds

3 large onions, cut in half and thinly sliced

2 tablespoons minced fresh ginger-root

1 small jalapeño pepper, seeded, deveined, and minced

1 tablespoon curry powder or *garam masala* (available at Indian and Oriental markets)

2 pounds cabbage (1 medium), quartered, cored, sliced ¼ inch thick

2 1-inch pieces cinnamon stick

½ teaspoon salt, or to taste

⅔ to 1 cup homemade chicken stock or canned broth

Freshly ground black pepper to taste

In a large sauté pan or skillet, bring the oil to rippling over high heat. Add the mustard seeds and cook, covered, until they begin to pop. Reduce heat to moderately high, lift the cover carefully, tilting it between you and the pan, and add the onions. Remove the cover and cook the onions, stirring, for 5 to 7 minutes, or until they are browned. Add the ginger and jalapeño and cook the mixture for 1 minute. Reduce heat to low, add the curry powder, and cook the mixture, stirring, for 1 minute.

Strew the cabbage over the onion mixture and press the cinnamon sticks down into the mixture. Sprinkle the cabbage with ½ teaspoon salt, add ⅔ cup stock, and bring to a boil over moderately high heat. Reduce heat to a simmer and cook the mixture, covered, for 5 to 6 minutes, or until the cabbage is crisp-tender, adding more stock to keep the mixture moist, if necessary, during the cooking time. Taste and adjust seasoning, adding salt and pepper to taste. Stir the mixture well, discard the cinnamon sticks, mound into a heated bowl, and serve.

ORECCHIETTE WITH GOLDEN ONION SAUCE

*Makes about 4 cups, enough for 1 pound of cooked
dried pasta; serves 4 as a main dish*

When onions are cooked in oil and butter over low heat, for a very long time, they develop an intense golden caramelized color and an aroma that will have neighbors knocking on your door hoping to be invited for dinner. A pasta sauce like this is not just for onion lovers; it's a sauce for everyone who appreciates extravagant flavor at a frugal price. Incidentally, *orecchiette*, the pasta shape this sauce was intended for, means "little ears" in Italian, and we are especially fond of them. If you can't find them, you'll have equal success serving this sauce over *fusilli*, medium shells, or any pasta shaped to hold sauce.

¼ cup light olive oil

4 tablespoons (½ stick) unsalted butter

3 pounds Spanish or yellow onions, thinly sliced (about 10 cups)

1 teaspoon sugar

½ teaspoon salt, or to taste

1 teaspoon freshly ground black pepper, or more to taste

2 tablespoons balsamic or white wine vinegar

½ cup dry white wine

1 cup homemade chicken stock or canned broth or vegetable stock

1 cup water

1½ cups grated Gruyère (about ¼ pound), or 1 cup freshly grated Parmesan plus additional Parmesan for serving at the table

½ cup minced fresh parsley

In a large sauté pan, melt the oil and butter over moderate heat. When the foam subsides, add the onions, cover, and cook, stirring occasionally, for about 45 minutes. Stir in the sugar, ½ teaspoon salt, 1 teaspoon pepper, and the vinegar, raise heat to moderately high and cook, uncovered, stirring and scraping often, for 15 or 20 minutes more, or until the onions are a deep golden color. Add the wine, stock, and water and bring to a boil over high heat. Reduce heat to a simmer and cook 5 minutes more. Add the Gruyère and stir until it is completely melted. Stir in the parsley, and taste and adjust seasoning, adding more salt and pepper, if necessary.

Meanwhile cook the *orecchiette* in boiling water until *al dente,* about 8 minutes. Drain well and add to the sauce in the pan, mix well over low heat, and serve with more Parmesan cheese to sprinkle on at the table.

NOTE: This sauce is also delicious on white beans. After preparing the sauce, empty two 19-ounce cans of white (cannellini) beans into a colander or large sieve, drain, and rinse under hot running water. Add the beans to the sauce, mix, heat through, and serve. Four to 6 diners can enjoy this as a main dish; 8 to 12 as a side dish or appetizer. It's also good cold or at room temperature—so think of it the next time you're preparing picnic fare or a summer supper.

FRIED ONIONS AND EGGS

Serves 4

When we served this to our kids when they were little, they would fight over who got the scrapings from the pan. This is such a plain dish, only two ingredients plus salt and pepper, but it is one of our favorite meals, if not the favorite. What is served in restaurants as an onion omelette is just not the same. The proportion of onions to eggs may seem excessive, and it is—that's what makes this dish so good! Those onions are sautéed until they are dark, dark brown, completely caramelized, a shadow of their former selves; then beaten eggs are added and both are scrambled together. What sticks to the pan, the part the kids fought over, is really the best part.

¼ **cup canola, peanut, or corn oil**

2 **to 3 pounds medium yellow onions, peeled and sliced ⅜ inch thick**

8 **large eggs**

½ **teaspoon salt**

½ **teaspoon freshly ground black pepper**

About 2 tablespoons water

In a large heavy skillet, bring the oil to rippling over moderately high heat. Add the onions all at once and cook, undisturbed, for about 3 or 4 minutes. At this point the onions on the bottom should have released some of their liquid and reduced the volume of onions in the pan. Stir, lifting the onions on the bottom to the top. Reduce heat to moderate and continue cooking, stirring frequently, for 20 minutes, or until the onions are a deep, dark brown and reduced to about one-third their former volume.

In a medium bowl, beat the eggs with a fork or a whisk. Add the salt, pepper, and water and beat again. Pour the egg mixture over the onions and cook, stirring and scraping, about 2 or 3 minutes, or until the eggs are scrambled and set. Serve immediately, scraping the brown bits left in the bottom of the skillet evenly over each portion.

NOTE: Eggs and onions are best, we think, accompanied by steamed potatoes and carrots together forced through a ricer and mixed with lots of butter.

Scrambled eggs (called "fried" in our family, thus the title above) and onions are often mixed with smoked salmon bits that have been sautéed for 1 or 2 minutes with the onions just before the eggs are added.

Sautéed chicken livers are another traditional addition, as are sautéed mushrooms.

ONION AND TOMATO RELISH WITH JALAPEÑO

Makes about 1½ cups; serves 4 to 6

What's a hamburger without ketchup and raw onion? Not much, as far as we're concerned. But a hamburger with this relish is something else again. Spicy and fresh-tasting, tantalizingly reminiscent of Southwest cooking, or maybe Cajun or Caribbean, it does wonders for a hot dog as well—or at the other end of the scale, a grilled steak. This is summer fare, though, not to be made unless the tomatoes are ripened on the vine!

2 vine-ripened tomatoes (about ¾ pound), finely chopped

1 large red onion, finely chopped

1 large fresh or pickled jalapeño pepper, seeded, deveined, and minced

2 tablespoons peanut, safflower, or canola oil

½ teaspoon salt

½ teaspoon freshly ground black pepper

½ teaspoon chili powder

In a bowl, combine the tomatoes, onion, jalapeño, oil, salt and pepper, and chili powder. Mix well and refrigerate, covered, at least 30 minutes or up to 24 hours before serving.

PARSNIPS

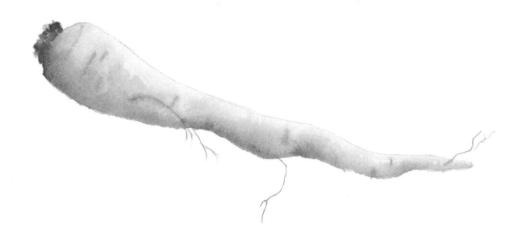

[*PASTINACA SATIVA*]

panais (Fr.)

pastinaca (It.)

chirivia (Sp.)

*I*t was the potato that almost did in the parsnip. Not that it was premeditated. As a matter of fact, the potato was the new kid on the block and didn't even know it would take the parsnip's place as the most valued companion of roasted beef, stewed birds, spit-turned lamb, goat, and pig at the dinner table. But it did. A sad story for the parsnip. A sort of *All About Eve* of the vegetable world. And all too true.

It all happened during the eighteenth century. The parsnip was the star of the European groaning board for a couple of thousand years, until the potato was discovered along with the New World. Though it took this new vegetable about two hundred years to grab the spotlight (see page 190), it ultimately turned the parsnip into a has been, an understudy at best.

That was truly a shame, because the parsnip is nothing like the potato and should be a star in its own right. Maybe not of the magnitude of the potato (which is much more versatile), but given a few leading roles instead of bit parts in soups and stews.

The first parsnip grew wild in northern Europe and parts of Asia. Like so many other roots it was domesticated thousands of years ago. It made its way south and eventually became a favorite of both the Greeks and the Romans. The Romans ate them for dessert with honey and fruit and in little cakes. Tiberius, the famous and infamous Roman emperor, had parsnip roots imported for him from France and Germany for his personal enjoyment at his villa on the Isle of Capri.

The root was so well thought of that in the Middle Ages babies were given one to suck on just as they are given pacifiers now. Their parents ate them, too, not for dessert as their forebears had, but with preserved fish like eel, salt cod, and herring. During the Renaissance and well into the eighteenth century, parsnips were one of the preferred vegetables at most meals, a true staple—until potatoes entered the competition. Parsnips traveled well though and, if no longer as welcome at European tables as the new and *exotic* South American tuber, they nonetheless became naturalized in the United States and Canada. They were widely used by the colonists in the same ways their English mothers had taught them—for puddings, wine, bread, casseroles, stews, purees, fried like potato chips, turned into croquettes, blanched then roasted with ribs of beef until they were brown, and especially in that English favorite from Elizabethan times, parsnip pie. In England, parsnip pie was (and still is in some places) served in early spring with a latticed top decorated with red primroses.

What a comedown this lovely root vegetable has had. Most people don't even know what one tastes like, and the only time we are likely to encounter it is as one of the vegetables in those plastic bags of "soup greens" at the supermarket. A lot of people love it without even knowing what it is they are eating.

Parsnips taste like no other root vegetable, with their own unique and singular characteristics. They are sweet but not cloying like sweet potatoes. They have a hint of parsley taste but a nutty flavor to go along with it—and a fresh aroma when they are cooking. They can sometimes have a slight bite, a peppery mouth-feel, but not the burn of a radish. Their texture is fibrous yet silky smooth. And they look like a husky, bleached-out carrot. They are filling, high in protein, and high in nonfattening carbohydrates.

Varieties

Make that singular. Parsnips may look long and slim, short and fat, or in any shape in between, but there is only one variety that you'll find on the produce shelf.

Availability

The best parsnips come to market after the first frost, even after a hard freeze. Here is another case—just as with many of the underground vegetables—of a wonderful *fresh* vegetable available when most others are not.

Storage

Store parsnips in a cold, humid atmosphere like your refrigerator. You'll find they have a long shelf life—weeks and weeks.

What to Look For

Judge quality as you would carrots. Choose smooth, creamy-colored roots free of cracks, cuts, nicks, or bruises. They should be of uniform medium size—about 4 to 5 inches long and 1½ to 2 inches in diameter, tapering to a point at the root end. Discard any with shriveled or wrinkled skins and brownish areas. Feel for firmness and toss back into the bin any that are flabby or limp, as well as those that are too short or too long.

Basic Preparation and Cooking Methods

Scrub them clean of clinging dirt and peel as you would a carrot. (Parsnips can be cooked first and then peeled, but we find them easier to peel when raw. The exception is when steaming. Parsnips can be steamed whole and the skins slipped off after they are cooked just tender.) The root cooks best and fastest when cut in half lengthwise and then into 1- or 2-inch pieces. Blanch them first for 5 minutes, then add them to a roast to absorb the juices and turn brown. Or you can just continue cooking them in salted water for 3 or 4 minutes more, and serve them buttered or sauced, mashed or pureed. Whole parsnips take longer to cook, 12 to 15 minutes, than those that are halved and quartered because the cooking time is shorter if the core is exposed. You can also slice and dice parsnips and sauté or fry them. But let's face it, most parsnips will end up in soups and stews. They are also wonderful cooked with and combined with carrots or potatoes or turnips.

nutrition

About 100g of peeled, cooked, and drained parsnips will yield: 81 calories, 1.32g protein, 19.53g carbohydrates, 2.2g fiber, 37mg calcium, .58mg iron, 29mg magnesium, 69mg phosphorus, 367mg potassium, 10mg sodium, and traces of zinc, copper, and manganese; 13mg vitamin C, .083mg thiamine, .051mg riboflavin, .724mg niacin, .588mg pantothenic acid, .093mg vitamin B_6, 58.2mg folacin, and no cholesterol. Note the especially high quantities of potassium, vitamin C, and folacin.

CRISP HERBED PARSNIP CHIPS

Serves 4 to 6

These chips are so good to snack on you might serve them often. If you do, try varying the dried herbs in the recipe to tilt the taste in different directions. Try pairing cumin and paprika, basil and marjoram, curry powder and a pinch of cayenne, avoiding the herbs that were used to flavor previous, accompanying, or subsequent dishes on your menu. Pass these chips with drinks or serve them as a snack.

1 **pound parsnips, peeled**	½ **teaspoon dried thyme, crumbled**
2 **tablespoons coarse (kosher) salt**	½ **teaspoon white pepper**
½ **teaspoon dried oregano, crumbled**	**Peanut or corn oil for deep-frying**

Shave the parsnips lengthwise into thin strips using a swivel-bladed vegetable peeler. Set aside. In a small bowl, combine the salt, oregano, thyme, and white pepper, and set aside.

In a deep fryer or heavy saucepan, heat 2 inches of oil to 375° F. Fry the parsnip strips in small batches until they are golden, and transfer them with a slotted spoon to paper towels to drain. Sprinkle the reserved herb mixture over the chips, and transfer them to a napkin-lined serving basket. Serve immediately.

NOTE: Herbed or plain, other root vegetables make wonderful chips. Try rutabagas, carrots, celeriac, turnips, beets, salsify, sweet potatoes—even ginger.

PARSNIP PUREE WITH PEAS AND SCALLIONS

Serves 6

This puree is especially delicious with a felicitous combination of flavors dominated, of course, by sweet, earthy parsnips. Plates will be cleaned, we guarantee.

1½ pounds parsnips, peeled and cut into 1-inch pieces

2 large boiling potatoes (about ¾ pound), peeled and cut into 1-inch pieces

4 tablespoons (½ stick) unsalted butter, cut into bits and left at room temperature

1 cup frozen peas

2 scallions, white and green parts, minced

½ cup milk, at room temperature
Salt and freshly ground black pepper to taste

Place the parsnips and potatoes in a saucepan and add enough cold water to cover by 1 inch. Bring the water to a boil and add salt to taste. Boil for 10 minutes, or until the vegetables are tender.

Meanwhile, in a small saucepan or skillet melt 1 tablespoon of the butter over moderate heat. Add the frozen peas and cook, stirring, for 1 minute, or until heated through; transfer to a bowl. Add the scallions, the remaining butter, and the milk.

Drain the parsnips and potatoes, return them to the pan, and steam them over moderate heat, shaking or stirring, for 30 seconds, or until any excess liquid has evaporated. Force the parsnips and potatoes through a ricer or a food mill fitted with the medium disk into the bowl containing the peas and scallions. Add salt and pepper to taste, and stir the mixture to combine well. Transfer to a warm serving bowl.

NOTE: Not that this puree needs anything more, but, if you like, 2 or 3 tablespoons grated Parmesan mixed in along with the salt and pepper before serving is an elegant addition.

PARSNIPS WITHOUT ORNAMENTATION

Serves 8

Parsnips have such a sweet, distinctive flavor that they can and should be served *au naturel* every so often, just so the taste can be savored unadorned. This dish proves the maxim: It is prudent to leave well enough alone.

⅔ cup water or canned chicken broth

¼ cup (½ stick) butter or margarine or a combination of both

1 teaspoon salt

½ teaspoon white pepper

2 pounds parsnips, peeled and shredded on a coarse grater

1 tablespoon chopped fresh parsley for garnish

In a large saucepan, bring the water, butter, salt, and pepper to a boil over moderately high heat. Add the parsnips. Cover, reduce heat to a simmer, and cook, stirring occasionally, for 10 minutes, or until tender. Nearly all the liquid will have been absorbed. Transfer to a warm serving dish and sprinkle with the parsley.

FROSTED SPICED PARSNIP CAKE

Serves 10 to 12

If you like carrot cake, you'll love this parsnip cake. It's fragrant with spices, moist and chewy, and offers the surprise of nuts and currants. We offer it with a cream cheese icing—but it's terrific served plain or with a dusting of confectioners' sugar to pretty it up. It's yet another in the growing list of dessert cakes made with vegetables that not even an inveterate hater of the healthy stuff (kids, for instance) can resist.

4 large eggs
2 cups granulated sugar
1½ cups canola or corn oil
2 cups all-purpose flour, sifted
2 teaspoons baking soda
½ teaspoon salt
2 teaspoons ground cinnamon
2 tablespoons minced fresh gingerroot

½ teaspoon powdered mustard
½ teaspoon freshly grated nutmeg
1 cup chopped pecans
½ cup currants
2 cups grated peeled parsnips
   (about 1½ pounds)
   Cream Cheese Frosting (recipe
   follows) or confectioners' sugar
   (optional)

Preheat the oven to 350° F.

Butter a 12-inch round cake pan.

In the large bowl of an electric mixer on medium speed, beat the eggs into the granulated sugar, 1 at a time, incorporating each thoroughly before adding the next. Beat the oil into the egg mixture, then add the flour, baking soda, salt, cinnamon, ginger, mustard, and nutmeg, beating to incorporate thoroughly.

With a spatula or with an electric mixer on low speed, fold in the nuts, currants, and grated parsnips, combining well.

Pour the batter into the prepared cake pan and bake in the center of the oven for 1 hour and 20 minutes. Remove the cake from the oven and let cool, faceup, on a wire rack. Invert the cake onto a serving platter and ice with Cream Cheese Frosting or dust with confectioners' sugar or serve plain.

CREAM CHEESE FROSTING

8 ounces cream cheese, at room
   temperature
¼ cup (½ stick) unsalted butter, at
   room temperature

1 cup confectioners' sugar
2 teaspoons vanilla extract, or 1
   tablespoon Frangelico liqueur
12 pecan halves (optional)

In the bowl of an electric mixer on medium-high speed, beat all the ingredients together until smooth. With a metal spatula, frost the top and sides of the cake. Decorate the top edge of the cake with the pecan halves, if desired.

PARSNIP MAPLE PIE WITH PECAN CRUST

Makes one 9-inch deep-dish pie

It's not often you see parsnips served as dessert these days although they were once considered an elegant way to end a meal in Europe. This is a delicious, spicy pie with a crust that, prebaked, can hold chocolate mousse, lemon chiffon, or dozens of other refrigerated fillings. It can also add new character to an oven-baked pumpkin or mince pie or an apple, peach, or pear tart. Serve accompanied by whipped cream or vanilla ice cream and additional maple syrup.

crust

1 cup pecans	½ teaspoon salt
2 tablespoons sugar	3 tablespoons ice water
1½ cups all-purpose flour	
6 tablespoons (¾ stick) cold un-salted butter, cut into pieces	

filling

2 pounds parsnips, peeled and cut in ½-inch dice	1 teaspoon cinnamon
1 cup half-and-half	1 teaspoon powdered ginger
3 large eggs, lightly beaten	¼ teaspoon ground cloves
¾ cup pure maple syrup	⅛ teaspoon ground mace
1 teaspoon maple extract	½ teaspoon salt

Preheat the oven to 425° F.

In a food processor, pulse the pecans with the sugar just until coarsely ground, then transfer to a bowl. Without wiping out the processor work bowl, blend together the flour, butter, and salt until the mixture resembles coarse meal. Add this to the pecan mixture along with the ice water. With a fork toss the mixture together until the water is incorporated, and press the dough into the bottom and up the sides of a 9-inch deep-dish pie pan, crimping the edge decoratively with your fingers. Prick the crust all over with a fork and chill it for 30 minutes.

Line the crust with foil, fill with dried beans or rice, and bake the crust in the middle of the oven for 7 minutes. Remove the beans or rice and foil, and bake the crust for 5 minutes more. Let cool before filling.

On a steamer rack set over briskly boiling water, steam the diced parsnips for 12 to 15 minutes, or until they are very tender. Remove the steamer rack and let the parsnips cool and dry. Force them through a ricer or a food mill into a bowl. You should have about 2½ cups.

Whisk in the half-and-half, eggs, maple syrup, maple extract, cinnamon, ginger, cloves, mace, and salt until the filling is smooth.

Preheat the oven to 350° F.

Pour the filling into the crust, smoothing the top with a rubber spatula. Bake the pie in the middle of the oven for 40 to 45 minutes, or until it is just set in the middle. Remove and let cool on a rack. Serve slices of the pie topped with whipped cream or vanilla ice cream and drizzled with the maple syrup.

NOTE: You can substitute 2½ cups sweet potato puree or carrot puree for the parsnips without changing the proportions of any of the other ingredients. Serving suggestions remain the same as well.

CREAM OF PARSNIP SOUP WITH FENNEL AND ONION

Makes about 8 cups; serves 6 to 8

Parsnips combine well with another vegetable little used in this country, anise-flavored fennel. Here they meld into a lovely soup in which the texture of the vegetables can be retained—or it can be smoothed away by pureeing them in batches in a blender or food processor. This soup can also be served cold, in which case you should cool the mixture without the yogurt, salt, and pepper. Just before serving, whisk in the yogurt and season well.

6 **tablespoons (¾ stick) unsalted butter**
1 **pound parsnips, peeled and cut into ¼-inch dice (a scant 3 cups)**
1 **pound fennel bulbs (about 1 large), cut into ¼-inch dice (about 3 cups), some chopped feathery tops retained for garnish**

1 **medium onion, finely chopped**
¼ **cup all-purpose flour**
5 **cups homemade chicken stock, canned chicken broth, or vegetable stock**
1 **cup plain yogurt, sour cream, or crème fraîche**
Salt and freshly ground black pepper to taste

In a soup kettle or large sauté pan, melt the butter over moderate heat and, when the foam subsides, add the parsnips, fennel, and onion. Cook, stirring often, for 15 minutes, or until the vegetables are softened. Add the flour and cook the roux, stirring, for 3 minutes.

Turn the heat to high and pour in the stock. Bring the liquid to a boil, stirring occasionally, then reduce the heat and simmer the mixture for 20 minutes.

Reduce heat to low and add the yogurt, salt to taste, and a generous amount of pepper. Stir until heated through, and divide the soup among heated soup plates. Garnish with the reserved fennel tops.

POTATOES

[*SOLANUM TUBEROSUM*]

spud

Irish potato

pomme de terre (Fr.)

aardappel (Dut.)

patata, tartuffo (Sp.)

kartoffel (Ger.)

patata (It.)

kartofel (Rus.)

cartof (Rom.)

> [The potato is] the most important, if less acclaimed, of all the Spanish
> discoveries and conquests.
> —Redcliffe N. Salman, *The History and Social Influence of the Potato*

P er unit of land and time, potatoes provide more protein and calories than any other food crop—five times more than wheat, corn, or soybeans. Even with unfavorable conditions such as limited irrigation and fertilizer, they yield about *10,000 pounds an acre.*

Amazingly, as valuable as the potato is as a food plant, only its tubers are harmless. All other parts of the plant contain poisonous substances which, although not always fatal if ingested, are certainly quite harmful. This is what comes of being part of the nightshade family, as in *deadly nightshade*. But, then again, tomatoes are also its close cousins, as are the sweet bell peppers, hot peppers, eggplant, and tobacco—all harmless except for tobacco. There are two thousand species in the potato's botanical genus, *Solanum*—a mere eight, with variations, are cultivated commercially.

Surprisingly, China grows 19 percent of the world's potatoes and potatoes were grown in Taiwan as early as 1650, only a century before being introduced in Europe. Russia got them in the seventeenth century by way of Peter the Great, who served them at royal banquets after being introduced to them in Holland. Russian peasants, however, considered them unclean and un-Christian, calling them Devil's Apples. It took royal edicts, heavy public-relations efforts, and just plain *threats* to earn potatoes their role as an essential part of the Russian diet.

Potatoes made their way to Europe via sixteenth-century Spanish explorers (read: exploiters), who brought potatoes back home from their travels to Peru, Ecuador, and Colombia. Spanish pigs were the first to enjoy them. Others in Europe grew them solely for their flowers and ornamental foliage, as did the Japanese, who first encountered potatoes in the seventeenth century, when Dutch seamen brought them. Not until Commodore Perry got the emperor to try the tubers did their uses stop being purely ornamental and become nutritional.

Like many foods, potatoes gained a reputation for having curative powers. They were prescribed for gout, sunburn (used topically), sore throat, lumbago, bruises, rheumatism (if carried on one's person), and toothache. The Irish were sure that potato cooking water would heal sprains and broken bones. This same water, the Dutch believed, could cause warts, yet those very same warts could be removed by rubbing them with a cut potato.

One thing potatoes were used for—and they worked, for good scientific reasons—was to prevent scurvy among ships' crews (and those left behind on land, too, who lacked vitamin C in their diets). As soon as Spain began shipping back the wealth plundered from the Peruvian mines and the South American Indians in general, potatoes became basic ships' stores, eaten to prevent scurvy, and consequently they began to be cultivated on both sides of the Atlantic.

However beneficial seafarers may have found potatoes, doctors well into the eighteenth century blamed them for causing all kinds of diseases: rickets, flatulence (beans and the cabbage family were upstaged), scrofula (a word read but not often looked up), syphilis (perversely, it was also supposed to cure it), indigestion, and leprosy (the French forbid the cultivation of potatoes because of this erroneous conjecture and not until late in the eighteenth century was the ban lifted).

In some towns in Massachusetts colony, potatoes were considered the spoor of witches. Why they were singled out as "bad seed" we're not sure. Perhaps it was because they were new, different, and matured unseen beneath the earth (the Devil's playground). Possibly the reason it took so long for people to trust the potato was that so many people, small farmers among them, suffered from eating the poisonous leaves and berries of the plant instead of the tubers.

It wasn't until the end of the eighteenth century that potatoes began to receive a modicum of respect as viable produce. Their chief champion then was French chemist Antoine-Augustine Parmentier. Does that name sound familiar? It should. To this day the elegant way to say potato soup is *potage Parmentier.* As a prisoner during the Seven Years' War in Germany, Parmentier subsisted mainly on potatoes, which, it was thought at the time, were only fit for pigs and criminals. He remembered this agricultural savior when he returned home, and after the famine of 1770 wrote a prizewinning paper on the potato, *Inquiry into Nourishing Vegetables That in Times of Necessity Could Be Substituted for Ordinary Food.* When Ben Franklin was serving the colonies in France, he dined at Parmentier's home on a menu consisting exclusively of potato courses, even the after-dinner liqueur (except for the liqueur, we've done the same at home and at friends' houses several times—try it!). Franklin probably passed

Parmentier's award-winning paper on to Thomas Jefferson who gave the paper a place in his library and potatoes a place in his garden.

By 1785 Parmentier was said to have presented Louis XVI a basket of potatoes for his birthday, along with a bouquet of potato flowers that Marie Antoinette immediately appropriated, placing blossoms and buds in her outsized coiffure. Apocryphal or not, the story circulated and potatoes and their flowers—believed to have received royal favor— became the rage, serving potatoes at court dinners *de rigueur*, and the populace of course followed suit. After his death, statues were erected in Parmentier's honor; potatoes are still planted on his grave in Paris and an annual banquet by the gastronomic society, the Academie Parmentier, fetes its patron.

Sir Francis Drake or Sir Walter Raleigh, in 1580 or 1586, brought potatoes to the attention of Queen Elizabeth I. She was seemingly indifferent but, in any event, John Gerard, the barber-surgeon-botanist, published his comprehensive tome *Herbal* in 1597 and used as his frontispiece an illustration of himself holding a handful of potato blossoms. Even so, potatoes didn't catch on and they idled in the British Isles for more than a hundred years, being turned at one point into starch to use as hair powder instead of wheat flour, which was in short supply. The scarcity of wheat due to crop failures was a boon to potato promoters. It wasn't until the 1830s that Great Britain embraced the potato to any extent, though by 1898 the *Journal of the Royal Agricultural Society* was hailing the potato as "the noble tuber."

If England was slow to enjoy the virtues of *Solanum tuberosum*, Ireland, only sixty miles or so across the Irish Sea, was not. Whether potatoes were washed up on Irish shores along with wrecks of the Spanish Armada or found their way there through Raleigh or Drake, they were firmly in residence when Oliver Cromwell invaded the island in 1649 and destroyed the food crops. Potatoes, crafty little devils, could be stored and, therefore, hidden from view (and of course hid themselves while growing). The tubers nourished the natives despite Cromwell's scorched-earth policy. Salman wrote later that, "In the potato, people discovered a new weapon with which to withstand the oppression of their conquerors. In the great struggle which followed, it was, we believe, the potato which saved them from extermination and gave them the opportunity to effect a temporary recovery. From now on it was to prove itself a shelter to the people against the economic weapons of their enemies."

Is it any wonder, then, that a century later the Irish were consuming about eight pounds of potatoes per capita, not in a month, nor a week, but every day! If you consider that an average baking potato weighs about half a pound, that's sixteen potatoes a day per person. If you also take into account that per capita includes small children and babies, some adults must have consumed from twenty-five to fifty potatoes daily. An old Irish saying went something like: There are only two things too serious to joke about in Ireland—marriage and potatoes.

In a land where farms were tiny for the most part, enough potatoes to sustain a family of five or six could be grown on a mere one and a half acres, and it didn't take the labor or know-how that nurturing grains did, as potatoes depend more on nature then nurture. By 1840 half the Irish population (about 9 million at the time) rarely ate anything else. Even the Great Potato Famine of 1846, the worst of many similarly tragic crop failures that preceded it, did not sway the Irish's faith in their beloved tuber.

Potatoes also enjoyed great favor in America, where they arrived variously via the West Indies in 1613 and Irish immigrants in 1719. By the mid-nineteenth century the railroads carried promotion people who exhorted farmers along their rights-of-way to grow potatoes. State and county fairs had potato-judging contests, potato races, potato chip–eating contests, baked-potato cooking contests, and potatoes were soon growing in almost every state of the Union, Alaska included (where potatoes were brought from Siberia by Russian fur traders as early as 1783. They could be grown to within seventy miles of the Arctic Circle. How's that for hardy!).

In Maine the potato industry got under way in 1890, helped by the railroad that was built to ship lumber. So ideal were the growing conditions here that while the average take from an acre of potatoes in Aroostook County in the 1920s was 266 bushels, the average for the rest of the country was only 108 bushels. Today Maine has less land planted in potatoes than Idaho but more than Washington, both of which outrank Maine in production. Our biggest producer? If you guessed California, you are smarter than we were before we started this book.

Idaho potatoes are drier, mealier, and fluffier than those from Maine, which makes them perfect for baking and french fries. Maine potatoes have a higher water content. They're known as all-purpose potatoes (the varieties: Chippewas, Irish Cobblers, Katahdins, Sebagos, and Green

Mountains), good for boiling, potato salad, mashing, roasting, and what have you. What you have in Idaho is a business that is no small potatoes—somewhere around $2 billion a year in Russet Burbanks and White Rose varieties. The Russet is the descendant of one developed in 1873 by Luther Burbank, who found a seedball in his mother's Massachusetts garden and took it from there. Although the potato was brought to Idaho in 1836 by the Reverend Henry H. Spalding, it was not the kind that, today, involves the labor of nearly 20 percent of all Idahoans.

In the United States we consume more than 5 billion pounds of processed french fries alone every year. That's in addition to the freshly made fries fried at home and in better restaurant kitchens.

Potato chips account for another whopping statistic: nearly $4 billion in annual sales. New brands seem to appear on supermarket racks every week. Once known generically as Saratoga Chips for the New York horse-racing village and spa where they were born, potato chips are said to have been invented out of pique. In the 1850s, it is believed, George Crum, the chef at a Saratoga restaurant called Moon's Lake House, learned that a diner—the story sounds better when the anonymous gourmand becomes the legendary railroad magnate, Commodore Cornelius Vanderbilt—had complained that the french fries coming from the kitchen were too thick for his tastes. Angered by the criticism, Crum (who was an American Indian) took a batch of fresh potatoes, sliced them paper-thin, and plunged them into a pot of boiling oil. Vanderbilt, or whomever Crum then served them to, must have made a lot of noise about how wonderful they were, because they became a nationwide sensation—and today they are available in every flavor from mouth-searing jalapeño pepper, to cheddar and onion, garlic, barbecue, and the currently faddish Cajun.

Mashed potatoes were first known in this country as a Pennsylvania Dutch dish—which they ate long before potatoes caught on in the rest of the colonies—early in the eighteenth century, and were even called Dutch potatoes or German potatoes until the 1850s. Though Jefferson served french fried potatoes at Monticello and the White House, they didn't become fashionable until the 1870s and weren't commonly sought after until the 1900s. In the 1920s, they became "french frieds" and in the thirties the *d* was dropped, making them french *fries*. Now everyone knows what you want if you just order "fries."

In the 1840s, slang for the mouth was "potato trap," which was probably shortened to just "trap" later on, as in the expression "Shut your trap." To be patient and "Hold your horses" became, synonymously, "Hold your potatoes" during the Gay Nineties—don't ask us why. In the Roaring Twenties a sexually appealing flapper was known as a "hot potato," which in the 1930s was transliterated into "hot patootie." A "potato" was a dollar in the thirties and "potato head," a stupid, clumsy jerk in the fifties; a toy with the name Mr. Potato Head arrived in the sixties. The 1980s have spawned the term "couch potato," meaning an inveterate television watcher who hardly ever moves from his or her seat in front of the boob tube. By the way, "Spuds," our nickname for potatoes, comes from an old English word for a narrow-bladed or pronged spade used in digging up roots, called a *spud*.

All this from a tuber originally the size of a peanut grown by mountain Indians in the Andes, because at the elevations at which they lived (over 10,000 feet) corn wouldn't grow. Some of those potatoes grew to the size of plums. These the Indians ate, planting the smallest of the crop. This had the effect, through unnatural selection, of causing their *papas* to grow smaller and smaller year after year.

The Indians cultivated potatoes in a wide variety of colors, in addition to the white-fleshed kind we know. They ranged from deep royal purple to blue, from pink to scarlet, and a buttery yellow. A yellow variety called a "kidney potato" was the first to be grown in the colonies. Now the many white potatoes on the market are being joined by some of the "antique" strains, whose bizarre colors intrigue those food fashionists who want to serve guests only the very latest thing. This recent development, we hate to tell them, is as old as the Andean hills.

Most greengrocers codify potatoes by area of origin—from Maine to California. They rarely know them by anything more enlightening than old, new, baking, or all-purpose. Sometimes, like wholesalers, they classify them simply as round whites, round reds, russets, and long whites. To discover the difference in specific species you must consult a good seed catalog. As a shopper and cook you can look basically for two types: new potatoes and old potatoes.

New Potatoes

Varieties

These are those thin-skinned round potatoes with red, pink, or pale tan, sometimes peeling, skins. While not immature, they have not been left in the ground to grow a more leathery skin and manufacture more starch. New potatoes have what is known as a "waxy" texture that holds its shape well and is a good bet for boiling (the tiny ones are especially good just rinsed and boiled whole in their skins, served with a sprinkling of parsley or dill, and a little butter), roasting, casseroles, and potato salads (warm or cold). There are several kinds of new potatoes: (1) New Whites have a long oval shape and almost transparent, pale skins, which often seem to be peeling. They are clean and sometimes have a slightly green coloring (solanine residue, eliminated in cooking and not harmful). They appear from May to September, depending upon where they are harvested. (2) New Reds are like their white cousins, but round in shape with slightly heavier skins. You'll find them in stores from April to the late fall—a longer season because the northern varieties are heartier and keep longer. Small reds are sometimes called Bliss or Baby Bliss. (3) Pea or Peewees and French Fingerlings are tiny reds or whites culled from the harvest—about the size of marbles. They're hard to find but worth looking for. Cooked and served whole, they are a rare treat.

Availability

The peak season for all types of new potatoes is from late winter right through late spring.

Storage

You can put them in the refrigerator for a few days—but no more, or their sugar content will increase. New potatoes, in any case, should be used within two weeks or they will lose their unique character—their newness.

What to Look For

Thin, papery, peeling skins; small size, under 3 inches; pink or yellow-tan color; and roundish shape.

Basic Preparation and Cooking Methods

Simmer or steam small new potatoes whole and unpeeled. Larger ones should be quartered, sliced, or cubed. Place in cold water to cover, bring to a boil, reduce heat to a simmer, and cook for 8 to 12 minutes (or steam for the same amount of time in a steamer basket). Test for doneness—neither crisp nor soft, just slightly *al dente*. Also try simmering tiny new potatoes in bouillon or stock instead of water. It adds little to the cost but a lot to the flavor. Use larger new, waxy potatoes for mashing, if you like a smooth, unlumpy result.

OLD POTATOES

Varieties

These are usually dirt brown, more substantial in size, and come round or long. Their starch content is higher than that of new potatoes, their texture is "mealy," and their skins thicker and tougher. High starch and low moisture content gives them a drier texture when baked. They are the ones to choose for mashing and for french fries. The russet—often called an Idaho—is the best known "old potato." Long whites are similar in appearance and are usually the ones in the market called all-purpose. They are not quite as fluffy as the russet when baked and, to our taste, do not have as distinctive and potatoey a flavor. Buy the type of potato that works best in the recipe you plan to prepare (the cold potato salad on page 214 works best with the all-purpose for instance, just because some of the pieces of boiled potato break up and add a decided creaminess to the texture of the salad). There are several kinds of old potatoes: (1) Idaho Bakers are unique and grow to white, fluffy-fleshed, thick-skinned perfection only in the volcanic ash and mineral-rich soil of the Idaho foothills. They are harvested in late summer and early fall, sorted, packed, stored, and shipped all over the United States for the following nine months. There are five commercial sizes: 70, 80, 90, 100, and 120 potatoes to the box. The 70s are enormous and must bake for almost 1½ hours. The 90s or 100s are deluxe and more than adequate in size. (2) Maines are the best for soups and mashed potatoes. They are left in the ground well past the first frost and are sold throughout the fall, winter, and spring. They are big and brown and dirty and must be thoroughly scrubbed or peeled before cooking. (3) California Russets also called California Leatherbacks have a rough-textured, leathery skin and are wonderful baked. The harvest season is short—the last few weeks of August, ending in early September. Look for dark skins and a long oval shape. Not available much after Idahos come back onto the market, look for them only the few weeks after Idahos run out.

Availability

Except the California Russets, you'll find these pretty much all year round because they can be commercially stored for up to twelve months.

Storage

Put them in a cool, nonhumid, dark place with good ventilation and you can store these potatoes for two or three months. Don't leave them in direct sunlight or they might start to grow, get sunburned, or soften. Moist environments, especially plastic bags, promote spoilage. Potatoes sitting in storage change in chemical content; the starch diminishes while the sugar increases. To reverse this chemical reaction, take the potatoes out of the storage bin, root cellar, or refrigerator and keep them at room temperature for a week or so before using them, even up to the point where the eyes begin to show little white sprouts. The starch content will have been restored along with the nutritional value, so the waiting period is worth it.

What to Look For

Select smooth, firm potatoes of even shape with mere dimples where the eyes are. If they give in to finger pressure and feel spongy, they have probably been frozen or improperly stored; reject them. They will have lost flavor, color, and mineral values, and their texture will be off when cooked. Irregular-shaped potatoes are fine, but are harder to peel. Don't buy any with discolored areas, cuts, bruises, or decay. Don't buy those with shriveled skins or sprouted eyes—they've been held too long. Green areas are called "sunburn" and indicate exposure to light and the production of a bitter-tasting toxin called solanine. If potatoes do have green areas on their skins or sprouted eyes (also containing solanine), simply cut them away—the solanine does not penetrate the whole potato. Sometimes growers and packers leave a protective layer of dirt on the skin to retard sunburn—just wash it off.

Basic Preparation and Cooking Methods

Potatoes should be scrubbed well before cooking. Cut away patches of green, if any, and any eyes that have begun to sprout. Peeled and cut potatoes begin to discolor quite quickly. If you are not using them immediately, cover them with cold water. Rinse or dry off, depending on end purpose, before using. For many recipes—even salads and casseroles—you don't have to peel potatoes except for aesthetic reasons. A good deal of the nutritional value is found just under the skin. *To bake potatoes,* dry them after scrubbing and pierce with a fork or the point of a knife in a few places to allow steam to escape. Rub with oil for a crisper skin or leave naked. Place them on an oven rack or baking sheet in a preheated 400° or 450° F. oven for 45 minutes to an hour. (If you are baking them with other dishes in a slower oven—350° to 375° F.—allow another 30 minutes of baking time.) A little overbaking is no problem. Never, ever wrap them in foil—the potato will be steamed, not baked. The best baked potatoes to our taste come out of a domed top-of-the-stove baker or from the oven when the potatoes are placed directly on the oven floor over the flame (gas ovens usually have the flame underneath the oven floor). Allow 20 minutes in a 400° or 450° F. oven on each side to crisp and char the skin, then place on the oven rack for the final 20 minutes. *Baked potatoes in a microwave* are not the same as those made in an oven, but they are faster. Use a low-moisture potato—Idaho Russets are best—wash but don't dry the potato, pierce with a fork at the center, wrap each in a microwave-safe paper towel to provide a moisture-controlled environment (the words of the Idaho Potato Commission). For ovens with cooking power of 500 to 700 watts, 1 8-ounce potato takes 4 to 5 minutes at full power; 2 potatoes 7 to 10 minutes; 3 potatoes 11 to 14 minutes; 4 potatoes 16 to 20 minutes. When microwaving several potatoes at once, arrange them like the spokes of a wheel or in a circle, end to end, about 1 inch apart. Wrap them separately. Though the potatoes may seem firm at the end of the cooking time, they will soften if allowed to stand on the counter for about 5 minutes. Overmicrowaving even for 1 or 2 minutes can make the potato soggy. Feel them to determine if more cooking is necessary.

nutrition

The potato is a carbohydrate-containing food. There are two kinds of carbohydrate categories: simple carbohydrates (refined sugar is one) and complex carbohydrates (the fruits, vegetables, and starches provide the other). Sugar is a source of energy, but nothing else. It offers no other nutrients and has what we call "empty calories." Potatoes fall into the category of complex carbohydrates which, while offering energy in the form of calories, are also jam-packed with vitamins, minerals, and pro-tein. They are virtually fat-free, have a minimum of natural sodium, and lots of fiber. Complex carbohydrates, contrary to popular belief, can help in weight-loss diets. Nothing satisfies like potatoes and their complex carbohydrate cousins. They make you feel "full" faster and help retain that feeling longer. You actually take in fewer calories while getting the kind of essential nutrients necessary for good health while on a restricted food-intake diet. They supply a steady source of energy rather than the spurt you get from simple carbohydrates.

One of the nice things about potatoes is that they come to you unrefined (wheat and other grains go through so much processing that often all that's left to eat is calories), just as nature made them. Like other tubers and roots, they are a storehouse of energy and nutrients that the above-ground plant feeds on, and they are, in effect, the "seed" of new plants. They have almost all you need to subsist on.

Because many of the potato's nutrients are in or just below the skin, you'll preserve these nutrients better if you boil, simmer, fry, roast, or sauté them in their skins. If you don't want to eat the skin for aesthetic reasons, yet want to retain most of the nutrients, peel them after cooking (this is only recommended for recipes that specify boiled potatoes, for obvious reasons). Studies show that a baked potato with its skin rivals our favorite, beans, in nutritional value and surpasses rice, pasta, and white bread (nutritional values without the skin are comparable). Boiled or baked potatoes in their jackets retain nearly all their vitamins.

A medium potato of 5 ounces has 110 calories (4 to 5 percent of the average calories recommended for adults daily), 6 percent of the recom-mended protein, 8 percent of the phosphorus, 20 percent of the vitamin B_6, 50 percent of the vitamin C (a medium Valencia orange has only 39 percent and a half grapefruit has about the same), 5 percent of the iron, 10 percent of the niacin, 8 percent of the folic acid (folacin), copper, and magnesium, 15 percent of the iodine, 2 percent of the riboflavin and zinc, 4 percent of pantothenic acid, and traces of calcium and vitamin A. A steak of comparable weight (5 ounces) has 500 calories, mostly from fat. The choice is obvious!

GOLDEN-FRIED POTATO WISPS DUSTED WITH GARLIC

Serves 4

In this recipe we use both the skins and flesh of the potatoes to make thin, narrow potato chips. If you've never tried them, the skins are almost better than the familiar chips. That's why, when we peel potatoes for a recipe, we scrub them first, collect the peelings, freeze them, and when we have enough, fry them up all by themselves. These garlicky chips are exactly right served with soup, a sandwich, or with any dish you'd ordinarily accompany with garlic bread.

4 large long oval white potatoes (about ½ pound each), scrubbed
Vegetable oil for deep-frying
Coarse (kosher) or table salt to taste

1 teaspoon minced garlic, or more to taste

Cut the potatoes lengthwise into ½-inch slices. Using a swivel-bladed vegetable peeler, shave long thin strips, including any skin, into a bowl of ice and water. Let them soak for 15 minutes, drain them well, and pat dry with paper towels. In a deep fryer or large saucepan, heat 2 inches of oil to 375° F. Fry the potatoes in batches for 1 minute, or until just golden, making sure the oil returns to 375° F. before adding the next batch. When done, transfer each batch with a slotted spoon to paper towels to drain. Sprinkle the potatoes with salt and garlic, while tossing gently. Serve warm.

GREAT MASHED POTATOES
WITH GARLIC AND ONIONS

Serves 4

- - - - - - - - -

Better than plain mashed potatoes. So much better, in fact, you could double the recipe and still run out. What's also nice to contemplate is that these mashed potatoes taste terrific even though they're not laced with butter and cream, chicken fat, or cheese. Without the optional butter they're completely cholesterol-free—but don't taste like it.

2 pounds yellow (Yukon or Finn-ish) potatoes or russet baking potatoes, peeled and cut into 1-inch pieces

4 large garlic cloves, peeled and quartered

1 large yellow onion, coarsely chopped

Unsalted butter to taste (optional)

Salt and white pepper to taste

In a steamer basket set over boiling water, steam the potatoes, onion, and garlic for 15 to 20 minutes, or until quite tender. Remove the steamer basket from the pan, reserving the liquid.

Force the potatoes, onion, and garlic through a ricer or food mill into a serving bowl (or transfer to a work bowl and puree with a potato masher). Stir in the butter, if desired, and ⅓ to ½ cup of the reserved hot cooking liquid, or just enough to achieve a nice smooth consistency. Season with salt and white pepper and serve immediately—or keep hot in a heavy-bottomed pan over low heat; stir well just before serving.

NOTE: Instead of the cooking liquid you can add the traditional hot cream or milk, but try these mashed potatoes our way first and see if the extra calories are necessary.

We will bury the following in this note, because we don't want to be the cause of anyone's demise (but what a way to go!): Unless you were brought up in an Eastern European or Jewish household, you probably have never tasted the most delicious of all mashed potatoes—the ones our mothers used to make mixed with the darkly browned onions and cracklings left from rendering chicken fat. If you don't have an addictive personality and are willing to risk your health to taste one of the most sublime dishes of all time, render about ¼ pound chicken fat with a couple of medium onions, sliced, a small chopped carrot, and a little water, all set over moderately low heat. When the fat has melted completely and the onions are very dark brown, mix it all, along with a lot of salt and pepper, into hot mashed potatoes. This is living—or its converse if one overindulges.

BARBECUED POTATOES IN GARLIC MARINADE

Serves 4 to 8

This is a marvelous way to serve potatoes outdoors. They're partially baked (this can be done way ahead) then marinated and grilled. The resulting crusty, golden brown nuggets are garlicky, tangy, and smoky tasting all at once. They can also be done indoors, under the broiler, if your tastebuds can't wait until cook-out weather.

4 large russet baking potatoes (about ½ pound each), scrubbed
1 cup Vinaigrette Dressing (page 216)

4 garlic cloves crushed through a press
Salt and pepper to taste

At least 1½ hours (or up to 24 hours) before placing potatoes on the grill, bake them at high heat (450° F.) for about 30 minutes or until they just begin to yield under finger pressure but are not cooked through. While hot, cut them in half lengthwise, then cut each half into quarters, Place the pieces in a mixing bowl or baking dish. Whisk the crushed garlic into the vinaigrette dressing and pour over the hot potatoes. Marinate for 1 hour or more, turning occasionally. Remove potatoes from vinaigrette (reserving the dressing left behind for another use) before placing on the grill. Grill the pieces for about 10 minutes on each side or until golden brown. Sprinkle with salt and pepper and serve hot.

BROILER-FRIED POTATOES WITH FRESH BASIL AND OLIVE OIL

Serves 4

- - - - - - - - -

A friend's Italian mother used to serve these potatoes at the lavish and multicoursed barbecues she made at her country house. First there would be Gorgonzola and butter–stuffed stalks of celery and fennel with drinks; then various homemade sausages; marinated mushrooms; tender raw asparagus under olive oil and slivers of Parmesan; seafood salad; marinated artichokes; several fresh and dried pasta dishes; thick slices of fresh tomatoes; deep-fried squash blossoms; barbecued steaks; slabs of liver and lamb from the grill. By the time platters of these crispy potato marvels were passed around we were so stuffed we could hardly eat another bite — but, of course, we did. As many of these potatoes as this gifted lady could provide, we could put away.

⅓ cup extra-virgin olive oil

4 medium Idaho baking potatoes, peeled and sliced ¼ inch thick

1½ teaspoons salt, or to taste

1 teaspoon freshly ground black pepper

½ cup chopped fresh basil

Preheat the broiler.

Line a baking sheet or jelly-roll pan with foil. Brush the foil with 2 tablespoons of the olive oil. In a medium bowl, drizzle the remaining olive oil over the potatoes, sprinkle with salt and pepper, and toss to coat well.

Arrange the oiled potato slices in the pan so that they just touch but do not overlap. Drizzle any oil remaining in the bowl over the potatoes and broil them 5 or 6 inches from the heat until golden brown, about 12 minutes. With metal tongs turn the potatoes over, taking care not to tear the foil, and broil them about 10 minutes longer. Check to prevent burning, and continue broiling 2 minutes more, or until golden brown.

Remove the pan from the oven, transfer the potatoes to a heated serving dish, sprinkle with the basil, toss lightly, and serve immediately.

CRUSTY FRENCH FRIES

Serves 4

Water can make the hot fat spray when deep-frying potatoes, and even experienced cooks can forget to dry them well. Sally received a nasty burn several years ago when, distractedly, she threw a handful of un-dried potatoes into hot fat and it erupted like "Old Faithful." In order to deter accidents like this, we dry off the potato strips and then dredge them in cornstarch, which prevents them from absorbing oil and gives them a crunchy crust as well.

4 baking potatoes (about ½ pound each), well scrubbed or peeled
1 cup cornstarch
  Salt and freshly ground black pepper to taste

Peanut, safflower, or corn oil for deep-frying

Cut the potatoes into long strips about ⅜ x ⅜ x 3 inches. Place them between layers of paper towels to dry.

On a flat dinner plate, mix the cornstarch with salt and pepper. Dredge the strips of potato a few at a time in the cornstarch and shake off the excess.

Heat several inches of oil in a pan until a frying thermometer reads 360° F. As they are dredged, add the potato strips to the hot oil without crowding, moving them around with a spoon or fork, until they are golden brown. Lift them out with tongs or a slotted spoon and drain on paper towels. Repeat, frying dredged potato strips (return oil to 360° F. before adding) in small batches. Sprinkle with salt, if you wish, and keep them hot in a warm, 300° F. oven, until all are done.

Potato Soup with Dill and Scallions

Serves 6

A family recipe, this classic potato soup has its origins in the Ukraine. Russians and Ukrainians invariably use dill in their soups, and dill is what gives this one its stature.

3 tablespoons unsalted butter

2 medium onions, chopped

1 tablespoon minced garlic

3 carrots (about ½ pound) peeled and cut into ¼-inch dice

6 all-purpose potatoes (about 2 pounds), peeled and cut into ½-inch dice

1 bay leaf

2 cloves

1 teaspoon salt, or to taste

1 teaspoon freshly ground black pepper, or more to taste

4 cups homemade chicken stock or canned broth

¼ cup snipped fresh dill

¾ cup chopped scallions, white and green parts, for garnish

In a soup pot or large sauté pan, melt the butter over moderate heat. When the foam subsides, sauté the onions and garlic, stirring frequently, until soft and transparent; do not brown. Stir in the carrots and sauté, stirring occasionally, for 2 to 3 minutes more. Add the potatoes and cook, stirring occasionally, for 5 minutes. Add the bay leaf, cloves, 1 teaspoon salt, and 1 teaspoon pepper, and stir in the stock. Raise the heat to high, cover, and bring to a boil, then reduce heat to a simmer and cook the mixture for 30 minutes, or until the potatoes are tender.

With a slotted spoon, transfer the vegetables in batches to a food processor and puree (coarse or smooth, depending on your taste). Return the puree to the soup pot and whisk to combine well. The soup may be made ahead to this point. When ready to serve, reheat over moderately low heat. To serve, taste and add additional salt and pepper, if needed, stir in the dill, ladle into heated soup bowls, and garnish each bowl with the chopped scallions. To serve chilled and creamed, add 1 cup plain yogurt, sour cream, or heavy cream along with the dill and stir to combine well.

POTATO CHIP SOUP (YES, POTATO CHIP SOUP)

Serves 8

Don't laugh. Although it may seem like one of those back-of-the-package recipes that are more to laugh at than to eat, it's not. It's really good. We should know; we've cooked it often and served it to family and friends for over three decades.

2 tablespoons peanut oil

2 medium onions, peeled, cut in half and thinly sliced

1 small celeriac, peeled and cut into ½-inch dice

1 large carrot, peeled and chopped

1 small turnip, peeled and cut into ½-inch dice

6 cups homemade chicken stock, canned broth, or water

3 tablespoons snipped fresh dill

1 6.5-ounce bag good-quality potato chips, salted or unsalted, crushed

1 teaspoon salt, or to taste

1 teaspoon freshly ground black pepper

1 cup milk or half-and-half

In a soup pot or large saucepan over moderately high heat, bring the oil to rippling. Add the onions and sauté for 3 minutes, stirring. Reduce heat to moderate and continue cooking, stirring occasionally, for 7 minutes more, or until the onions are golden brown. Stir in the celeriac, carrot, and turnip and cook the mixture, stirring frequently, for 5 minutes.

Add the stock and bring to a boil, then reduce heat to a simmer. Stir in 2 tablespoons of the dill and the potato chips and cook the mixture, covered, for 20 to 30 minutes, or until the vegetables are very tender.

In a blender or food processor, puree half the soup (in batches, if necessary) and return it to the pot. Stir in the salt, pepper, and milk; return the soup to a simmer and cook 2 minutes longer. Ladle the soup into bowls and garnish with some of the remaining dill, or transfer the soup to a tureen and serve it at the table, garnishing each bowl with a little dill.

RUSSIAN POTATO AND FARMER CHEESE-FILLED PIROGI IN SOUR CREAM DOUGH

Makes about 30 to 36 pirogi

- -

You can serve these Russian/Polish pastries as a first course or a main course. They are often eaten (read: devoured!) topped with lots of melted browned butter or sour cream mixed with snipped dill, but there is no law against nestling them beneath a garlicky tomato sauce or meat sauce. We've often had them with sautéed onions or sprinkled with Parmesan cheese and olive oil. The classic sour cream dough is the preferred enclosure for these little half-moon shapes called in Russian *poloomyesyats*. They can be boiled as they are in this recipe or spread on a greased and lightly floured cookie sheet, brushed with an egg wash, and baked in a 400° F. oven for about 15 minutes, or until they are golden brown.

pastry dough

- - - - - - - - - - -

3½ cups sifted unbleached all-purpose flour
1 teaspoon baking powder
1 teaspoon salt
½ cup (1 stick) unsalted butter, cut into small pieces

2 large eggs, beaten
1 cup (8 ounces) sour cream
1 large egg yolk beaten with 1 teaspoon cold water (for egg wash)

filling

- - - - - - -

1½ pounds Idaho potatoes, peeled and quartered
3 tablespoons olive oil
1 medium to large onion, minced
¾ pound farmer or pot cheese

1½ teaspoons salt, or to taste
1 teaspoon freshly ground black pepper
½ cup (1 stick) unsalted butter

In a medium bowl, thoroughly combine the flour, baking powder, and 1 teaspoon salt. With your fingers or a pastry cutter, working quickly, rub the flour mixture and ½ cup butter together until it resembles coarse meal. In another bowl, beat the eggs and the sour cream together until they are combined well; add the mixture to the flour and butter and stir together with a wooden spoon (or use your hands, they're much more effective).

When well combined, turn the dough out onto a floured surface and knead until it is smooth and pliable (about 3 minutes), adding more flour, if necessary, to prevent sticking. Divide the dough in half, and shape each half into a ball. Lightly flour them and chill for 30 minutes or longer.

To prepare the filling, place the potatoes in a medium saucepan and cover with cold salted water. Bring to a boil over high heat, reduce heat to moderate, cover, and cook until tender, about 15 to 20 minutes. Meanwhile, in a small skillet or sauté pan, bring the olive oil to rippling over moderate heat. Add the onion and cook, stirring occasionally, until the onion is soft and just beginning to turn golden, about 5 to 8 minutes.

Drain the cooked potatoes and, in a medium bowl, mash them with a potato masher. Add the sautéed onions, farmer cheese, and 1½ teaspoons salt and the pepper and mix well.

On a floured surface with a floured rolling pin, roll each piece of dough as thin as possible, no thicker than ⅛ inch. Using a 3-inch-round cookie cutter or glass tumbler, press out circles of the dough. Gather the scraps together, roll out again, and cut into more rounds.

Fill each circle with 1 teaspoon of the potato filling. Brush the edges with the egg wash, fold the dough over into half-moons, and press with your fingertips to seal. Press again with the tines of a fork (it looks pretty and ensures the seal). Place the pirogi on a floured towel.

In a large kettle or saucepan, bring several quarts of salted water to a boil over high heat. Add half the pirogi and cook for 3 minutes after they rise to the surface. With a slotted spoon, transfer the first batch to a heatproof serving dish to keep warm in a low oven while you cook the remaining pirogi.

Meanwhile, in the same small skillet used to sauté the onion, cook ½ cup butter over moderate heat until it starts to brown, about 3 or 4 minutes. Drizzle the butter over the pirogi and serve.

Rösti
Potatoes—Traditional
Swiss Fried Potato Cake

Serves 4 to 6

This is *the* potato dish of German-speaking Switzerland where most people eat it at one meal or another every day of their lives. To make it properly, the potatoes should be shredded on a shredder the Swiss use especially for this dish. We would guess that you won't be eating this every day, so you will probably use the shredding side of your four-sided grater, or the shredding disk of your processor. If you possess neither of these pieces of equipment, cut the potatoes into fine julienne strips. For some reason the Swiss think *rösti* tastes best when the potatoes are cooked a day ahead. Not being Swiss, we think they're just dandy made the same day.

2 pounds all-purpose or new potatoes, scrubbed	¾ teaspoon salt
4 tablespoons (½ stick) unsalted butter	2 tablespoons hot water or hot beef or chicken broth

Cook the potatoes in boiling salted water to cover until just tender, about 15 or 20 minutes, depending on the size of the potatoes. Drain and cool. (This can be done the day before.) Peel and shred the potatoes.

Melt the butter in a large skillet over moderate heat and, when the foam subsides, add the potatoes and salt. When the potatoes are heated through, reduce the heat to simmer and continue cooking, turning frequently with a spatula, until the potatoes are soft and golden. Press the potatoes with a spatula into a flat cake, sprinkle with the hot water or broth, cover, and cook until the potatoes are crusty and golden on the bottom, about 15 to 20 minutes. Shake the pan frequently to avoid sticking. If they should happen to stick, loosen them carefully without breaking the crust until they slide in the pan and add a little more butter. Turn onto a hot serving dish, crusty side up, and serve immediately.

NOTE: If you are like us, the more crust the better, so instead of serving, slide the potatoes back into the skillet, crusty side up, and cook about 5 to 10 minutes longer. Slide back onto the platter and serve immediately in wedges.

VARIATIONS

1. In and around Berne they often make *rösti* by cooking 3 slices of diced bacon with 1 medium onion, minced, in the skillet before adding the potatoes. The onions are cooked until they are transparent and begin to turn golden. The Bernese do not brown the bacon or the onions. Because the *rösti* are cooked in the bacon fat, the butter can be cut back to 2 tablespoons. Continue as above.

2. Add ½ cup diced or shredded Gruyère, Emmentaler, or Jarlsberg to the potatoes as they cook, along with ½ teaspoon or more freshly ground pepper.

3. Not traditional, but delicious nonetheless, is to cook the sausage meat from two links of Italian sweet or hot sausage in 2 tablespoons of the butter before adding the potatoes, mix through, and continue the recipe. Sautéing 1 cup diced fennel with the sausage adds still another distinctive flavor to this classic.

4. Dried fruits are not traditionally added to *rösti*, but they are to other rural Swiss potato dishes and they can work equally well here. To the original recipe, add 1 medium onion minced and sautéed in 2 tablespoons of the butter until transparent; then mix in 1 cup dried sliced pears or apples (soaked in warm water for 30 minutes and drained). Sauté for a few minutes more and mix in the potatoes. Continue as above.

EVERYBODY'S FAVORITE
POTATO PANCAKES

Makes 16 to 20 pancakes

Lots of pepper makes our potato pancakes special. And, of course, not being niggardly with the onions. We don't peel the potatoes either, nor do we add flour or matzo meal. One egg for 3 pounds of potatoes is enough to just hold them together, more makes them too wet. We make these pancakes often and never use a recipe—but for this book we had to measure and test. Feel free to go overboard or underboard on any of the ingredients. It doesn't seem to hurt. The amount the recipe makes depends on the size of your spoon.

6 medium baking potatoes (about 3 pounds), well scrubbed
1 large onion (about 2½ inches across), peeled
1 large egg, lightly beaten
2 teaspoons salt, or to taste
1 tablespoon freshly ground black pepper

Peanut, safflower, or canola oil for frying
Apple sauce as an accompaniment (optional)
Sour cream as an accompaniment (optional)

Grate the potatoes on a flat grater set over a large sieve fitted over a medium work bowl. Let the potatoes drain through the sieve into the bowl for a minute or two, then carefully pour off the accumulated liquid, retaining the starch that has settled to the bottom. Stir the grated potatoes into the starch. Grate the onion into the potato mixture. Add the egg, salt, and pepper and mix to combine well.

Preheat the oven to 300° F. Line a jelly-roll pan with a double thickness of paper towels.

In a large sauté pan or high-sided skillet, bring ¼ inch of oil almost to the smoking point over high heat. Reduce heat to moderately high and spoon about 2 tablespoons (or a large work spoon) of the batter into the pan. Repeat until the pan is full but not crowded. Reduce heat to moderate and cook the pancakes about 5 minutes, or until the bottoms are browned and crisp. With a spatula, turn the pancakes and cook the other side 3 to 5 minutes more, or until browned and crisp. Repeat with the rest of the batter. Transfer each batch when done to the jelly-roll pan to drain. Keep the pancakes warm in the oven until all are ready. Serve immediately with or without applesauce or sour cream.

NOTE: The potatoes may be grated by cutting them in chunks and pulsing them a few times in the food processor. This can be done in batches along with the onion that has been cut into large dice. The result should be drained in a sieve over a work bowl, the liquid drained from the bowl, and the starch retained and mixed into the potato-onion mixture as above.

Potato pancakes can also be a main course, especially if ¼-inch slices of all-beef frankfurters are stirred into the batter. Sliced salami or kielbasa can stand in for the frankfurters, if you'd rather.

Draining the liquid from the potatoes precludes needing to add flour, matzo meal, or bread crumbs to the batter. We find pancakes made with these additions can have the texture of library paste.

Instead of grating the potatoes, try shredding them. This gives the potato pancakes a lacy look and texture. Still grate the onions, however.

Making potato pancakes can keep the cook at the stove and away from the table out of earshot of the complements. Our sister-in-law, Barbara, devised a way to feed potato pancakes to a large crowd and still hear the accolades: Fry the pancakes up to 6 hours ahead and let them drain on double layers of paper towels. They will become limp and soggy, but don't worry. Just before serving, in a large sauté pan, get fresh oil very hot and refry the pancakes for a few seconds on each side to heat them through and give them a very crispy crust. Dozens of them can be refried within 15 or 20 minutes and held in a 300° F. oven until all are refried, and none will become soggy. Other friends have fried big batches ahead of time and recrisped them on cookie sheets in a very hot, 425° F., oven for 10 minutes. We've had no luck with this method, but perhaps we're too impatient to get to those pancakes and don't leave them in the oven long enough.

POTATO CAKES FLAVORED WITH MACE

Serves 6 as a side dish

These little potato cakes can be made in individual ramekins or in a muffin tin. Mace makes the difference. It is a highly aromatic spice that comes from the same tree as nutmeg. Nutmeg is the seed of the yellowish fruit of this tree; mace is the bright scarlet, netlike, fragile membrane surrounding the shell that encases the nutmeg seed inside the fruit. Dried and ground mace is usually orange in color.

2 pounds red or white new potatoes, peeled and coarsely grated (about 4 cups), turned into a sieve and allowed to drain

6 tablespoons unsalted butter, melted

¾ teaspoon salt

½ teaspoon white pepper

¼ teaspoon ground mace

Preheat the oven to 475° F.

Scrape the grated potatoes into a large bowl and mix in the melted butter, salt, pepper, and mace. Pack the potato mixture into 6 buttered ⅔-cup ramekins or a buttered 6-cavity muffin tin. If using ramekins, set them on a rimmed baking sheet. Bake the cakes until just browned around the edges, about 30 to 40 minutes. Remove the ramekins or muffin tin and let cool slightly. Loosen the sides of each cake with a small sharp knife and invert them onto a rimmed baking sheet and remove the ramekins or muffin tin. Brush the inverted cakes with any butter left in the molds. (The recipe may be prepared to this point and kept at room temperature for up to 2 hours in advance.) Reduce the oven temperature to 400° F. and bake until well browned and crisp, about 20 to 25 minutes. Serve hot.

POTATO AND WHITE BEAN SALAD WITH WHITE BEAN AND ROASTED PEPPER DRESSING

Serves 6

Potatoes are good for you. Beans are good for you. Together, we guess, they're better for you. All we can guarantee is that this salad is delicious with its unique, savory dressing.

1 **large red bell pepper**	2 **tablespoons red wine vinegar**
1½ **pounds small red new potatoes**	1 **tablespoon green peppercorn Dijon mustard**
3 **cups canned white cannellini beans, drained and rinsed well**	¼ **cup light olive oil**
3 **scallions, white and green parts, thinly sliced**	2 **tablespoons canola or safflower oil**
1 **teaspoon salt, or to taste**	1 **tablespoon Maggi seasoning**
½ **teaspoon freshly ground black pepper, or more to taste**	

Roast the pepper under the broiler at the end of a fork directly over a gas flame, turning until charred all over. Place the pepper in a paper or plastic bag, twist closed, and let steam for 10 minutes. Slip the skin off the pepper, core, seed, devein, and cut into small pieces.

Place the potatoes in a large saucepan of cold salted water and bring to a boil over high heat. Reduce heat to a simmer and cook until just tender, about 10 to 15 minutes, depending upon the size of the potatoes. Let the potatoes cool slightly, and cut into quarters. In a large serving bowl, toss the potatoes together with 2½ cups of the beans (reserving remaining ½ cup for the dressing), the scallions, 1 teaspoon salt, and ½ teaspoon pepper.

In a food processor, combine the vinegar, mustard, olive oil, canola oil, Maggi seasoning, reserved beans, and roasted pepper pieces. Puree for about 30 seconds. Pour the dressing over the potato and bean mixture and toss to coat. Taste and adjust the seasoning, adding more salt and pepper, if needed, and serve at room temperature.

CREAMY POTATO, CELERIAC, AND ONION SALAD

Serves 6 to 8

Most commercial potato salads and many made by home cooks have the consistency of library paste. All it takes is liquid to change that. If restaurants and delis who, naturally, want to make a profit on their food would just add a little water—not even costly milk or stock or wine—to their potato salad they would keep more friends and customers. Water also saves on the quantity of mayonnaise necessary to loosen up the salad. This in turn saves on calories and cholesterol. Try it. Even if you never liked potato salad before, we almost guarantee you'll become a convert.

2 pounds all-purpose potatoes (preferably yellow Yukons or Finnish)

1 medium to large celeriac (about 1 pound)

1 large Bermuda onion, finely chopped

2 teaspoons salt

1 teaspoon freshly ground black pepper

3 tablespoons chopped fresh parsley or snipped fresh dill

2 tablespoons powdered mustard

1 teaspoon Maggi seasoning

½ cup cold water

1¼ cups homemade mayonnaise (page 107) or good-quality bottled mayonnaise

Wash the potatoes thoroughly and place them in a large saucepan with cold water to cover. Bring to a boil over high heat, then reduce heat to a simmer and cook the potatoes, covered, for 25 minutes, or until the potatoes are tender but firm. Drain and cool.

Meanwhile, peel and cut the celeriac into quarters, and slice each quarter into ⅛-inch-thick triangles.

When the potatoes are cool enough to handle, peel them and slice them crosswise into ⅛-inch-thick rounds. In a large bowl, combine the potatoes, celeriac, onion, salt, pepper, and parsley and toss to combine.

In a small bowl, whisk the mustard and Maggi seasoning with the water until dissolved. Gradually whisk in the mayonnaise until the dressing is smooth. Pour the dressing over the potato mixture and toss with a wooden spoon until combined well. (Don't be concerned if you break up some of the potatoes; these bits will combine with the dressing to make a creamier texture.) Chill for several hours or, preferably, for 24 hours, to meld the flavors before serving.

NOTE: You can add 2 tablespoons capers or chopped olives to the salad or 1 or 2 tablespoons anchovy paste. When opting for these additions, it might be wise to add the salt to taste gradually after the salad has been mixed.

POTATO AND MUSSEL SALAD
WITH BASIL VINAIGRETTE

Serves 6

‑‑‑‑‑‑‑‑‑‑

Mussels are one of the most economical offerings in the fish market. Potatoes are equally thrifty. How is it, then, that together they make an almost opulent salad? This one is best at room temperature or only slightly chilled, so if you must make it ahead of time and refrigerate, let it sit out on a kitchen counter at least 30 minutes before serving.

vinaigrette

‑‑‑‑‑‑‑‑‑‑‑

¼ cup freshly squeezed lemon juice

1 tablespoon Dijon mustard (preferably tarragon-flavored Dijon, if possible)

1 tablespoon Maggi seasoning

Salt and freshly ground black pepper to taste

¾ cup olive oil

¼ cup minced fresh basil

3 tablespoons minced fresh parsley

salad

‑‑‑‑‑‑

2 pounds small new potatoes, scrubbed

5 pounds mussels

1 celery rib, thinly sliced

3 radishes, thinly sliced

1 cup frozen peas, thawed

2 cups cherry tomatoes, cut in half

2 scallions, white and green parts, very thinly sliced

In a bowl, whisk together the lemon juice, mustard, Maggi seasoning, and salt and pepper to taste. Add the oil in a thin stream, whisking until it is combined and emulsified. Whisk in the basil and parsley. Set aside.

In a steamer set over boiling water, steam the potatoes, covered, for 8 minutes, or until they are just tender; transfer to a large bowl. Toss the potatoes with ½ cup of the reserved vinaigrette while they are hot, and let them cool.

Scrub the mussels well in several changes of water, scrape off the beards, and rinse the mussels in a colander. In the steamer, if it is large enough, set over boiling water, or in a large saucepan with 1 cup boiling water, steam the mussels, covered, over moderately high heat for 5 to 7 minutes, or until they open. Transfer them with a slotted spoon to a bowl and let them cool.

Remove the mussels from their shells, discarding any that have not opened. Add the mussels to the potatoes, along with the celery, radishes, peas, tomatoes, scallions, and the remaining vinaigrette. Toss the salad well and taste and adjust the seasoning, adding more salt and pepper if necessary. Serve at room temperature or slightly chilled in a bowl or mounded on a platter that has been lined with lettuce leaves.

Potato and Onion Spanish Omelette, Fragrant with Dill and Fennel

Serves 4 to 6

Whenever we thought of having a Spanish omelette, we usually thought better of it because what came to mind was the leftover vegetables disguised with a fresh tomato and some onion, all bound with beaten eggs—a concoction that our mothers made. It was sort of watery and made Spanish food a revelation to us when we finally tasted the real thing. This one is Spanish, we assure you, *so* Spanish it should actually be called a *tortilla*. But that smacks of Mexican or Tex-Mex food, which this isn't.

2 tablespoons fennel seeds

4 tablespoons light olive oil

6 medium russet potatoes (about 2 pounds), peeled and cut into ½-inch dice

2 medium onions, thinly sliced

8 large eggs

8 large garlic cloves, peeled and minced

2 tablespoons snipped fresh dill
Salt and freshly ground black pepper to taste

In a small dry skillet over moderate heat, toast the fennel seeds, stirring frequently, about 3 minutes, or until fragrant. Transfer to a small bowl.

In a 12-inch ovenproof skillet or sauté pan, bring 3 tablespoons of the oil to rippling over moderate heat. Add the potatoes and onions and cook, stirring frequently, for 5 minutes. Add ½ cup water, cover, and cook about 5 minutes, or until the potatoes are just tender. Uncover and continue cooking until the water evaporates. Add the remaining oil.

Meanwhile, in a medium bowl, beat the eggs lightly and add the reserved fennel seeds, garlic, dill, and salt and pepper to taste. Pour the egg mixture over the potato-onion mixture, spreading it evenly with a wooden spoon or spatula. Cook 1 minute. Reduce heat to low, cover, and cook until the eggs are almost set, about 8 minutes.

Meanwhile, preheat the broiler. Uncover the skillet and broil the omelette until the eggs are just set, watching carefully. Invert the omelette onto a warm platter and serve it cut in wedges.

GARLIC-ROASTED POTATOES WITH KALAMATA OLIVES PROVENÇALE

Serves 4

In southwestern France, garlic is referred to as "the poor man's truffle." To us, garlic is far superior to truffles and much more versatile. Taste what it does to potatoes in this recipe and never envy the rich again!

2 pounds small (1 inch in diameter) new red potatoes, scrubbed and quartered

2 tablespoons minced garlic

4 tablespoons light olive oil

½ teaspoon dried red pepper flakes, or ¼ teaspoon hot paprika

1 teaspoon salt, or to taste

½ teaspoon freshly ground pepper, or more to taste

20 Kalamata or other brine-cured black olives, pitted and chopped

2 tablespoons minced fresh parsley

Preheat the oven to 425° F.

In a baking pan, toss together the potatoes, garlic, oil, red pepper flakes, 1 teaspoon salt, and ½ teaspoon pepper until the potatoes are coated and evenly seasoned. Roast the potato mixture in the oven, stirring occasionally, for 25 minutes, or until golden brown.

Remove the pan from the oven and stir in the olives and parsley. Taste and adjust the seasoning, adding more salt and pepper if needed, and transfer to a warm serving dish.

NOTE: If you like, substitute ¼ cup chopped sun-dried tomatoes for 10 of the olives. Or omit the olives altogether and substitute 2 tablespoons small capers and 2 scallions, both white and green parts, thinly sliced. You can even sprinkle Parmesan over these potatoes and move them a few miles over the border from Provence into Italy. The most important ingredients are the potatoes, garlic, and oil. Anything and everything else can be changed to suit your palate or the ingredients you have on hand.

POTATO PIE WITH SMOKED SALMON, SCALLIONS, AND CREAM

Serves 4 to 6

This is a dish we invented to use up leftover smoked salmon we happened to have in the freezer. It uses some familiar elements as well and brings them all together in a new way. It also is a method of stretching an expensive ingredient like smoked salmon so that a little can serve a lot of people. Try this potato pie for Sunday breakfast or for a late supper. It can be made ahead to several different points in the recipe and given a final baking or reheating just before serving. A good-quality store-bought frozen crust works well in this recipe, if you don't want to spend time making your own.

Pastry for a Two-Crust (9-inch) Pie Shell (page 146)

1½ pounds Maine, Long Island, or other all-purpose potatoes, peeled and thinly sliced

2 tablespoons snipped fresh dill

½ teaspoon freshly ground black pepper, or more to taste

½ cup chopped scallions, white and green parts

¼ pound sliced smoked salmon, cut crosswise into ¼-inch strips

1 tablespoon unsalted butter

4 hard-cooked large eggs, peeled and thinly sliced

½ cup crème fraîche or heavy cream

1 egg yolk

1 teaspoon cold water

Line the bottom of a 9-inch pie pan with half the pastry and chill along with the remaining pastry until ready to use.

Rinse the potato slices in cold water to remove excess starch. Drain and pat dry with paper towels. Toss with the dill and pepper. Layer overlapping slices of potato in the pastry shell, using half the potatoes. Sprinkle scallions over the potato layer. Sauté the smoked salmon in the butter for 30 seconds, and spread it over the potato slices and scallions. Arrange the egg slices over the salmon, and top with the rest of the potato slices. Spread with the crème fraîche and refrigerate.

Preheat the oven to 400° F.

Roll out the remaining dough into a circle to fit the top of the pie. Beat the egg yolk with the cold water, brush the edges of the pastry with the egg wash, cover the pie with the circle of dough, and crimp and seal the edges. Brush the top with the remaining egg wash and cut several narrow leaf-shaped slits in it. Bake for 20 minutes. Reduce the oven temperature to 350° F. and bake 50 minutes more. Reduce the temperature to 300° F. and continue baking another 10 minutes. Remove the pie from the oven and allow it to rest for at least 5 minutes before cutting and serving. Or, if you like, let the pie rest for up to 1 hour and serve warm or at room temperature.

POTATO SAUCE ON PENNE VELLA

Serves 4

A Sicilian friend, Enza Vella, gave us this recipe that uses two of our favorite starches in one dish. Paradise! Enza suggested basil leaves as the herb, but confided that she goes out into her garden the day she makes the sauce and picks whatever looks good to her. The really unusual thing about this recipe is the way the potatoes are cooked. The technique is like that for risotto: Liquid is added gradually and each addition is allowed to be absorbed by the potatoes before the next is added. Consequently, the potatoes become part of the velvety sauce.

⅓ cup light olive oil

1 medium onion, coarsely chopped

1½ to 2 pounds russet baking potatoes (about 4), peeled and cut into ½-inch dice

2 cups homemade chicken stock or canned broth

1 cup chopped fresh basil

1 pound penne

Salt and freshly ground black pepper to taste

Several whole basil leaves for garnish

½ cup freshly grated Parmesan or Pecorino cheese

In a medium saucepan over moderately high heat, bring the oil to rippling. Stir in the onion, reduce heat to moderately low, and sauté the onion, stirring frequently, for 7 to 10 minutes, or until it is translucent and golden. Stir in the potatoes, coating them with the oil, and continue sautéing lightly, stirring occasionally, for 8 minutes.

Meanwhile, in another saucepan bring the stock to a gentle simmer over moderately low heat. Add ⅓ cup of the hot stock to the potato mixture. Cook without stirring. When the stock has been absorbed, add another ⅓ cup, stirring occasionally with a wooden spoon to break up the potatoes into coarse pieces. When the second addition of stock has been absorbed repeat once more, adding ⅓ cup stock. When cooked through and creamy, stir in the remaining 1 cup stock all at once and add the chopped basil. Continue simmering, stirring occasionally, for 8 or 9 minutes more.

While the sauce is simmering, prepare the penne. In a large kettle of boiling salted water over moderately high heat, cook the penne, stirring frequently, for 8 minutes, or until *al dente*. Drain and transfer to a serving bowl.

Season the potato sauce with salt and pepper to taste, pour it over the penne, and toss to combine well. Garnish with several basil leaves and serve. Pass the Parmesan or Pecorino at the table.

POTATO AND TOMATO STEW WITH PANCETTA

Serves 4 to 6

We make this Italian stew with canned Italian tomatoes and their juice—it's a simple, easy side dish that goes well with any main course, especially grilled meats and fish. If you can find pancetta (at Italian specialty food stores), please use it. If not, use lean, smoked bacon.

¼ pound sliced pancetta or lean bacon
2 tablespoons olive oil
1 medium onion, thinly sliced
1 large garlic clove, minced
1 pound can Italian tomatoes with their liquid

2 pounds all purpose potatoes, peeled and cut into ½-inch cubes
Salt and freshly ground pepper to taste
½ cup chopped fresh basil leaves

In a 10-inch sauté pan or skillet over moderate heat, sauté the pancetta until golden. Drain on paper towels. Pour fat from pan and return pan to moderate heat. Add olive oil and heat until rippling; stir in the onion and garlic and sauté until transparent, about 4 to 5 minutes. Add the tomatoes with their juice, the potatoes, salt and pepper, and cook, stirring occasionally, for about 20 to 25 minutes or until potatoes are tender. If the stew gets a little dry, add a few tablespoons of hot water or stock. Just before removing from the heat, fold in the basil. Serve hot.

POTATO AND CELERIAC PIE
FILLED WITH *SEA SCALLOPS* AND
SAUTÉED CABBAGE

Serves 4 generously

This is another way we have of stretching an expensive ingredient to feed several diners—yet not one of them would ever think that we're economizing. Here we use bay scallops, but you could substitute shrimp, fresh salmon, swordfish, or any firm-fleshed fish. You could also devise your own filling using things like crumbled sautéed sausage meat and 4 lightly fried eggs, cubed ham, and loosely scrambled eggs with scallions—and turn this into an elegant brunch or Sunday breakfast dish. Whatever filling you think up, be sure it is just barely cooked through, not overdone, because it will keep on cooking while the potato-celeriac crust becomes crisp. Master the method and you can be as creative as you like with the fillings.

1 tablespoon unsalted butter

3 cups thinly sliced cabbage

1 teaspoon freshly squeezed lemon juice

1 teaspoon distilled white vinegar

¾ teaspoon minced fresh thyme, or ¼ teaspoon dried, crumbled Salt and freshly ground black pepper to taste

½ to ¾ pound sea scallops, cut into quarters, or whole bay scallops, tossed in 1 teaspoon vegetable oil to coat

½ cup minced onion (1 medium)

1 pound all-purpose potatoes, peeled and grated (about 2 cups), turned into a sieve and allowed to drain

1 cup grated celeriac

1 tablespoon plus 1 teaspoon vegetable oil

Preheat the oven to 350° F.

In a large heavy skillet or sauté pan, melt the butter over moderately high heat. When the foam subsides, cook the cabbage, covered, stirring occasionally, for 10 to 15 minutes, or until crisp-tender. Stir in the lemon juice, vinegar, thyme, and salt and pepper to taste, and transfer to a bowl; set aside. Return the pan to the heat and when it is very hot add the scallops, stirring until they are just opaque. Stir them into the reserved cabbage.

In a large bowl, combine the minced onion, the well-drained grated potatoes, grated celeriac, ½ teaspoon salt, and ½ teaspoon pepper.

Heat a 10-inch ovenproof skillet over moderate heat, add 1 tablespoon oil, and heat it to rippling. Add half the potato-celeriac mixture and spread it evenly over the bottom of the skillet with a spatula. Spoon the cabbage-scallop mixture over it with a slotted spoon (leaving any accumulated liquid behind) and spread it evenly in a circle leaving a 2-inch border of potato around the filling. Carefully spread the remaining potato-celeriac mixture over the top and, with a spatula, press it into a domed shape. Continue cooking over moderate heat for 4 minutes. Place the skillet in the center of the oven and bake for 7 minutes; remove, loosen the pie with a spatula, and invert it onto a platter. Add the remaining 1 teaspoon oil to the skillet, slide the inverted pie back into the pan, and place the pan over moderate heat for 5 minutes, or until the second side is nicely browned. Serve in the skillet or invert the pie onto a warm serving platter. Cut into wedges and serve immediately.

Colcannon-Stuffed Potato Shells with Leeks and Bacon

Serves 4

Colcannon is a humble Irish dish usually made with boiled potatoes and cabbage or kale. We like the idea a lot, but spiff it up a bit (an Irish cousin tells us that once again we are gilding the lily) by baking the potatoes and adding a couple of seasonings that might be considered un-Irish. In any case, preparing colcannon like this can take it out of the side-dish category into main-dish fare—preceded with a bowl of soup, perhaps, and accompanied by some mixed greens or a sliced tomato and chopped onion salad. It can also stand on its own as a luncheon dish, and with scrambled eggs it becomes an elegant Sunday brunch offering.

4 **Idaho or russet baking potatoes (about ½ pound each)**	4 **garlic cloves, coarsely chopped**
¼ **pound kale, tough stems removed, leaves washed well, drained, and coarsely chopped (about 2½ cups firmly packed)**	1 **cup milk**
	3 **tablespoons unsalted butter**
	½ **teaspoon mace or caraway seeds**
	Salt and freshly ground black pepper to taste
2 **medium leeks, trimmed, leaving 2 inches pale green, washed well and sliced into ½-inch rounds**	4 **slices lean bacon (preferably Irish), cooked until crisp, drained, and crumbled**

Bake the potatoes following the procedure on page 197. While the potatoes are baking, in a heavy saucepan combine the kale, leeks, garlic, milk, butter, mace, and salt and pepper and bring to a boil over high heat. Reduce heat to moderate and simmer the mixture, covered, stirring occasionally, for 15 minutes, or until the vegetables are just tender. Transfer the vegetables to a bowl with a slotted spoon and boil the liquid remaining in the pan until it is reduced to about ½ cup.

When the potatoes are done, reduce oven temperature to 350° F.

While the potatoes are still hot, cut a thin lengthwise slice from the top of each one (discard or save for another use, like fried skins), scoop out the potatoes leaving a ¼-inch-thick shell, and force the potato flesh through a ricer or food mill fitted with the medium disk. Mix the potato flesh into the vegetables, along with two-thirds of the bacon and enough of the cooking liquid to reach a nice consistency. Divide the mixture among the potato shells, mounding it generously. Sprinkle the remaining bacon bits evenly over the colcannon and, if necessary, heat the potatoes in a baking dish, covered, in the oven for 15 minutes, or until they are just heated through. Serve hot.

NOTE: Another of our favorite stuffings would be spinach and sour cream. Cook the spinach in the water that clings to the well-washed leaves for 3 minutes, or until wilted. Add a few grindings of nutmeg and force the spinach, along with the scooped-out potatoes, through a ricer. Mix in ½ pint of sour cream, and mound the mixture back into the shells. Serve with a dollop of sour cream on top.

FLAVOR-OF-THE-DAY MASHED-POTATO DINNER ROLLS

Makes about 30 rolls

We hardly ever have leftover mashed potatoes, but when we do we more than likely use them up in another recipe, like this one. These rolls are moister than most just because of the potatoes. They're extra flavorful, too, because of the garlic or onions (boiled or sautéed) or dill or caraway or what-have-you that seasoned the original mashed potatoes. That's why we named them "Flavor of the Day." But, of course, you can always use mashed potatoes made from scratch or make more than you need (½ cup is all that this recipe calls for) for a meal. The rolls, like almost all baked goods, freeze well: Just cool them, wrap in aluminum foil, or store in plastic freezer bags. They'll keep for weeks. When ready to use, place frozen or thawed rolls in a preheated 325° F. oven for a few minutes to crisp up.

1 envelope (¼ ounce) active dry yeast	1¼ teaspoons salt
¼ cup lukewarm water	1 large egg
½ cup hot mashed potatoes	½ cup lukewarm milk
8 tablespoons plus 1 teaspoon unsalted butter	3 cups all-purpose flour
3 tablespoons sugar	2 or 3 tablespoons caraway seeds, dill seeds, poppy seeds, or minced onion for garnish

Combine the yeast and warm water in a small bowl. In the large bowl of an electric mixer, beat the hot mashed potatoes with 5 tablespoons plus 1 teaspoon of the butter, the sugar, salt, and egg. When beaten well, beat in the yeast mixture. Add the warm milk and the flour alternately, and beat well. Turn the dough out on a lightly floured surface and knead by hand for 5 minutes, adding only enough flour to prevent the dough from becoming overly sticky.

Put the dough into an oiled bowl and turn to coat completely, cover with plastic wrap or a dish towel, and set aside in a warm place to rise until doubled in bulk, about 1½ hours. When the dough has risen, remove the wrap and punch down the dough. Place it on a lightly floured surface and divide into 2 pieces. Roll out 1 piece of the dough ¼ inch thick. Cut into rounds with a 2½-inch cutter or glass tumbler. Repeat with second piece of dough.

Melt the remaining 3 tablespoons butter and pour it into a shallow soup plate or bowl. Dip one side of each round in the butter, fold the dough over, buttered side in, to make a half-round. Place the rolls, seam side up and touching each other slightly, in two 9 x 9-inch baking pans. Sprinkle the garnish over the rolls, cover them with plastic wrap, and let stand until doubled in bulk, about 1 hour.

Preheat the oven to 375° F.

When the rolls have risen, place them on the middle rack of the oven and bake for 18 minutes, or until golden. Serve warm.

CHOCOLATE MASHED-POTATO CAKE

Serves 8 to 10

In our cookbook *The Brilliant Bean,* we developed several cakes in which we substituted bean puree for flour. They were inventions that were notably successful, at least as far as we and our readers were concerned. The cakes were moist—we dislike dry cakes that rely on icing for moisture—and they offered better nutrition, with plenty of soluble fiber, vitamins, and minerals—the good stuff that's processed out of white flour. Mashed potatoes work the same way, and because of their starch content, the cake has a wonderful "crumb." This cake is moister, more nutritious, and just as flavorful as those made with flour.

5 ounces semisweet chocolate

1 tablespoon instant espresso powder

2 tablespoons Frangelico liqueur

½ cup (1 stick) unsalted butter

4 large eggs, separated, at room temperature

½ cup granulated sugar

1 cup unseasoned mashed potatoes (about ½ pound peeled, boiled potatoes), at room temperature

½ cup finely ground hazelnuts

Pinch of salt

Confectioners' sugar

Preheat oven to 350° F.

Grease an 8-inch springform pan and line the bottom with a round of wax paper.

In a small saucepan set over the lowest possible heat, or in the top of a double boiler over simmering water, melt the chocolate, espresso powder, the Frangelico, and butter. Stir to combine, and set aside to cool.

In the large bowl of an electric mixer set at medium speed, beat together the egg yolks and granulated sugar for about 3 minutes, or until the mixture is thick and pale yellow. Reduce speed to low, pour in the cooled chocolate-butter mixture, and continue beating until just blended, about 1 minute. Add the mashed potatoes and hazelnuts and beat on low speed until just combined.

In a separate bowl, beat the egg whites with a pinch of salt until stiff.

With a spatula fold the whites gently but thoroughly into the chocolate batter. Pour the batter into the prepared springform pan and bake in the middle of the oven for 35 minutes, or until the sides are firm; the cake will be soft in the center.

Remove from the oven and cool in the pan for 1 hour. Run a thin knife around the sides of the cake to loosen it, remove the sides of the pan, and let the cake cool completely.

Invert the cake onto a serving plate and peel off the wax paper. Sprinkle with confectioners' sugar.

NOTE: We often serve this cake with whipped cream sweetened with more Frangelico or, alternately, set each slice on a pool of pureed frozen raspberries. You can do both, if you like.

RADISHES

[*RAPHANUS SATIVUS*]

red—var. sativus (syn. radicula)

white—var. mougri

black—var. niger

Red, white, and black radishes were all eaten by the Egyptians about four thousand years ago, 2000 B.C But even before the Egyptians, the Chinese were cultivating black radishes, the Indians and some Indonesians grew white radishes, and Turks and Persians and other Middle Eastern peoples were enjoying ruby reds.

It's the red radish (also available in white) that is most familiar to us and most commonly seen in our markets. But a little scouting and insisting often turns up the other two varieties. Each has a distinctive taste and bite. The reds are round, crispy, and can burn your tongue; the whites (sometimes with tan or beige skins) are longish, sweeter, and blander; the blacks have a denser, drier texture, can look like black beets or white carrots, have an earthier flavor, and come in beige as well as black, charcoal-brown, and white. If you are thoroughly confused, you are not alone. Even botanists are not sure if radishes from the Orient are the same botanical variety as those cultivated in Europe and the United States. There is no confusion about the flavor of radishes, however. They have a freshness of flavor rivaled by few underground vegetables.

The reason radishes often taste "hot" is because they are a member of the crucifer family, which includes such nonwallflowers in the flavor area as mustard, watercress, and horseradish, and such nonvegetables as—the wallflower. The enzyme that produces the spicy, peppery mouthfeel reacts with another enzyme to form a mustard oil that, like mustard itself, imparts a burning sensation. Because this enzyme occurs mostly in the skin of the radish, peeling can moderate its effects. But who would want to—it's their surprise that is part of radishes' appeal. One never knows until one bites into a radish whether it will be mild, hot, or shockingly stinging. Some black radishes can be as impossibly "hot" as horseradish and make your eyes tear, and your lips and tongue burn.

Varieties

You are familiar with the red, globe-shaped radish available at any produce stand in leafy bunches or clipped of their greens and packed in cello bags. The long and slender white radish, called the Icicle, also comes both ways and has a crisp texture and zesty flavor when fresh. Black radishes look exactly like huge black beets. When peeled, the flesh is ivory-white.

Availability

Fresh bunched red radishes are best in late spring and throughout the summer, but they are always available at major markets throughout the year. The white Icicles come to market slightly later. Cello-packed red or white radishes can be had at any time—but they are neither firm nor bright and should only be used when those with the green tops aren't to be found. Black radishes are widely used in Eastern Europe and can usually be found in markets that have a Russian or Polish or even German clientele. They have a long shelf life and can stay fresh-tasting for months on end if they have had their leaves and roots removed.

Storage

Bunched radishes are harvested, packed in chipped ice, and shipped to market. They should be sold and eaten within days of arriving at the store, otherwise the green tops begin to yellow, a warning flag that the radishes they are attached to are less than garden fresh. (Besides, you get less for your money with inedible yellow tops. Fresh radish greens are delicious in a salad.) Once in your kitchen, cut off the greens immediately and store them separately for salad use. This lengthens the life of the radishes by another

week, and explains why so many stores sell radishes without their tops. The same applies to white radishes. Trimmed black radishes, as mentioned, keep for months in your vegetable crisper.

What to Look For

Red or white radishes should be bright, firm, and crisp-looking with few if any cracks (which ruin the appearance but not the quality) and deep green leaves. Choose black radishes that are hard to the touch. If they feel soft, they can be woolly in the middle.

Basic Preparation and Cooking Methods

Radishes are best raw, but they can be cooked like turnips and combined with other vegetables as well. Clip off the tops and root ends and slice or serve whole. The French serve red radishes with fresh butter. The English often have them at breakfast with bread and butter. We like them in salads, on the relish tray, chopped as a garnish for cold soups, steamed, sautéed, added to stir-fried dishes as you would water chestnuts, and boiled and mashed with potatoes. Black radishes are wonderful sliced thin, refreshed in ice water, patted dry, salted, and served with beer. Or do as they do in Eastern European countries: Slice them thin, ice them, pat dry and before serving drizzle with chicken fat, sprinkle with salt and pepper, and accompany with black bread. Radishes of any color add a nice crunch to cold meat sandwiches or fish salads.

---

nutrition

These figures are for common red radishes. White and black radishes will be a little higher in some nutrients and a little lower in others—but nothing significant. In 100 grams there are: 17 calories, .6g protein, .54g fiber, 21mg calcium, .29mg iron, 9mg magnesium, 18mg phosphorus, 232mg potassium, 24mg sodium, .3mg zinc, .04mg copper, .07mg manganese, 22.8mg vitamin C, .005mg thiamine, .045mg riboflavin, .3mg niacin, .088mg pantothenic acid, .071mg vitamin B_6, 27mg folacin, 8IU vitamin A and, of course, no cholesterol.

Radishes and Scallions with Raspberry Vinegar Glaze

Serves 4

It's not often that one eats cooked radishes, but they are surprisingly good, especially with the savor of raspberry vinegar. Serve them with chops, sautéed calves liver, grilled or richly sauced chicken, or as part of a vegetarian dinner.

2½ tablespoons sugar

⅓ cup raspberry vinegar

1 tablespoon unsalted butter

½ teaspoon salt, or to taste

¼ teaspoon pepper, or more to taste

½ cup water

1 pound radishes (without stems and leaves), trimmed

2 tablespoons minced scallion greens

In a sauté pan, skillet, or saucepan just large enough to hold the radishes closely in one layer, combine the sugar, vinegar, butter, ½ teaspoon salt, ¼ teaspoon pepper, the water, and the larger radishes. Bring to a boil, covered, over moderately high heat, then add the smaller radishes, reduce heat to a simmer, and cook, covered, for 10 minutes. Uncover and simmer the radishes 5 to 10 minutes more, or until they are just tender.

With a slotted spoon, transfer the radishes to a bowl and keep them warm, covered. Raise heat to moderately high and boil the liquid in the pan until it is reduced to about ¼ cup, or is thickened to the consistency of a glaze. Return the radishes to the pan, taste and adjust the seasoning with salt and pepper, as needed, then tip and swirl the pan to coat the radishes thoroughly with the glaze. Transfer to a serving dish, sprinkle with the scallions, and serve.

Radish, Fennel, and Endive Salad with Mustard Vinaigrette

Serves 6

It seems that no one ever eats salad at our dinner table without exclaiming over the dressing. When we reveal the proportions—which are quite normal, we assure you—they think we are holding back on an ingredient. Their dressings do not taste like ours even though the recipes are the same. The same except for one addition learned from our good friend and the best cook we know, Thalia Gubler, a.k.a. Deedee. Maggi seasoning makes the difference—either sprinkled over the salad before it is dressed and tossed or added to the dressing when it is blended. Try it. It makes such an incredible difference, you'll never again make salad dressing without it. It's no secret. The Swiss have been using it for decades. Deedee is married to a Swiss, Walter, who insists a bottle of Maggi be kept on the table along with the salt and pepper.

3 tablespoons Dijon mustard

2 tablespoons red wine vinegar
  Salt and freshly ground black
  pepper to taste

1 tablespoon Maggi seasoning, or
  more to taste

6 tablespoons light olive oil

24 radishes, trimmed and thinly
  sliced (about 2 cups)

4 fennel bulbs, trimmed and thinly
  sliced crosswise (about 4 cups)

1 Belgian endive, thinly sliced
  crosswise

2 tablespoons minced fresh parsley

6 large curly-leafed lettuce leaves,
  rinsed and spun dry

In a blender or food processor combine the mustard, vinegar, salt, pepper, and Maggi seasoning. With the motor running, add the oil in a thin stream until it is well combined and emulsified.

In a salad bowl, toss together the radishes, fennel, endive, parsley, and the vinaigrette. Arrange a lettuce leaf on each of 6 salad plates and divide the radish, fennel, endive salad among them.

SOLE WITH RADISHES AND SNOW PEAS IN LIME VINAIGRETTE

Serves 4

- - - - - - - - -

This is an elegant warm-weather dish. It's served almost at room temperature and combines several textures and flavors. Everything can be done ahead except the baking of the sole. And because this only takes about 7 minutes, dinner can be ready very quickly. We would serve the sole with buttered new potatoes in their jackets at room temperature and perhaps a tomato and onion salad, if tomatoes are in season.

2 tablespoons freshly squeezed lime juice

1 teaspoon freshly grated lime rind

1 tablespoon Dijon mustard

1 teaspoon Maggi seasoning
   Salt and freshly ground black pepper to taste

⅓ cup light olive oil

4 sole fillets (6 ounces each)

White pepper to taste

½ pound snow peas, trimmed, stringed, and cut diagonally into ½-inch pieces

½ cup finely chopped radishes

1 3-inch-long strip of lime rind cut lengthwise into fine julienne strips

In a small bowl, whisk together the lime juice, grated rind, mustard, Maggi seasoning, and salt and black pepper to taste. Add the oil in a thin stream, whisking until the vinaigrette is well combined and emulsified. Set aside.

Preheat the oven to 400° F.

Season the fillets with salt and white pepper and arrange them in a buttered jelly-roll pan. Cover them with a sheet of buttered foil and bake for 7 minutes, or until they just flake.

Meanwhile, in a saucepan over high heat, bring salted water to a boil and blanch the snow peas for 5 seconds. Drain them, refresh immediately under cold water, and pat dry.

With a large spatula, transfer the fillets to 4 plates, sprinkle them with the snow peas, chopped radishes, and julienned rind, and spoon the vinaigrette over them. Let the fillets cool for 5 minutes before serving.

RAMPS

[*ALLIUM TRICOCCUM*]

wild leek

Come late March and early April in the Appalachian Mountain area, the ramp season begins, drawing ramp fanatics from as far away as Hawaii. The foraging and ensuing feast was started in Richwood, West Virginia, by the Society of the Friends of the Ramp in 1921. The annual celebration draws upward of 3,500 people who consume some 180 bushels of ramps.

The ramp is a wild onion that grows in moist woodland areas in soil made rich by decaying leaves. Its habitat is the eastern United States and Canada from Quebec to as far south as Georgia. The flat, broad, dark green leaves (looking demurely like lily-of-the-valley) with slender bulbs beneath, appear in the spring and are gone by summer, when a leafless stem replaces the leaves and several greenish-white flowers appear at the tip.

Ramps are often called wild leeks, but bear little resemblance to their cultivated cousins, especially when it comes to taste. Leeks are mild; ramps taste like onions that have been "pumping iron." The most pungent of the *Allium* family, they are strong—too strong for some tastes. Ramps are usually cooked; raw ramps are recommended only to the stoutest of hearts or those with a congenitally stuffed nose. Even the cooked plant is potent. The smell lingers in a household for days afterward and stays on the breath for two or three days at least.

The American Indians ate ramps, which probably grew in profusion in the hardwood forests of the Midwest, and some people believe that Chicago got its name from the Indian word that refers to the pungent smell of the ramp, *checagou*. Chicago is lucky. There are lots of worse smells it could have been named after.

Varieties

There seems to be only one variety of ramp—powerful.

Availability

Ramps grow wild and can be searched out toward the end of winter and in early spring in their native habitat, the forested areas of the eastern and midwestern United States. They are hardly ever found in greengrocers, even the most esoteric ones.

Storage

Just-picked ramps can last a week or more, unwashed and refrigerated.

Their aroma permeates everything, though, and so we don't recommend keeping them on hand. The pungent smell can penetrate many layers of plastic wrap and spoil the flavor of other foods.

What to Look For

Just follow your nose.

Basic Preparation and Cooking Methods

Ramp's hearty flavor withstands any kind of cooking method without weakening. They are wonderful in stews, pot pies, and braised. They are not recommended raw or in salads; their pungency can overwhelm almost any other ingredient.

nutrition

See "Scallions," page 261.

RAMP CHAMP OR RAMPS MASHED WITH POTATOES

Serves 4 to 6

You can make champ in the Irish way, with scallions, or with American ramps instead—a version with a much more forceful taste. The method is similar: the ramps, standing in for scallions, are simmered in milk and beaten into the potatoes, so that none of the flavor or nutrition is lost.

3 pounds large boiling potatoes, scrubbed

1½ cups chopped ramps, including the green tops

1½ cups milk

½ cup (1 stick) unsalted butter, or less to taste, cut into pieces

1 teaspoon salt, or to taste

½ teaspoon white pepper, or more to taste

Place the potatoes in a large saucepan with cold water to cover. Bring to a boil over high heat, reduce heat to a simmer, and cook 25 to 30 minutes, or until tender.

Meanwhile, in a small saucepan, combine the milk and ramps. Bring the milk to a simmer over moderate heat, reduce heat to moderately low, and simmer the mixture gently for 15 minutes, or until the ramps are softened.

Drain the potatoes, return them to the pan, and steam them, covered, over moderate heat, shaking the pan frequently, for 5 minutes, or until any excess water has evaporated. Peel the potatoes, and mash them in a mixing bowl while they are hot. Beat in the butter to taste. Lift the ramps from the milk with a slotted spoon and stir them into the potato mixture with enough of the hot milk to make the potatoes fluffy but not thin. Add the salt and pepper, taste and adjust seasoning, and mound into a warm serving bowl. Serve hot.

RUTABAGAS

[*BRASSICA NAPOBRASSICA; BRASSICA CAMPESTRIS* VAR. *NAPO-BRASSICA*]

yellow turnip

Swede, Swedish turnip or turnip root

cabbage (Eng.)

chou-navet (Fr. and Can.)

Russian turnip

Bulgarian turnip

Canadian turnip

Rutabagas are probably the least expensive vegetable at your produce stand. Except for its thin skin, there is absolutely no waste, the texture is about as smooth as a new potato, and the taste is delightfully earthy. In addition, it mixes well with other root vegetables, has a lovely golden color, and is packed, jam-packed, with nutrients.

So why is it so unloved?

It certainly doesn't have a long history of being strictly a peasant food or a reputation for being fit only for animal fodder. As a matter of fact, it doesn't have an ancient history at all. A crossbreed of cabbage and turnip, it was first referred to by the Swiss botanist Caspar Bauhin in 1620 and attributed to his developmental skills.

Most people think the rutabaga is a sort of giant turnip, but it is actually a weedy, tuberous relative of the cabbage whose globular stem, with a little help from Bauhin's genius, swelled underground to quite remarkable size. He apparently promoted it until it became one of the most popular vegetables in northern Europe, especially in winter—its nicknames stemming from the countries where it finds its way into the most saucepans. Consequently, you won't hear it called the American turnip, as it hardly finds its way into our saucepans at all. Indeed, it sells so slowly in this country that it comes to the market with a thin wax coating to preserve its shelf life. Even without the paraffin preservative (which should be peeled off with the skin before cooking), it is more durable and keeps better than almost any other vegetable you can name.

Rutabagas are grown extensively where the weather is cool—in Sweden, Russia, the British Isles, France, and, where most of ours come from, Canada. Some Canadian varieties have a particularly subtle, delicate flavor and can be quite sweet. When Canadian varieties are out of season, markets get their rutabagas from California (where else?), but they are not nearly as tasty.

About the size of a softball, a rutabaga will be dark purple about two-thirds of the way down from the stem end and dull yellow from there to the root. Peeling reveals creamy yellow flesh denser than a potato's. Most people dislike them without ever having tasted them (could it be the name that's off-putting?), and they can be somewhat sharp if they are not of good quality. A potato mashed with the rutabaga takes care of this.

There are many delicious ways to prepare rutabagas. You can simply cut them in cubes or chunks and place these around a roast instead of potatoes—or in addition to them. Boil or steam them with carrots and potatoes and mash them with butter, a little cinnamon, salt, and pepper. Blanch slices for 5 minutes and use them for tempura. Add pieces to vegetable soup. Mix mashed rutabagas with butter, cream, and a little nutmeg, sprinkle with brown sugar, and bake for 15 or 20 minutes. You'll think you're eating acorn squash—but without the fibers.

Try rutabagas if you never have. They really are delicious—and so cheap that if the investment doesn't pay off to your taste it won't hurt very much. We wouldn't ask you to do the same with truffles.

Varieties

Although rutabagas are not labeled as to country of origin, many of those you'll find at the greengrocers' come from Canada. These are sweeter and finer than those from California. Some local rutabagas from the Northeast and Midwest are also of good quality. Ask your produce manager.

Availability

Canadian rutabagas are in season from October through July. The California product takes up the slack. Farm stands and specialty markets in the Northeast and Midwest often have local product.

Storage

Rutabagas can keep in your refrigerator for more than a month. When fresh, they can be stored in a root cellar, packed in sand or sawdust, for up to a year. The wax coating you'll find on all but local farm varieties is there to prevent dehydration, shriveling, and waste. It preserves freshness even in your refrigerator, so don't remove the wax until you're ready to prepare the rutabaga. Then just peel it away along with the skin.

What to Look For

Choose a tuber between 4 and 6 inches in length, almost round in shape, that feels heavy for its size, and is without bruises or cracks. We've never seen them in stores with stems and leaves attached, but if you do they will most likely be unwaxed and fresh from the earth. Incidentally, the wax is perfectly safe and you can see and feel that it is there, unlike the thin coating given cucumbers, which can sometimes be undetectable.

Basic Preparation and Cooking Methods

After peeling with a swivel-bladed peeler, use a sharp knife to slice the tuber in half. Then cut it in slices or 1-inch cubes, depending on its end use.

You can braise, boil, or steam rutabagas; use slices or cubes in soups, stews, or with roasts. Mash cubes alone or with a potato and, perhaps, a carrot. Sauté blanched slices or fry them in batter for tempura. Braising should take 15 to 20 minutes, boiling 20 to 25 minutes, steaming 25 to 30 minutes. Cooking time will vary a little depending on the size of cubes. Sliced rutabagas will take even less time to cook.

nutrition

We were not kidding when we said rutabagas are jam-packed with nutrients. Besides being a low-calorie (only 36 per 100g), high-carbohydrate food (8.13 per 100g), rutabagas contain all the necessary minerals, every vitamin except B_{12} and A, and all the amino acids but proline. The minerals per 100g are: calcium 47mg, iron 0.52mg, magnesium 23mg, phosphorus 58mg, potassium 337mg, sodium 20mg, zinc 0.34mg, copper 0.04 mg, manganese 0.17mg. The vitamins per 100g are: vitamin C 25mg, thiamine 0.09mg, riboflavin 0.04mg, niacin 0.07mg, pantothenic acid 0.16mg, vitamin B_6 0.10mg, folacin 20.5mg. Extra bonus: no cholesterol.

GRATIN OF RUTABAGA WITH FRESH ROSEMARY

Serves 6 as a side dish

Gratins are moist on the inside, crisp and crusty on the outside. We like to use fresh rosemary whenever it is available, but ½ teaspoon or so of dried rosemary works almost as well in this particular dish. The cream mellows and blunts the sometimes sharp edge of the rutabaga and the garlic adds a subtle, indefinable note that binds all the flavors together.

1 pound rutabaga, peeled, cut in half, and sliced very thin with a *mandoline* or food processor

2 tablespoons all-purpose flour

1 teaspoon chopped fresh rosemary

1 cup freshly grated Parmesan

Salt and freshly ground black pepper to taste

1 cup heavy cream

½ cup homemade chicken stock or canned broth

2 teaspoons minced garlic

In a steamer basket set over boiling water, steam the rutabaga slices, covered, for 3 to 4 minutes, or until crisp-tender. Lift out the basket and allow the rutabaga to drain and cool; pat the slices dry with paper towels.

Preheat the oven to 375° F.

Butter an 11- or a 12-inch oval gratin dish or a 1½-quart baking dish. Arrange one-third of the rutabaga slices evenly over the bottom and sprinkle them with 1 tablespoon of the flour, ½ teaspoon of the rosemary, ⅓ cup of the Parmesan, and salt and pepper to taste. Arrange half the remaining rutabaga slices over the Parmesan, sprinkle with the remaining flour and rosemary, ⅓ cup of the remaining Parmesan, and salt and pepper to taste. Arrange the remaining rutabaga over the Parmesan and season with salt and pepper.

In a small saucepan over moderately high heat, combine the cream, chicken stock, and garlic and bring the mixture just to a boil. Pour it evenly over the rutabaga layers, and sprinkle the top with the remaining Parmesan. Cover with foil and bake in the preheated oven for 30 minutes. Remove the foil and bake for 20 minutes more, or until the top is golden brown. Let the gratin stand for 5 minutes before serving.

CREAMED RUTABAGAS WITH CARAMELIZED ONIONS

Serves 4 to 6

Rutabagas are versatile and economical. So if you add an extravagance like heavy cream to them you are adding only pennies to an already thrifty dish and should not feel guilty. About 1 pound of browned and sliced sweet Italian sausage can also be added 5 minutes before the rutabagas are completely cooked to make a really satisfying meal-in-one—especially if you substitute ¾ cup canned chicken broth for the water to thin the sauce slightly, and serve it all over pasta.

1½ **pounds yellow onions, cut in half and thinly sliced**	½ **teaspoon salt, or to taste**
¼ **cup (½ stick) unsalted butter**	½ **teaspoon freshly ground black pepper, or more to taste**
1½ **pounds rutabagas, peeled and cut into ½-inch dice**	¾ **cup heavy cream**
	½ **cup water**

In a large sauté pan or saucepan over moderate heat, melt the butter and, when the foam subsides, cook the onions, stirring frequently, for 20 to 25 minutes, or until they are browned (caramelized). Stir in the rutabagas, ½ teaspoon salt, ½ teaspoon pepper, the cream, and water. When the liquid begins to bubble, reduce heat to moderately low and gently simmer, stirring occasionally, for 15 to 20 minutes, or until the rutabagas are tender. Taste and adjust the seasoning, adding more salt and pepper if desired, and serve from a heated bowl.

NOTE: We have suggested above that, with the addition of Italian sausages, this recipe can become a sauce for pasta. Well, as a matter of fact, it makes a good pasta topping without the sausages. If there is not enough sauce for you, increase the liquids until you have a consistency you prefer. Remember, though, pasta shapes absorb more sauce than strands of spaghetti.

RUTABAGA AND WATERCRESS PUREE

Serves 4
- - - - - - - -

Watercress isn't an underground vegetable, of course, but when cooked quickly in a little chicken stock and seasoned simply with salt and pepper, it is one of our favorites. Here it gives the usually earthy rutabaga a refinement and elegance it never achieves on its own—as a delightful accompaniment to game, fish, and poultry.

1½ pounds rutabagas, peeled and cut
    into ½-inch dice
1 bunch watercress
2 tablespoons unsalted butter

¼ cup half-and-half or lowfat milk
   Salt and freshly ground black
   pepper to taste

In a steamer set over boiling water, steam the rutabagas for 30 minutes, or until tender. In a saucepan, bring water to a boil over high heat and blanch the watercress for 1 minute; drain and refresh under cold running water, then squeeze it dry.

In a food processor, puree the rutabaga with the watercress until smooth. Melt the butter in a small skillet over moderate heat, and when the foam subsides, cook the puree, stirring, for 1 minute. Stir in the half-and-half until well combined, and season with salt and pepper. Cook, stirring, for 2 minutes more, or until the puree is hot. Transfer the puree to a heated bowl, press decorative depressions around the edges with the back of a soup spoon, and serve.

RUTABAGA AND POTATO TERRINE STRIPED WITH SCALLION PUREE

Serves 8 to 10 as a side dish or appetizer

This terrine is not only pretty to look at with its pastel layers of cream and pale orange and pinstripes of kelly green, but it tastes as good as it looks. We usually serve it as a side dish, but it could be a starter or part of a buffet table, served at room temperature.

2 pounds rutabagas, peeled and cut into 1-inch cubes
Salt to taste
1½ pounds large boiling potatoes, peeled and cut into 1-inch pieces
½ cup milk
4 tablespoons (½ stick) unsalted butter, cut in half and at room temperature

White pepper to taste
1½ cups coarsely chopped scallion greens
1 cup homemade chicken stock or canned broth

Place the rutabagas in a saucepan with enough water to cover by 1 inch. Bring to a boil over high heat, add salt to taste, reduce heat to a simmer, and cook for 20 minutes, or until tender. Place the potatoes in another saucepan with enough water to cover by 1 inch and bring to a boil over high heat. Add salt to taste, reduce heat to a simmer, and cook for 15 minutes, or until tender. Drain the rutabagas and return them to the saucepan, covered, over low heat to steam, shaking the pan, for 1 minute. Drain the potatoes and return them to the saucepan, covered, over low heat to steam, shaking the pan, for 1 minute.

Force the rutabagas through a ricer into a bowl, add 2 tablespoons of the butter, and salt and pepper to taste; combine the mixture well and reserve, covered.

Force the boiling potatoes through a ricer into another bowl, add the milk and the remaining 2 tablespoons butter, and salt and pepper to taste; combine the mixture well and reserve, covered.

In a saucepan, combine the scallion greens and stock. Bring the stock to a boil over high heat, reduce heat to a simmer, and cook the mixture for 10 to 15 minutes, or until the stock is reduced to about ¼ cup. Puree the scallion mixture in a blender or food processor, and return it to the saucepan. Boil it over moderately high heat, stirring, until it is very thick.

Preheat oven to 375° F.

Butter a 9 x 5 x 3-inch loaf pan and spread 1 cup of the rutabaga mixture over the bottom. Spread 1 cup of the potato mixture over it, and spread half the scallion puree over the potato layer. Repeat in the same manner, ending with a layer of the scallion puree. Place the loaf pan into a larger pan, add enough boiling water to reach halfway up the sides of the terrine, and bake, covered with foil, for 50 minutes to 1 hour. Cool for 10 minutes. Invert the terrine onto a work surface and cut into slices. Or invert onto a serving platter and slice at the table. Serve hot, warm, or at room temperature.

SALSIFY

[*TRAGOPOGON PORRIFOLIUS*]

oyster plant

vegetable oyster

scorzonera (It. & Sp.; bot.: Scorzonera

hispanica)

black salsify

salsifis (Fr.)

Salsify, a member of the prodigious daisy family, is an absolutely delicious root which, unfortunately for Americans, is not particularly well known here. It is cultivated in the United States on a very casual basis and is available only at markets that specialize in "gourmet" produce, and at some enlightened farmers' markets. It was at the Union Square Greenmarket in New York City that we first encountered it in any quantity.

Two centuries ago, Thomas Jefferson, who was an enthusiastic and inquisitive agriculturalist, experimented with many exotic (at the time) vegetables. One of them was salsify, also called oyster plant because of its taste, which even Jefferson thought tasted like oysters.

Maybe oysters tasted different in the eighteenth century or our particular taste buds are different now, but we don't taste a similarity. The only thing we can figure out is that oysters are supposed to be a food that improves a man's virility and, once upon a time, so was salsify.

What *does* it taste like? A little like a cooked turnip but subtler, a little like parsnip, a little like parsley root. Its taste is similar to several of its cousins, but different.

Though salsify was, before World War II, a fairly common vegetable on many produce stands, it is little used now. As a matter of fact, up until 1975 it was practically on the endangered species list at American tables. Since then it has been making a slow, plodding comeback — and until it gains wider acceptance will continue to carry a rather high price tag.

In shape it resembles a very long, very thin parsnip or carrot — but not in color. (If it isn't the taste or the sexual-potency fables, maybe it's the color that gave it its nickname — salsify can turn grayish when peeled and exposed to air and it darkens like potatoes and many other root vegetables.) Salsify has a dirt-colored skin except for *scorzonera,* called black salsify because of its black skin. It is a native of the southern parts of Europe, but has been cultivated here since the eighteenth century and has even become naturalized in many parts of the United States (meaning it is considered a weed by many). It is a pretty plant, quite flamboyant when in flower, with daisy-shaped purple blossoms that open in the morning and close before noon. In Great Britain the plant is also called in the vernacular "John-go-to-bed-at-noon."

In Europe, where salsify has always been a favorite, the young leaves and tight little heart are popular in raw salads. They can also be blanched, braised, steamed, or boiled. Salsify tastes best served with butter or a delicate sauce and a little salt and pepper. Don't mask the flavor with heavy seasonings; keep it subtle.

The roots grow about 10 or 12 inches long and a bit over an inch in diameter on top. The skin, as we said, is usually dirt-colored but can also be grayish white or grayish yellow. The flesh beneath is always white. Canned salsify is available imported from France. It's not bad as canned vegetables go—but be careful, from the photograph on the label you might mistake it for white asparagus.

Varieties

The dirt-colored salsify is the most common here although you may encounter *scorzonera* (black salsify) from time to time. They both taste alike and look exactly the same once they're peeled, and have the very same texture. Incidentally, the name *scorzonera* derives from the Catalan word for viper. Centuries ago, in Spain, it was used as an antidote for the bite of the poisonous reptile (it's also called "viper's grass" there).

Availability

Salsify is usually planted in the spring in the more temperate parts of the country; the seeds won't germinate in heat. The roots are harvested in late summer or in the fall after the weather has turned cold—or left in the ground to winter and dug (they can't be pulled) in early spring. These are the times you'll be most likely to find the root in the market—late summer, fall, winter, and early spring.

Storage

The roots will keep well for a week or two in the crisper drawer of your refrigerator, wrapped loosely in paper towels or in an open plastic bag.

What to Look For

Long, thin, carrot-shaped roots with light brown skins (black, if it's *scorzonera*) and shallow lateral indentations like parsnips or carrots. Often they will have thick root hairs protruding downward from top to bottom. They are usually sold trimmed of greens in bunches of 6 to 8—priced by the bunch most often, but sometimes by the pound.

Basic Preparation and Cooking Methods

Salsify can be peeled or scraped with a swivel-bladed vegetable peeler before cooking, cut into 2-inch lengths, and dropped immediately into acidulated water (water to which a few drops of lemon juice or vinegar has been added) so that the pieces do not discolor. It can also be cooked first and peeled afterward. In either case, start with cold salted water with a little lemon juice or vinegar added, bring to a boil, reduce heat to a simmer, and cook until just tender, about 15 minutes—*do not overcook or it will become mushy.* You can also cook the pieces in broth, or sauté them in butter or oil. Salsify can be mashed or riced with butter; combined with mashed potatoes or pureed with carrots; or served chilled, marinated in a vinaigrette dressing.

---

nutrition

Cooked salsify is low in calories (we don't mean to imply that raw is high, it's not), about 68 calories to a 100g serving. This same size serving will contain: 2.73g protein; 15.37g carbohydrates; 1.49g fiber; 47mg calcium (that's high); .55mg iron; 18mg magnesium; 56mg phosphorus; 283mg potassium (a lot); 16mg sodium; 4.6mg vitamin C; .056mg thiamine; .173mg riboflavin; and .392mg niacin. And no cholesterol.

SALSIFY AND BEET SALAD UNDER HORSERADISH CREAM

Serves 4

Serve this salad as a first course or to accompany slabs of cold poached fish. In the past we made this salad with hearts of palm, but when we discovered salsify we discovered a most satisfying substitute. Salsify can also stand in for artichoke hearts. We don't mean to imply that it can't stand on its own; it certainly can.

1½ pounds salsify
½ cup plus 2 tablespoons freshly squeezed lemon juice
Salt to taste
4 large lettuce leaves
4 canned whole beets, quartered and sliced ¼ inch thick, chilled

⅓ cup heavy cream or half-and-half
2 teaspoons homemade or bottled white horseradish
Freshly ground black pepper to taste
2 tablespoons light Tuscan olive oil

Trim the salsify, scrub well, peel, and cut into 1-inch lengths, dropping them immediately into a large saucepan with 1 inch of water, 2 tablespoons lemon juice, and 1 teaspoon salt. Cover and bring to a boil over high heat, then reduce heat to moderate and cook for 12 to 15 minutes, or until just tender. Drain, then chill for at least 1 hour or overnight.

Before serving, line 4 salad plates with the lettuce leaves and divide the salsify among the plates, arranging it decoratively. Scatter the beet pieces evenly over the salsify. In a glass or ceramic bowl, whisk together the cream, the remaining 1 cup lemon juice, horseradish, and salt and pepper to taste until the mixture is frothy, about 10 to 15 seconds. Add the olive oil, drop by drop, whisking after each addition. Keep whisking until the dressing is well combined and emulsified. Drizzle the dressing over the salad and serve.

SALSIFY WITH BROWN BUTTER, GARLIC, AND CAPERS

Serves 4

Salsify is done here Provençale style, which means with garlic. The browned butter and capers is our touch. It's a taste we acquired when we used to eat brains sauced this way. Salsify works just as well and doesn't clog our arteries like brains would.

1½ pounds salsify

2 tablespoons freshly squeezed lemon juice

1½ teaspoons salt, or to taste

4 tablespoons (½ stick) unsalted butter

1 tablespoon minced garlic

1 tablespoon tiny capers or chopped large capers

½ teaspoon freshly ground black pepper

2 tablespoons minced fresh parsley

Trim the salsify, scrub well, peel, and cut into 1-inch lengths, dropping them immediately into a large saucepan with 1 inch of water, the lemon juice, and 1 teaspoon salt. Cover and bring to a boil over high heat, then reduce heat to moderate and cook for 12 to 15 minutes, or until just tender. Drain.

Meanwhile, brown the butter in a saucepan over moderate heat, about 3 minutes. Watch carefully that it does not burn. Add the garlic and sauté until it turns golden, about 2 minutes. Add the capers, cooked salsify, ½ teaspoon salt, and the pepper and stir to combine well and heat through. Shower with parsley and serve.

GILDED SALSIFY

Serves 4

As we've said, salsify is so good it needs no gilding. Why try to improve on a good thing then? Because this is a cookbook, and that's what we're supposed to do. The gilding here is kept to a minimum, however, and is used merely to enhance a simple root, proving to guests that you've exerted a little effort on their behalf.

1½ pounds salsify
  2 tablespoons freshly squeezed
     lemon juice
  1 teaspoon salt
  1 tablespoon unsalted butter

  2 tablespoons fine white bread
     crumbs
  2 tablespoons minced fresh parsley
     Freshly ground black pepper to
     taste

Trim the green tops from the salsify, scrub well, peel, and cut into 1-inch lengths, dropping them immediately into a large saucepan with 1 inch of water, the lemon juice, and 1 teaspoon salt. Bring to a boil over high heat, covered, reduce heat to moderate, and cook for 12 to 15 minutes, or until just tender.

Meanwhile, cook the butter in a small skillet over moderate heat until it is golden brown, about 2 to 3 minutes. Add the bread crumbs and stir until the butter is absorbed.

When the salsify is tender, drain it and mash with a potato masher, or put through a ricer. Stir in the bread crumbs, parsley, and salt and pepper to taste. Combine well and mound in a warm serving dish.

Or, when the salsify is tender, drain and pile the little logs in a heated serving dish. Add the salt, pepper, and parsley to the buttered bread crumbs in the skillet, combine well, and sprinkle over the salsify.

PEPPERY SALSIFY AND GARLIC SAUCE FOR LINGUINI

Makes about 5 cups, enough for
1 pound of linguini; serves 4

What a way to warm your insides—with two of the best of the underground vegetables combined with pasta. Easy on the budget and so satisfying, especially for pasta freaks and salsify aficionados like us. We hope this recipe will make you a convert as well.

1½ pounds salsify
2 tablespoons freshly squeezed lemon juice
1 teaspoon salt
1 pound linguini
4 flat anchovy fillets, or to taste, chopped

¼ teaspoon dried hot pepper flakes, or more to taste
¾ cup light olive oil
½ cup minced fresh parsley
Freshly ground black pepper to taste

Trim the green tops from the salsify, scrub well, peel, and cut in ½-inch lengths, dropping them immediately into a large saucepan with 1 inch of water, the lemon juice, and 1 teaspoon salt. Bring to a boil over high heat, then reduce heat to moderate and cook for 10 minutes, or until just crisp-tender. Drain in a colander and refresh under cold water.

Bring 4 quarts of water to a boil in a large kettle. Add the linguini, stirring frequently, and cook for 8 minutes, or until *al dente*. Drain.

Meanwhile, in a large heavy sauté pan or skillet, cook the garlic, anchovies, and red pepper flakes in the oil over moderately low heat, stirring, until the garlic turns golden. Add the salsify and parsley, and cook the mixture, stirring, until heated through. Add salt and pepper to taste, and toss the sauce with the drained linguini. Serve immediately.

Sauteed Salsify with Two Peppers

Serves 4

Although salsify was a semipopular vegetable before the Second World War, the last half-century since has seen it lose favor. Cookbooks stopped giving recipes for it. The new, creative chefs forgot about it. Home cooks found that it was too much trouble to search out (it wasn't, and still isn't, at the local supermarket). We'd like to see it make a comeback. If kiwis can do it, salsify certainly can! Maybe this recipe will help.

1 **pound salsify**
2 **tablespoons freshly squeezed lemon juice**
3 **tablespoons olive oil**
  Salt and pepper to taste
1 **red bell pepper, cut into ½-inch dice**

1 **fresh jalapeño pepper, seeded, deveined, and minced**
2 **tablespoons minced shallots**
2 **tablespoons minced fresh coriander**
2 **sprigs fresh coriander for garnish (optional)**

Trim the green tops from the salsify, scrub well, peel, and cut into ½-inch lengths, dropping the pieces immediately into a bowl containing 2 inches of water and the lemon juice.

In a heavy sauté pan, bring the oil to rippling over moderately high heat. Drain the salsify and pat it dry, then add it to the oil and sauté, stirring and turning it frequently, for 10 to 12 minutes, or until crisp-tender and slightly browned. Season the salsify with salt and pepper and transfer it to a plate with a slotted spoon.

In the same sauté pan, cook the bell pepper over moderate heat, stirring for 1 minute. Add the jalapeño and cook the mixture, stirring, for 1 minute more. Stir in the shallots and cook the mixture, stirring, for 1 minute, or until the bell pepper is crisp-tender. Stir in the reserved salsify and cook, stirring, until just heated through. Remove the pan from the heat and stir in the minced coriander and salt and pepper to taste. Transfer the vegetables to a warm serving bowl, garnish with the coriander sprigs, and serve.

SCALLIONS

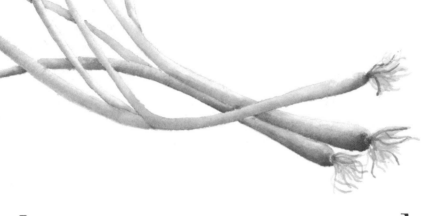

[*ALLIUM FISTULOSUM*]

spring onion

green onion

stone leek

cibol

*D*epending on the authority, scallions are described as (1) young onions harvested before they mature into a bulb, and (2) a separate part of the onion family, like leeks or shallots, that are nonbulb-forming. We subscribe to this second version. Scallions are not shallots; they are not leeks; they are not onions; they are not chives. They are unique. They are scallions.

Their nicknames may add to all the confusion. They are the first of the onion clan to appear in the spring, so they are called by some spring onions. They are mostly green leaves with a tight white stalk, so others named them green onions. They look something like a baby leek, though appearances deceive, yet they still picked up the name stone leeks. Cibol is a variation of the Spanish (*cebolla*), Portuguese (*cebola*), Italian (*cipolla*), and Yiddish (*tsibele*) words for onion, yet this nononion is nicknamed for its cousin.

As cookbook authors, we have had lengthy discussions with our editors about what to call scallions. What they knew them as, and wanted them called, always depended upon the region of the United States they were brought up in. Scallion is the original, traditional name stemming from the Latin *caepa Asclonia* onion (the confusion is ancient history) of Ashkelon, that Biblical port city in Palestine where the Philistines resided and where chives, according to food lore, first bloomed.

Scallions are completely edible from their hollow green leaves to the root ends of their white stalks. For years American recipes have almost always specified using only the white parts of the scallions. In our recipes both white and green parts are always used; why discard perfectly edible food, especially when it tastes so good and looks so pretty and fresh?

Whatever the scallion is or isn't, it remains a delightful, zingy addition to both uncooked and cooked dishes. Americans, with their traditionally bland palates, perversely eat scallions raw more often than cooked. Although we love raw scallions, they are terrific braised, sautéed, steamed, added to cooked dishes for a milder-than-onion flavor and where their deep green color helps make a dish look more pleasing. Of course, in Oriental cooking the green leaves are always used and are highly prized, just as they are in our kitchen. At our table, hardly a soup is served that doesn't appear—and isn't more appealing—with chopped scallions strewn over the top for garnish and added flavor.

Oriental cooks have always used both the white stalk and the green leaves of scallions. The scallion is the oldest and most used ingredient in

Chinese cooking. In Japanese cooking only two members of the onion family are used, and both happen to be varieties of scallion.

Scallions have been improved in flavor over the past few decades. Newer varieties are quite mild, almost sweet compared to those of years gone by. The best scallions and the biggest crops are produced in California, but Ohio, New Jersey, and Texas have sizable harvests as well. Those from California are shipped year-round with root hairs and tops clipped for packing. Other states produce scallions for local consumption. In Louisiana, shallots are not allowed to bulb nor the tops to die and are harvested as "scallions." In some areas, white bulb onions are grown specifically to inhibit bulbing and are harvested when young in the spring (perhaps these are the *real* spring onions). At our farmer's market in Manhattan we have purchased "red scallions," which are really red onions taken from the ground before they have a chance to mature. Their flavor is indistinguishable from common "white scallions."

Varieties

It would be tedious to repeat here what we have just said in the previous paragraphs. All you have to know is: If it looks like a scallion, it will taste like a scallion, whether it is really an immature onion or shallot or a true scallion.

Availability

The peak season for scallions is May through July, but you'll find them sold fresh year-round.

Storage

Fresh scallions last at least a week when refrigerated unwashed. Some of the outer leaves may turn limp and yellow if the bunch is stored too long. Just discard these and trim well before using. Do not try to freeze fresh scallions, the results will be virtually unusable. Besides, good quality scallions are always available, so why bother?

What to Look For

Head for bright, dark green leaves with firm white stalks with no wilt or rot. The bunch of 6 to 8 plants should look crisp and straight or slightly curved. Root hairs at the stalk end should be white. Avoid browned roots and yellowed tops—these scallions are beyond their prime.

Basic Preparation and Cooking Methods

Rinse individual stalks under cold water, trim 1/16 inch off the roots end, and remove any wilted or yellowed tops. Pull off any slimy-feeling thin membranes surrounding the white stalk. If the scallions are to be served whole, you might trim the green leaves to an even length for appearance' sake. Or they can be sliced into various lengths, chopped, or minced for cooking or garnishing. Save any decent leaf trimmings for soup or stock flavoring.

---

nutrition

Depending on its length and thickness, a scallion stalk has only 4 to 10 calories; with all that satisfying flavor, scallions should be high on dieters' lists of snack foods. In 100g of raw scallions there are only 25 calories, 5.55g carbohydrates, .84g fiber, 60mg calcium, 1.89mg iron, 20mg magnesium, 33mg phosphorus, 257mg potassium, 4mg sodium, .44mg zinc, .06mg copper, 45mg vitamin C, .07mg thiamine, .14mg riboflavin, .2mg niacin, .144mg pantothenic acid, 13.7mg folacin, 5,000IU vitamin A. All the amino acids but cysteine, and no cholesterol.

SCALLION BUTTER FLAVORED WITH CURRY

Makes approximately ⅔ cup

Keeping flavored butters in the freezer makes it simple to add instant, vivid flavor to grilled or broiled meats, fish, poultry, or sandwiches. This one, spread on triangles of toast or cocktail breads, can be used as a base for canapés of egg, smoked fish, or vegetable pâtés. We also like it on chicken or turkey sandwiches, or melted as a quick sauce for boiled shrimp.

½ cup plus 2 tablespoons (1¼ sticks) unsalted butter, at room temperature

1 cup minced scallions, white and green parts

1 tablespoon curry powder or *garam masala* (available at Indian stores and some specialty food shops)

1 teaspoon freshly squeezed lemon juice, or more to taste

½ teaspoon salt, or to taste

½ teaspoon white pepper

In a small skillet, melt 2 tablespoons of the butter over moderately low heat. When the foam subsides, cook the scallions until softened. Add the curry powder and cook the mixture, stirring, for 30 seconds. Remove from the heat and let cool in the skillet.

Meanwhile, in a small bowl, cream the remaining ½ cup butter. Add the lemon juice, scallion mixture, and salt and pepper and blend with a spatula or whisk until thoroughly combined. Chill the butter for 15 minutes, or until slightly firm and malleable. Transfer the scallion butter to a 12-inch length of wax paper and roll it into a log 1 to 1½ inches in diameter. Twist the ends of the wax paper and chill the butter until firm enough to unwrap and slice. Or you can twist the ends of the wax paper, chill the butter until firm, seal the wrapped log in a plastic freezer bag, and place in the freezer. It keeps up to 2 months frozen. With a warm knife, slice as much as is needed from the frozen log, then refreeze the remainder.

CHILLED CRUSHED SCALLION AND SOUR-GRASS SOUP WITH RED RADISH

Serves 6

This soup will cool you off better than an icy shower on the hottest summer day! Scallions, sorrel (sour grass), and radishes are all at their best in summer, which is why this soup is the perfect choice for lunch, supper, or a picnic. It's our own variation on a traditional Russian sorrel soup called *schav* and it is also a feast for the eyes, combining the cooling colors of green and white with an accent of red.

8 cups water

2 pounds fresh sour grass (sorrel) leaves, washed, stems removed, coarsely chopped

1 10-ounce package frozen chopped spinach
Juice of 1 lemon

2 bunches scallions, both white and green part, trimmed and sliced

2 tablespoons salt

1 heaping teaspoon freshly ground black pepper

1 pint sour cream or plain yogurt

6 red radishes, thinly sliced

1 small cucumber (preferably Kirby), quartered lengthwise and thinly sliced

In a soup pot or large saucepan, bring the water to a rolling boil. Add the sour grass, frozen spinach, and lemon juice. Cover, reduce heat to a simmer, and cook for 20 minutes. Remove from heat and allow to cool to room temperature. Refrigerate for 2 hours, or up to 24 hours.

Place the sliced scallions in a metal or glass bowl large enough to hold the finished soup and sprinkle with the salt. With the flat bottom of a heavy, 8-ounce glass tumbler, press down and crush the scallions, twisting the tumbler as you press, until all the slices have released their juices, are limp, and the salt has dissolved. Scrape any scallions sticking to the tumbler back into the bowl, and mix in the pepper.

Add the sour cream to the scallion mixture and stir until well blended.

Add the sour grass and its liquid to the sour cream–scallion mixture, 1 cup at a time, stirring to combine well after each addition.

Ladle the soup into cooled soup bowls, and garnish with the radishes and cucumber slices.

NOTE: In the unlikely event that there is any leftover soup, it will keep, covered tightly, in the refrigerator for 4 or 5 days. The sour grass–spinach mixture can be kept frozen for up to 2 months. On the day it is to be served, thaw, return to the refrigerator to chill, and combine just before serving with the scallion–sour cream mixture.

SCORCHED SCALLIONS

Serves 6

We first had grilled scallions at a tiny joint some friends took us to about fifteen minutes after we had deplaned for the first time in Mexico City. A revelation! So simple, yet so delicious. They were really marvelous—and always are whenever we've had them since, in Mexico or in the United States. Serve with grilled meats, chicken, or fish—or serve as a starter with Mexican food

24 thick scallions, trimmed to about 10-inch lengths

1 tablespoon vegetable oil, or more if needed

Salt and freshly ground black pepper to taste

Preheat the oven to 500° F.

Coat the scallions all over with the oil, arrange them in one layer in a jelly-roll pan, and sprinkle them with salt and pepper to taste. Roast in the top third of the oven for 5 minutes, or until just tender. Turn the broiler on high and place the jelly-roll pan with the scallions 2 inches from the heat. Broil for 1 to 2 minutes, or until the scallions begin to char. Alternatively, coat scallions as above and place on charcoal or gas-fired grill for 7 minutes, turning once, or until charred.

SCALLION, CREAMY BLUE CHEESE, AND TOASTED ALMOND SANDWICH FILLING

Makes about 1¾ cups; filling for 4 to 6 sandwiches

You can use this as a sandwich spread or as an hors d'oeuvre on triangles of cocktail pumpernickel, toast, or on crackers. It can stand alone in a sandwich or can be combined with sliced chicken, turkey, strips of daikon, or paper-thin rounds of kohlrabi or tomato.

½ pound Blue Castello, Saga Blue, or other triple crème blue cheese

3 tablespoons plain yogurt

¾ cup whole blanched almonds, toasted and cooled

1 cup sliced scallions, white and green parts

½ teaspoon white pepper

1 tablespoon freshly squeezed lemon juice, or to taste

In a food processor, puree the cheese and yogurt until creamy. Add the almonds and process, pulsing, until the almonds are finely ground. Add the scallions, pepper, and lemon juice and blend the mixture just until it is combined well. Spread the mixture on lightly toasted pumpernickel, or mound it in a decorative bowl and surround it with cocktail bread triangles and/or crackers.

SHALLOTS

[*ALLIUM ASCALONICUM*]

eschalots

Spanish garlic

échalote (Fr.)

schalotte (Ger.)

scalogna (It.)

ascalonia, chalota, escalma (Sp.)

Shallots, like garlic, form a cluster of bulbs rather than a single one like an onion. This distinguished member of the lily family is much more subtle in flavor than its cousins, but again, like an onion, varies in intensity with the soil and climate in which it is grown. Some say its flavor is akin to a very mild onion with a touch of garlic added, but shallots have a distinct flavor of their own. They are easily grown—even in your kitchen window. Just plant a clove in a pot of sandy soil and watch it thrive, reproducing itself over and over again.

Although often pricey, shallots are generally available at both green-grocers and supermarkets. Usually you will find shallots sold near the onions and potatoes, often displayed in small net bags or in pint containers. You'll recognize them by their papery, copper-colored skins (they also come in a greenish white or in deep mauve) and the pointed, arrow-shaped cloves that are held together in loose clusters. The cloves themselves, when peeled, are grayish or purplish in color.

Although many staple sauces of French cuisine demand shallots, they are almost more important to the cuisines of Southeast Asia: Thailand, Vietnam, Laos, Malaysia, and Indonesia cannot do without them. There shallots might be charred over a flame before being used, sliced, fried crisp and sprinkled over a dish for a textured garnish, or pounded to a paste with chile peppers, lemon grass, and other seasonings.

Unlike onions, garlic, and scallions, shallots are never "hot" and never disturb the balance of flavors in any sauce or gravy. Raw shallots won't add bite to a salad or salad dressing, won't overpower seafood or shellfish. They can even be prepared on their own as a vegetable dish simmered or roasted right in their skins—just peel them and serve alone or mix with another vegetable, such as green beans, snow peas, or potatoes; or mash them with a little salt and pepper and use as a cracker spread.

Varieties

You'll find the refined shallot in three different colors at your market, the most common being the hard, shiny coppery bulbs. But you may also come across the greenish white or purplish varieties. The purple seems strongest to our taste, but even these are mild compared to other, more robust relatives in the onion family.

Availability

Shallots are available twelve months of the year, but those available in July or August are not quite as good as those harvested in the cooler months. Most shallots on the East Coast come from New Jersey and Long Island. But you'll also find them imported from France and South America (usually in late spring). They are also grown on the West Coast, supplemented by imports from Southeast Asia.

Storage

Shallots are surprisingly sturdy. They keep well for months at a time if bought fresh. Even if they've been stored for a long time before being sold they will still keep for several weeks in a dark, airy place or loosely wrapped in paper towels in the refrigerator. If they begin to sprout, use them quickly, as they can sometimes turn bitter.

What to Look For

Select hard, shiny bulbs with brittle, parchmentlike skins. Discard those that are bruised, beginning to sprout, withered, dried out, or soft.

Basic Preparation and Cooking Methods

Shallots cook quickly and don't need high heat. They can be blanched, boiled, or roasted right in their skins—the skins slip off easily. Otherwise, slice off a bit of the root and tip end and use the knife or your fingernails to peel off the skin. Use shallots raw in salads and salad dressings, or sauté, simmer, or steam them for 5 to 10 minutes before adding to a cooked dish. Do not brown shallots deeply; unlike onions they will turn bitter.

---

nutrition

Shallots are used in such small quantities that their nutritional qualities hardly matter—and as a matter of fact, they are not particularly loaded with any vitamins or minerals, except potassium: 100g contains 334mg. Instead, use shallots to make other foods with lots of nutritional value taste even better.

SHALLOT BUTTER FOR SAUCES

Makes a generous 2 cups

Keep this butter on hand to make quick and superb sauces. Use a quantity of it whisked with pan juices and a little wine (red or white, whatever is appropriate) and serve it with meats, fish, or vegetables. It will keep for up to 2 months in the freezer, but we doubt you'll have it around for that long.

8 shallots, minced	2 tablespoons minced fresh parsley
1 tablespoon minced garlic	½ teaspoon white pepper
¼ cup dry sherry or dry white wine	½ teaspoon salt, or to taste
1 cup (2 sticks) unsalted butter, at room temperature	Dash of allspice

Combine the shallots, garlic, and white wine in a small stainless-steel or enameled saucepan. Bring to a boil over high heat and cook until the liquid is reduced to 1 tablespoon, about 3 minutes. Remove from the heat and allow to cool.

Pour the cooled mixture into a food processor and add the butter, parsley, white pepper, salt, and allspice. Process, scraping down the sides once or twice, until thoroughly blended, about 30 to 40 seconds.

Scrape the shallot butter onto a large sheet of plastic wrap, and with a rubber spatula, shape it into a smooth cylinder about 1½ inches in diameter. Fold over the plastic wrap, roll up the cylinder of butter, and twist both ends to seal. Or wrap it in smaller portions in a similar manner.

Label it with the date and store in the refrigerator for up to 2 weeks, or in the freezer for 2 months.

CREAMED SHALLOT AND ENDIVE SOUP WITH BACON

Serves 4 to 6

Belgian friends turned us on to this soup years ago. The original recipe had more endive and less shallots, but over the years the proportions have changed (to feature one of our favorites) and this version emerged. It's a lovely, rich soup with unique flavor characteristics that hold up even when it is served cold.

2 tablespoons unsalted butter

8 shallots, minced

1 pound Belgian endive (about 6), rinsed and thinly sliced cross-wise

4 cups homemade chicken stock or canned broth

1 cup heavy cream or half-and-half

4 slices of lean bacon, cooked crisp and crumbled

1 teaspoon minced fresh chervil, or ¼ teaspoon dried, crumbled

¼ teaspoon salt, or to taste

½ teaspoon white pepper

1 large egg yolk

2 tablespoons milk
Fresh parsley or basil leaves for garnish (optional)

In a large sauté pan or soup pot, melt the butter over moderate heat and cook the shallots, stirring, until they are softened. Add the endive and cook the mixture, stirring frequently, for 3 minutes. Add the stock and cream and bring to a boil over high heat, then reduce heat to a simmer and cook for 5 minutes.

Stir in the bacon, chervil, and salt and pepper. In a small bowl, whisk together the egg yolk and milk, and pour the mixture into the soup in a thin stream, whisking the soup as you pour. Transfer the soup to a tureen, or ladle it into heated soup bowls. Garnish with the parsley or basil leaves.

NOTE: You can reserve half the crumbled bacon and use it as a garnish to sprinkle over individual servings instead of the parsley or basil leaves.

HOT SHALLOT MOUSSES
BATHED IN STILTON AND
WALNUT SAUCE

Serves 4

This may seem like an elaborate recipe (especially to guests) but it really is quite simple. It's an elegant way to start a dinner menu and allows shallots to star for a change instead of playing their usual supporting role.

mousses
----

4 large outer leaves of cabbage or iceberg lettuce, spines removed
1 tablespoon unsalted butter
1 tablespoon light olive oil
1 pound shallots, peeled and coarsely chopped

1 medium onion, chopped
⅓ cup homemade chicken stock or canned broth
1 large egg, lightly beaten
¼ cup half-and-half
   Salt and white pepper to taste

sauce
----

1 tablespoon unsalted butter
1 tablespoon light olive oil
1 tablespoon minced garlic
2 tablespoons dry white wine
1¼ cups half-and-half
2 ounces Stilton cheese, crumbled

3 tablespoons chopped walnuts
¼ cup homemade chicken stock or canned broth
   Salt and white pepper to taste
4 walnut halves for garnish (optional)

In a large saucepan of boiling salted water, blanch the cabbage leaves for 1 minute. Carefully remove the leaves with tongs and pat dry with paper towels, reserving the hot water. Line four ½-cup ramekins with the blanched leaves, allowing some of the leaves to hang over the sides about 1 inch. In a saucepan, heat 1 tablespoon butter and 1 tablespoon olive oil over moderately low heat. When the foam subsides, cook the shallots and onion until they are softened, about 2 minutes. Add ⅓ cup stock and cook the mixture, stirring, for 3 or 4 minutes more, or until almost all of the liquid has evaporated. In a blender or food processor, puree the mixture until it is smooth, and let it cool in the container for 10 minutes.

Preheat the oven to 300° F.

When the shallot and onion mixture has cooled, add the egg and ¼ cup half-and-half and blend until well combined. Season to taste with salt and pepper. Spoon the mixture into the lined ramekins. Fold the overhanging cabbage leaves over the mousse, put the ramekins in a baking pan and add enough hot water (from blanching the leaves) to the pan to reach halfway up the sides of the ramekins. Bake the mousses in the middle of the oven for 35 to 40 minutes, or until they are firm to the touch. Remove the ramekins from the pan and let them cool for 10 minutes.

While the mousses are cooling, heat 1 tablespoon butter and 1 tablespoon olive oil in a saucepan over moderate heat. When the foam subsides, cook the garlic for 1 minute, or until it is just softened. Add the wine and continue cooking, stirring, for 1 minute more, or until the liquid is reduced to about 1 teaspoon. Add 1¼ cups half-and-half, raise the heat to high, and bring the mixture to a boil; lower heat to moderate and boil the mixture, stirring, for 8 to 10 minutes, or until the liquid is reduced to about ¼ cup. Add the Stilton, walnuts, ¼ cup broth, and salt and pepper to taste, and stir well to combine.

Invert the mousses onto individual serving plates and spoon the sauce around them. Decorate each mousse with a walnut half, if desired.

CRISP BROWNED SHALLOTS SHOWERED ON BUTTERED NOODLES

Serves 4

- - - - - - - -

Sometimes a simple side dish is best. The shallots can be fried ahead of time and combined with the noodles just before serving. The noodles' texture—a little slippery—melds well with the semicrisp rings of browned shallot. The contrast of pale golden noodles against the dark gold of the shallots doesn't hurt either. Its eye appeal can cause your taste buds to work overtime.

Peanut, safflower, or canola oil for frying

¾ pound large shallots, peeled and thinly sliced crosswise

½ pound medium egg noodles

2 tablespoons unsalted butter

Salt and freshly ground black pepper to taste

1 teaspoon poppy seeds

In a large sauté pan or heavy skillet over moderately high heat, bring ½ inch of oil to rippling. Add the shallots and fry, stirring occasionally, for 2 to 3 minutes, or until they are golden. Transfer them with a slotted spoon to paper towels to drain.

In a large saucepan over high heat, bring salted water to a boil and cook the noodles for 7 to 9 minutes, or until *al dente*. Drain them well and return them to the pan. Over low heat toss the noodles with the butter, salt and pepper to taste, and the poppy seeds. Mound the noodles in a heated serving dish and sprinkle the shallots in a circle around the edge.

CARAMELIZED SHALLOT VINAIGRETTE SAUCE

Makes about 1 cup

One usually thinks of vinaigrettes as dressing for salads or as marinades. This one is hearty enough to stand alone as a sauce. We like it to dress up steamed vegetables such as string beans or potatoes, to sauce polenta or cannellini beans, or to team with roast or grilled meats and poultry.

½ cup plus 2 tablespoons light olive oil

5 medium shallots (4 ounces), peeled and thinly sliced

½ teaspoon salt, or to taste

¼ cup white wine vinegar

1 tablespoon Dijon mustard

1 tablespoon Maggi seasoning

½ teaspoon fresh thyme or marjoram or ¼ teaspoon dried

Freshly ground pepper

In a medium sauté pan or skillet over moderate heat, bring 2 tablespoons of the oil to rippling. Add the shallots, sprinkle with salt, and cook, stirring frequently, until dark golden brown, 8 to 10 minutes. Add 2 tablespoons of water and cook a few seconds more, stirring, until the water evaporates. Set aside to cool slightly.

Meanwhile, in a medium bowl whisk together the remaining oil with the vinegar, mustard, Maggi seasoning, and thyme. Stir in the shallot mixture and pepper to taste. Pour into a covered jar or plastic container with a tight fitting lid and let mellow for 2 or 3 days in the refrigerator. Bring to room temperature, shake or stir, and serve.

SWEET POTATOES

[*IPOMOEA BATATAS*]

boniato (Cuban)

batata (Sp.)

white sweet potato

Cuban sweet potato

camote (Latin Am.)

The sweet potato, *Ipomoea batatas*, is absolutely no relation to the potato and belongs to an entirely different family, one related to the morning glory. The only kinship the two have is the derivation of the word *potato*, which is a skewed European version of the Indian word for sweet potato, *batata*. So much for the botanical expertise of the early explorers and conquistadores.

Potatoes are tubers, emanations of the roots of the plant, not the root itself. Sweet potatoes, on the other hand, are true roots, or at least a part of the root—the edible part. They are sometimes called by the misnomer *yams*. (True yams are a completely different botanical category of vegetable. Neither tubers nor roots, they are rhizomes like ginger; see page 330 for more on yams.)

Although true yams are inferior food to sweet potatoes, they, nevertheless, seem to have a better image in this country because you'll see sweet potatoes often called yams in greengrocers and even at farmers' markets.

Sweet potatoes are native to the Western Hemisphere only and were discovered along with the discovery of the New World. The West Indians on Hispaniola introduced them to Columbus on his second voyage.

Unlike potatoes, when sweet potatoes were brought to the Old World from the New, they were an overnight success. Henry VIII, who ruled England in the early 1500s, got them as part of Catherine of Aragon's dowry. He could eat two dozen at one sitting, it was reported, and had them turned into sweetened and very spicy pies. He tried to have them grown in England after his divorce from Catherine cut off his source, but although they bloomed, they withered on the vine in the cool English summer.

The Spanish court had a definite taste for what they called the "root fruit," and unlike England, had the proper climate to begin cultivating a local supply. (Sweet potatoes are not grown from seed but from sprouts cut from roots of prior crops or from the vines. A sweet potato vine was a popular houseplant in the 1920s, 1930s, and 1940s. It grows quickly and easily when set on its side in a dish with water coming up halfway.)

The sweet potato diaspora, like the dispersion of so many other New World agricultural products, happened with the explorers. The Spanish ships of discovery brought it from the Americas to Europe, the Pacific, and the Philippines. The Portuguese took it from there to India, China, Japan, and Malaya.

It seemed to have a penchant for confusing people wherever it settled. In parts of Japan it is known as the "Chinese potato," in parts of China it is called the "Japanese potato." The Japanese use the sweet potato as one of the vegetables to dip in batter and fry for tempura. The Indians use it similarly for *pakoras*.

Sweet potatoes are so loved on some Pacific islands that they have all but supplanted other staples, and in places like New Guinea they often represent 90 percent of the local diet. They could do worse.

The Incas and Mayas in Central and South America cultivated several types used variously as food or artists' coloring material. De Soto found them growing along the Mississippi in what is now Louisiana. They were grown by the colonists in Jamestown, Virginia, in 1648, and were a dietary staple when other food was in short supply during the Revolutionary War.

It was in the seventeenth-century English colonies that the sweet potato was first cultivated in North America. It was called simply a "potato" then. Not until 1740, about twenty years after the introduction of the white potato by the Irish into Massachusetts, was the longer term *sweet potato* used or necessary to differentiate between the two "potatoes."

Varieties

Only two main types of sweet potato are of commercial importance in the United States, although within these types there are literally hundreds of varieties. Most of them have the familiar yellow-brown or orange-brown skin and ocher, bright orange, yellow-red, or reddish-violet flesh. One is so pale it could pass (uneaten) as a white potato. Most taste sweet, but the degree of sweetness varies from variety to variety. They range in shape from round or oval to long, slender, and tapered on the ends. They can grow in length to 10 inches and in diameter up to 5 inches.

The two varieties you'll find in the bins at your market are dubbed by wholesalers and growers as "moist" (red) or "dry" (white). These designations have little to do with their water content and refer mainly to the climate and soil in which they were grown. Moist types are the ones most often erroneously called *yams* because of their color. They have darker brownish red skins and vibrant orange-red flesh. They also have a higher starch content that converts to sugar as they cook, resulting in a sweeter end product. The dry sweet potato has a light brown-yellow skin with golden or pale yellow to white flesh. They convert less starch to sugar and are decidedly less sweet when you eat them. They're also a bit more fibrous than the tender reds.

Availability

Sweet potatoes are available all year because of curing and storage methods—but the peak season for red or moist types is late summer through March. September through November are the best months for white or dry kinds. Winter and spring are the prime seasons for sweeter stored roots of both varieties, because the curing process that helps the sweet potato to keep actually makes them sweeter. The freshly dug roots are held in controlled high-heat, high-humidity areas for about a week, allowing conversion of starch to sugar and dextrins.

What to Look For

Seek out firm sweet potatoes with bright, smooth, shallowly dimpled skins. Medium sizes that are fat in the middle and tapered at both ends are easiest to handle in the kitchen. Don't buy those with knobs, indentations, bruises, blemishes, or signs of sprouting. Odd shapes will be hard to peel and cut without waste. Damaged, decayed, shriveled, or discolored skins

and soft spots can affect the taste of the potato even when the bad parts have been cut away. Check, too, for cuts, holes, and worms.

Storage

Sweet potatoes keep better at room temperature than in the refrigerator. Try to store them in a cool, dry place with good ventilation and they will keep for 2 or 3 weeks.

Basic Preparation and Cooking Methods

Like white potatoes, sweet potatoes can be baked, boiled, fried, sautéed, mashed, scalloped, or what have you. Most basic cooking methods are suitable for both.

Before cooking, scrub the skin well and check for woody areas. Cut these away. Bake whole sweet potatoes in their skins in a 400° F. oven for 40 to 45 minutes, longer if you like, depending on size. (You really can't overbake sweet potatoes—their skins just get crisper and thicker.) Pierce the skin with a fork to allow steam to escape. Because of piercing and tiny, unseen fissures in the skin, sticky juices can ooze out during baking, burn on the oven floor or rack, and be a mess to clean up afterward, so we bake sweets on a cookie sheet, in a shallow baking pan, or on a sheet of aluminum foil—not directly on the oven floor or rack. When a fork goes into the flesh easily or the sides give to finger pressure, the sweet potato is ready to eat plain or with a little butter, salt, and pepper.

You can peel raw sweet potatoes, cut them into slices or cubes, and simmer in a covered pot in a little water, no more than an inch. They should be done in 12 to 20 minutes for slices, 10 to 15 minutes for cubes. If they over-cook for a few minutes, it's not a disaster, as long as the water doesn't all cook away. They can also be boiled in their skins to preserve nutrients. Boil for 20 to 30 minutes and remove the skin when cool enough to handle.

The lighter-colored dry varieties generally take a bit longer to cook than the orange-fleshed types.

Sweet potatoes take well to micro-waving. Pierce the skin, place on a paper towel to catch any juices, and microwave a single potato at full power for 5 to 8 minutes. To do multiples, arrange them in a circle or like the rays of the sun and microwave for 8 to 10 minutes for 2; 10 to 13 minutes for 3; 13 to 17 minutes for 4. Turn the pota-toes over once and give them a quarter turn twice during cooking. They will probably feel slightly firm when you remove them from the microwave at the end of the cooking time; just let them sit on the counter for a few min-utes to soften.

nutrition

The sweet potato has more calories, minerals, and vitamin A than the white potato—but less protein. A 5 x 2-inch sweet potato with its skin has 172 calories, 2.3g protein, .9g fat, 29.2g carbohydrates, 41mg calcium, 61mg phosphorus, .9mg iron, 13mg sodium, 315mg potassium, 11,920IU vitamin A, .13mg thiamine, .08mg riboflavin, .8mg niacin, and 30mg vitamin C. They provide almost three times the recommended daily al-lowance of vitamin A—a white potato has none at all. You get three-fifths of the RDA of vitamin C, along with a nice bit of color on your plate.

BOURBON-SPIKED SWEET
POTATO AND APRICOT PURÉE

Serves 4 to 6

Even though we might have a sweet tooth, the thought of another Thanksgiving dinner with a sweet potato casserole filled with pineapple, blanketed with brown sugar and toasted marshmallows makes our teeth ache. Sweet potatoes are sweet enough on their own without the addition of cloying sweeteners. Fruit *is* a nice flavor complement, but we believe a tart, somewhat sour fruit is called for. We happen to love apricots, especially dried. When we had some left over after making an apricot cheesecake, we came up with this puree. It's sweet and slightly tart at the same time, and the bourbon lends an added edge. Thanksgiving is our favorite holiday and now we have another family favorite to serve.

2½ pounds sweet potatoes, peeled and cut crosswise into ½-inch slices

¼ cup packed, coarsely chopped dried apricots

4 tablespoons (½ stick) unsalted butter, at room temperature

1 tablespoon Dijon mustard

2 tablespoons bourbon
Salt and freshly ground white pepper to taste
Fresh mint leaves for garnish (optional)

In a steamer set over boiling water, steam the sweet potatoes and the apricots, covered, for 20 minutes, or until the potatoes are very tender. Puree the mixture in a food processor with the butter, mustard, bourbon, and salt and pepper (in batches, if necessary), until the puree is smooth. Mound the puree in a serving bowl and decorate with the mint leaves, if desired.

NOTE: The puree can be held in a low oven (300° to 325° F.) for 30 minutes before serving, if covered loosely with foil.

The puree can be frozen and reheated in a preheated 375° F. oven for 45 minutes to 1 hour. Cover tightly with foil.

This recipe can be doubled or tripled without affecting the flavor.

TWO-TONED SWEET POTATO AND POTATO GRATIN

Serves 6 to 8

This is a pretty way to serve sweet potatoes—wedges are a sunny orange and white—and one that's a little less sweet because of the white potatoes and cheese. The addition of nutmeg and a little mustard is a felicitous touch. You can substitute turnips for the potatoes, if you like, for an even more piquant undertone.

¾ pound sweet potatoes (about 2 medium), peeled

¾ pound boiling potatoes (about 3 medium)

½ teaspoon powdered mustard

½ teaspoon salt, or to taste

½ teaspoon freshly ground black pepper

1½ tablespoons all-purpose flour

1 cup shredded Jarlsberg

1½ teaspoons freshly grated nutmeg

1 large egg

2 tablespoons cold unsalted butter, cut into pieces

Using a food processor, a *mandoline,* or by hand, slice the sweet potatoes very thin, as if for potato chips. Peel the boiling potatoes and slice them in the same manner. In a small bowl, combine the mustard, salt, and pepper with the flour. Butter a 13- to 14-inch oval gratin dish or a 2-quart shallow baking dish, and arrange half the white potatoes in the dish, sprinkling them with ⅓ cup of the Jarlsberg and ½ teaspoon of the nutmeg. Cover the layer with half the sweet potatoes and sprinkle with half the flour mixture. Repeat with remaining layers. You will end up with 2 white potato layers and 2 sweet potato layers.

Preheat the oven to 375° F.

In a medium bowl, whisk the egg. In a small saucepan over moderately high heat, scald the milk, and add it in a thin stream to the egg, whisking. Pour the custard over the potato layers. Sprinkle the remaining ⅓ cup Jarlsberg and ½ teaspoon nutmeg evenly over the top, dot with butter, and bake the gratin in the middle of the oven for 45 minutes, or until the potatoes are tender and the gratin is bubbling and golden brown. Let the gratin stand on a kitchen counter for 5 to 10 minutes to get crusty before serving.

ORANGE-LEMON SWEET POTATO PUREE WITH PECAN TOPPING

Serves 4

For this recipe we use what most greengrocers call "yams," the reddish-fleshed "moist" sweet potatoes that are more intensely sweet than the "dry" yellow-fleshed variety. Lemon juice and orange zest add just the right acidic undertones. The chopped pecans are a southern contribution that offers a pleasant texture along with a welcome, toasty taste.

2 pounds "yams," well scrubbed

4 tablespoons (½ stick) unsalted butter, at room temperature

3 tablespoons freshly squeezed lemon juice, or more to taste

2 pieces orange zest (3 x ½ inch), cut into thin julienne strips

¼ cup water

Salt and freshly ground black pepper to taste

2 tablespoons chopped toasted pecans

Place the "yams" in a large saucepan with enough salted water to cover them by 2 inches and bring to a boil over high heat. Cover, reduce the heat to a simmer, and cook the "yams" for 20 to 30 minutes, or until they are tender.

Drain the "yams," let them cool just until they can be handled, and peel off the skins. Force them through a ricer or food mill back into the pan, and add the butter, lemon juice, orange zest, and water, stirring to combine. Heat the puree over moderately low heat, stirring frequently, until heated through (add more water or orange juice to thin, if necessary). Season the puree with salt and pepper and transfer it to a heated serving dish. Sprinkle the top with the chopped pecans and serve.

NOTE: You can substitute toasted walnuts for the pecans, or even chopped, salted, dry-roasted peanuts. But pecans are our choice.

BROWNED-BUTTER SWEET-POTATO CLOVERLEAF ROLLS

Makes 18 rolls

- - - - - - - - - - - - - - -

We first used browned butter as shortening in a tart shell. The flavor it gives to such pastry, startlingly nutty, challenges the best you've ever tasted. For pâté brisée and tart shells, you need solid shortening, so the butter is browned and then chilled and resolidified in the refrigerator. In this recipe for rolls, room-temperature liquified butter is called for, so it is browned first (not dark brown, just a nice, pale tan), then cooled but not chilled.

6 tablespoons unsalted butter	⅓ cup milk
3 tablespoons sugar	1 teaspoon salt
¼ cup lukewarm water	¾ cup mashed cooked sweet pota-
2½ teaspoons (1¼-ounce package) active dry yeast	toes (¾ pound fresh)
2 large eggs	3½ to 4 cups all-purpose flour

In a small saucepan, melt 4 tablespoons of the butter over moderate heat. When the foam subsides, reduce heat to moderately low and brown for 2 to 4 minutes, until it turns a caramel color. Do not let it burn. Remove the pan from the heat and set aside to cool.

In a small bowl or cup, stir together 1 tablespoon of the sugar and the lukewarm water, sprinkle the yeast over the mixture, and let it proof for 5 minutes, or until foamy.

In a large bowl, whisk together the eggs, the remaining 2 tablespoons sugar, the milk, melted browned butter, salt, sweet potatoes, and yeast mixture until well combined. Stir in 3 cups flour, 1 cup at a time, and turn the dough out onto a floured surface. Knead the dough, incorporating as much of the remaining 1 cup flour as necessary to prevent the dough from sticking, for 8 to 10 minutes, or until smooth and elastic.

Form the dough into a ball, put it in a well-buttered or oiled large bowl, and turn it to coat with the butter or oil. Let the dough rise, covered with a dish towel or plastic wrap, in a warm place for 1 hour, or until it is double in bulk.

Preheat the oven to 400° F. Brown the remaining 2 tablespoons butter, as above.

Turn the dough out onto a floured surface, cut off pieces of dough about the size of a walnut, and form them into balls. Put 3 balls of dough into each of 18 buttered or oiled ⅓-cup muffin tins, brush the tops of the rolls with the melted browned butter, and let the rolls rise, covered loosely, in a warm place for 30 to 45 minutes, or until they are almost double in bulk.

Bake the rolls in the middle of the oven for 12 to 15 minutes, or until they are golden brown. Serve warm.

NOTE: The rolls can be frozen after baking. Cool and wrap tightly in foil. Reheat, frozen, in the foil wrapping in a preheated 400° F. oven for 25 to 30 minutes, or until heated through.

SWEET POTATO SOUP WITH YOGURT AND CARAWAY

Serves 6

If you can find Russian black caraway seeds (a.k.a. *chernishkas*) at good spice shops or a friendly bakery, by all means use them in place of the ordinary kind. They look like coal mined for a dollhouse and add a dry, spicy flavor to the soup.

2 tablespoons light Tuscan olive oil

1 medium onion, finely chopped (about 1 cup)

2 carrots, peeled and thinly sliced (about ⅔ cup)

2 celery ribs, thinly sliced (about ⅔ cup)

1 bay leaf

2 large sweet potatoes (1½ pounds), peeled, quartered lengthwise, and thinly sliced

2 boiling potatoes (about ½ pound), peeled, quartered, and thinly sliced

5 cups homemade vegetable stock or vegetable broth

½ cup dry white wine or dry vermouth

Freshly grated nutmeg to taste

Salt and white pepper to taste

1½ teaspoons caraway seeds (preferably black)

6 teaspoons sliced scallions, green part only, or snipped fresh chives

6 tablespoons plain or lowfat yogurt

In a large sauté pan or heavy saucepan, bring the olive oil to rippling over moderately high heat. Add the onion, carrots, celery, and bay leaf, reduce heat to a simmer, and cook, stirring occasionally, for 6 to 8 minutes, or until the vegetables are softened. Add the sweet potatoes, boiling potatoes, stock, and wine, increase heat to moderately high and bring the mixture to a boil. Reduce heat to a simmer and cook, covered, for 20 to 25 minutes, or until the potatoes are tender. Remove from the heat and discard the bay leaf.

In a blender or processor, puree the mixture in batches, transferring the puree to a bowl. If it is too thick, add a little water. Season with nutmeg and salt and pepper, and return to the sauté pan.

Fold the caraway seeds and scallions into the yogurt.

Over moderately high heat, stir the soup until it is hot. Ladle it into warm soup bowls, and top each serving with a dollop of the yogurt mixture. Serve immediately.

GINGERED SWEET POTATOES WITH SHERRY AND WALNUTS

Serves 4

- - - - - - - - - -

A fast, delicious way to prepare sweet potatoes that substitutes ginger marmalade and sherry for the ubiquitous brown sugar—and to good advantage. The bright flavor of ginger and the mellowness of the sherry highlight the natural sweetness of the potatoes, rather than adding more.

1 **pound sweet potatoes (preferably orange-fleshed "yams"), peeled and cut into ¼-inch dice**

3 **tablespoons unsalted butter, cut in small pieces**

3 **tablespoons ginger marmalade**

½ **cup medium-dry sherry**

2 **tablespoons chopped walnuts, lightly toasted**

Salt and freshly ground black pepper to taste

1 **teaspoon grated lemon zest (optional)**

In a steamer set over boiling water, steam the sweet potatoes, covered, for 5 minutes, or until just tender. Remove from the heat and set aside.

In a sauté pan or skillet, combine the butter and ginger marmalade over moderate heat, stirring, until the butter has melted and combined with the ginger marmalade. Stir in the sherry and cook the sauce until it is well combined and slightly thickened.

Lift the sweet potatoes from the steamer and stir them into the ginger-sherry sauce. Add the walnuts and salt and pepper to taste. Toss the mixture to coat with the sauce and cook until just heated through. Transfer the potato mixture to a warm serving bowl and sprinkle with the lemon zest, if desired.

SPICED SWEET POTATOES WITH APPLE, PEAR, AND CURRANTS

Serves 4 to 6

Sweet potatoes combine well with fruits and spices. In this recipe the fruits retain their shape and some of their crispness to lend a nice texture in counterpoint to the softness of the sweet potatoes.

½ cup currants

¼ cup water

1 tablespoon orange-flavored liqueur, such as Triple Sec or Grand Marnier

1 pound sweet potatoes (about 3), peeled and cut crosswise into ⅓-inch slices

4 tablespoons (½ stick) unsalted butter

1 tart apple, such as Granny Smith, peeled, cored, quartered, and sliced ¼ inch thick

1 firm pear, such as Bosc, peeled, cored, quartered, and sliced ¼ inch thick

¼ teaspoon ground cinnamon

¼ teaspoon ground allspice

¼ cup freshly squeezed orange juice

Salt to taste

In a small bowl, soak the currants in the water combined with the orange liqueur for 20 minutes.

In a steamer set over simmering water, steam the sweet potatoes, covered, for 15 to 20 minutes, or until they are just tender.

In a large sauté pan, melt 2 tablespoons of the butter over moderate heat. When the foam subsides, cook the apple, stirring, for 2 minutes. Stir in the pear, cinnamon, allspice, and orange juice and cook the fruit mixture, covered, for 2 minutes more. Stir in the sweet potatoes, the currants with their soaking liquid, and salt to taste. Reduce heat to a simmer and cook the mixture, uncovered, for 3 minutes. Blend in the remaining 2 tablespoons butter and serve.

SWEET POTATO-ORANGE CUSTARD PIE

Makes one 9-inch deep-dish pie

Grated raw sweet potatoes are used in this dessert pie that originates in the South, perhaps Louisiana. It has a wonderfully silky texture that contrasts nicely with the crunchy, nutty crust. This pie bakes for 45 minutes to 1 hour, so it is wise to have an aluminum-foil collar or frame ready to place over the edge of the crust to prevent it from overbrowning. We use one of those aluminum-foil pie plates that a supermarket frozen crust comes in, with the center cut out. It works perfectly.

1 prebaked Pecan Crust (page 184)

5 ounces (1¼ sticks) unsalted butter or margarine

1 cup dark brown sugar

2 large eggs, lightly beaten

2 cups peeled, grated raw sweet potato (about ¾ to 1 pound)

3 tablespoons grated orange zest

1 tablespoon freshly squeezed lemon juice

½ teaspoon powdered ginger

½ teaspoon ground mace

¼ teaspoon freshly grated nutmeg

¼ teaspoon ground cloves

Preheat the oven to 350° F.

In the large bowl of an electric mixer, cream together the butter and brown sugar at medium speed. Add the beaten eggs and grated sweet potatoes and continue to beat until well combined. Beat in the orange zest, lemon juice, ginger, mace, nutmeg, and cloves until incorporated thoroughly. Pour half the custard mixture into the cooled prebaked crust, and place the pie on a cookie sheet and place in the bottom third of the oven. Pour in the remaining custard carefully, barely to the rim of the crust. If necessary, don't use all the custard. Bake for 45 minutes or more, or until the custard is firm when you shake the pan.

Let the pie cool to room temperature, then refrigerate for 1 to 3 hours before serving.

NOTE: You can also test the pie by inserting a small sharp knife into the very center. It should come out clean. Cover the cut with a few strategically placed pecan halves or some cinnamon sugar.

SPICED SWEET-POTATO DESSERT LOG WITH CREAM FILLING

Serves 8 to 10

We invented a dessert roll like this several years back using pumpkin puree where we now use sweet potatoes. The original had chopped crystallized ginger flecked through the whipped-cream filling. Sweet potatoes are more assertive than pumpkin, so we suggest flavoring the whipped cream with a nut- or fruit-flavored liqueur instead. Plain sweetened whipped cream works just as well. A dusting of confectioners' sugar is the only decoration.

sheet cake

1 16-ounce can sweet potatoes in light or heavy syrup
¼ cup all-purpose flour
1 teaspoon baking powder
5 large eggs, separated
¾ cup granulated sugar
1 teaspoon powdered ginger

1 teaspoon ground cinnamon
½ teaspoon ground cloves or allspice
¼ teaspoon freshly grated nutmeg
⅛ teaspoon salt
⅛ teaspoon cream of tartar
   Confectioners' sugar for dusting

filling

1 cup heavy cream
2 tablespoons confectioners' sugar

2 tablespoons nut- or fruit-flavored liqueur or Stone's Ginger Wine (available at most liquor stores)

Preheat the oven to 350° F.

Butter a 16 x 11-inch jelly-roll pan; line it with wax paper, and butter and lightly flour the paper.

Drain the sweet potatoes, rinse well, and pat dry with paper towels. Puree the sweet potatoes in a food processor, or put through a food mill or ricer. Measure 1 level cup and set aside. (A 16-ounce can of sweet potatoes will yield about 1¼ cups; the excess can be saved for another use or discarded.)

Sift the flour with the baking powder.

In the large bowl of an electric mixer, beat the yolks at high speed for about 3 minutes, or until they are frothy. Gradually add ½ cup of the granulated sugar and continue to beat the mixture for 3 minutes or more, or until it ribbons when the beater is lifted. On low speed, mix in the sweet potato puree, the flour mixture, ginger, cinnamon, cloves, and nutmeg. Beat just until all the ingredients are combined.

In a separate bowl, beat the egg whites with the salt and cream of tartar at high speed until they hold soft peaks. Gradually beat in the remaining ¼ cup sugar, 1 tablespoon at a time. Beat the whites until they hold stiff peaks.

With a rubber spatula, fold one-quarter of the whites into the sweet potato mixture, gently but thoroughly. Fold the remaining whites into the mixture until there are no traces of white. Pour the batter into the lined jelly-roll pan and spread evenly with the spatula. Bake in the center of the oven for 20 minutes, or until the cake shrinks from the sides of the pan. Cool for 30 minutes, then invert the cake onto a clean sheet of wax paper sprinkled with confectioners' sugar. Carefully peel the wax paper from the inverted cake.

In a chilled bowl, beat the heavy cream until it thickens. Add the 2 tablespoons confectioners' sugar and continue to beat until the cream holds stiff peaks. Add the liqueur and continue to beat just until incorporated.

Spread the cream mixture evenly over the cake and, lifting the wax paper on one long edge, roll the cake tightly, lengthwise. Using the wax paper as a sling, transfer the log to a serving platter. Remove the wax paper carefully. Chill for at least 1 hour. Sprinkle with confectioners' sugar and slice in 1½- to 2-inch servings.

TARO

[*COLOCASIA ANTIQUORUM*]

coco, baddo, and eddo (W. Ind.)

dasheen (S.A.)

Taro has been cultivated for so long that it no longer exists in its wild state. It is so ancient that prehistoric man counted it as a staple of his diet. It provided starch in the diets of Chinese and Southeast Asians even before they started to use rice, and it was there in tropical Asia that it originated and from whence it spread around the world.

At the time of Christ, taro reached Egypt and it has been prized there for two millennia. The Spanish, in a reversal of their usual process, introduced it to the New World's tropical areas, where it has become a staple as well. Centuries ago, long before European ships ventured into uncharted seas, cultivation of taro began in the South Pacific, where island people soon became dependent upon it. Conditions were so right for its growth that the plant has escaped cultivation and spread.

On some islands in the West Indies, notably Barbados, Jamaica, and Trinidad (where it is variously called *coco, baddo,* and *eddo*), the leafy tops of the plant are called *callaloo* and are the basis of an "indigenous" soup of the same name. (The greens have shown up recently at our farmers' market—but not the root!) Most West Indians and South Americans know it as *dasheen,* a corruption of the French *de la Chine*—from China— and it appears under that name in many southern produce markets. However, Asian and Hispanic markets elsewhere in this country display it as taro root.

Today the plant is grown extensively in North Africa, Italy, and the Middle East, besides many other countries from Cuba to Hawaii to Japan—wherever there is wet soil and a long growing season. It is a universal starchy food in the world's tropical regions and is used there in place of or in conjunction with rice, potatoes, yams, and other root vegetables.

Taro is not eaten raw—its taste is too bitter, too sharp from the calcium oxalate crystals, which can be toxic and can only be destroyed by cooking. It is always cooked either by itself or added, after blanching, to stews usually rich with meat and fat. Cooked this way its flavor is reminiscent of potatoes but nuttier, somewhere between an artichoke and a chestnut.

Tourists in Hawaii and other Polynesian islands hardly ever leave without tasting poi, a creamy, pasty, purple-gray mass of fermented taro paste. This initiation to the bland, sourish concoction is usually their last. Poi seems to be an acquired taste, although some travelers find it quite palatable. Everyone finds it perfectly digestible. They should—the

Kanaka language, spoken almost everywhere poi is eaten, has no word for indigestion.

The tubers you'll find in U.S. markets are about the size of medium white potatoes. They are barrel-shaped and have a hairy brown skin with lateral pinstripes and warty lateral buds. Paring the skin reveals flesh that is white to creamy to gray, often speckled with purple. Larger varieties sometimes have a piece of the top sliced off. There is nothing wrong with them. Because long ago taro ceased producing seeds, the method of propagation is through the planting of these tops.

Varieties

There is only one species of taro but there are plenty of varieties—over forty-five in Hawaii and two hundred or more in the West Indies, though these diverse varieties have more to do with the leaves and shoots than with the tubers. Taro from Hawaii, which may appear in mainland markets, are usually smaller (only 2 or 3 inches in length) than those imported from elsewhere. They are usually more expensive as well.

Availability

All seasons.

Storage

Taro does not keep well, only for a week at most in the refrigerator.

What to Look For

Firm tubers without cracks or soft spots. Warty lateral buds are normal. As noted, taro with a slice off the top is being used to propagate the species. Its taste and freshness are unimpaired.

Basic Preparation and Cooking Methods

Taro may be steamed, sliced, and fried like potato chips; french fried; mashed; pan-browned; parboiled for 10 minutes, then baked or added to stews; it sometimes ends up as dessert. Taro takes a little longer to cook than a potato and its consistency is a little moister. Though pale in color when raw, taro turns from grayish to purplish when cooked. Cut off the ends and peel it deeply, removing the skin and any hidden blemishes. Place the peeled taro in cold water until ready to use. Cooked taro should be served very hot, directly from the stove or oven, otherwise it can turn thick and waxy in texture. Plan to baste taro with a good deal of fat while baking or roasting—or to serve it with lots of butter or gravy—because it tends to dry out. We find that taro can absorb more oil than eggplant! Frying seems to suit it best.

nutrition

Taro has its pluses—per 100g, it is high in calcium (43mg), magnesium (33mg), phosphorus (84mg), and potassium (591mg); but also relatively high in calories (107) and low in protein (1.50g). It's a good carbohydrate food (26.46g), but somewhat low in vitamins (4.5mg vitamin C). It has traces of saturated fats, monosaturated fats, and polyunsaturated fats—but no cholesterol.

TARO AND ONION SOUFFLÉ PIE

Serves 6

This is not a real soufflé, of course, but it is light and fluffy and makes an unpretentious and pleasingly nutty-tasting side dish that's perfect for family dinners.

2 pounds large taro
Salt to taste
1¼ cups milk, or more to cover
1¼ cups water, or more to cover
4 tablespoons (½ stick) unsalted butter
1½ pounds large red onions, thinly sliced (about 3 or 4)

⅓ cup dry white wine
¼ cup freshly grated Parmesan
2 large eggs, beaten
Freshly ground black pepper to taste
2 to 3 tablespoons bread crumbs

Peel the taro with oiled hands or with rubber gloves. Cut it into 2-inch chunks and place them in a bowl with cold water to cover.

In a large saucepan, combine the drained taro, 1 teaspoon salt, the milk, and water. Bring to a boil over moderately high heat, adding more water and milk to cover, if necessary, then reduce heat to a simmer and cook, uncovered, about 25 to 30 minutes, or until tender.

Meanwhile, melt 2 tablespoons of the butter in a skillet or sauté pan over moderate heat. When the foam subsides, add the onions and sauté, stirring frequently, for about 7 to 10 minutes, or until they begin to brown. Add ¼ cup water and the wine and, when the mixture begins to simmer, cover and reduce heat to moderately low. Continue simmering, stirring occasionally, for 30 minutes.

When the taro is tender, drain it in a fine sieve, reserving the liquid. Force the taro through the medium disk of a food mill into a bowl, and stir in enough of the reserved cooking liquid to make a smooth, medium-thick puree (there will probably be about ½ cup liquid left over). Add the remaining 2 tablespoons butter, the Parmesan, beaten eggs, and salt and pepper to taste, and stir to combine well. Set aside.

Preheat the oven to 350° F.

Butter an 8-cup (2-quart) soufflé dish and sprinkle with the bread crumbs. Drain the onions, if necessary, and stir half of them into the taro mixture, reserving the rest. Spoon the mixture into the soufflé dish and bake in the upper third of the oven for 30 minutes, or until puffed, lightly brown, and firm on the surface. Remove from the oven and distribute the reserved onions over the top of the soufflé. Serve hot.

PANFRIED TARO, ITALIAN STYLE

Serves 6

- - - - - - - -

No, taro is not usually found on Italian tables. But the vegetable takes well to Italian methods for cooking potatoes, so we offer this pleasing dish that combines it with rosemary and parsley for a continental twist.

2 **pounds large taro**	1 **tablespoon unsalted butter**
2 **tablespoons olive oil**	2 **tablespoons minced fresh Italian**
1 **large onion, thinly sliced**	**flat-leaf parsley**
2 **teaspoons fresh rosemary, or 1**	**Salt and freshly ground black**
teaspoon dried	**pepper to taste**

Peel the taro with oiled hands or with rubber gloves. Cut it into 2-inch chunks and place them in a bowl with cold water to cover.

In a large saucepan, bring 4 cups salted water to a boil over high heat. Add the drained taro pieces, add more water to cover, if necessary, and return to a boil. Reduce heat to a simmer and cook, uncovered, until tender, about 25 to 30 minutes.

Meanwhile, in another large saucepan over moderate heat, bring the oil to rippling. Add the onion and sauté, about 5 minutes, or until limp and translucent. Stir in the rosemary and sauté for 1 minute more.

Drain the taro and cut it into ¼-inch slices. Stir the taro slices into the onion mixture, add the butter, parsley, and salt and pepper to taste, and sauté, stirring frequently, for 5 to 7 minutes, or until the taro starts to brown and form a crust. Serve immediately, very hot.

TRUFFLES

[*TUBER MAGNATUM* (MAGNATE OR TYCOON'S TRUFFLE)]

Italian white truffle
piedmont truffle
Italian truffle
tartufo bianco
tartufo d'alba (It.)

[*TUBER MELANOSPORUM*]

black, French, or perigord truffle
truffe de France
truffe des gourmets
truffe de perigord
truffe noir
truffe vraie (Fr.)

Truffles are among the most expensive, if not *the* most expensive, foodstuffs in the world. This was brought home to our son, Matt, when he was eight years old and decided to buy truffles as a Mother's Day present for his mother, who had never tasted them except in pâté. With the ten dollars he'd saved, he went to our local gourmet store, Balducci's, in Greenwich Village, picked the smallest can off the shelf, and took it to the checkout counter. When he handed it to the clerk, she rang up a fifteen-dollar tab for the one-ounce tin of Italian white truffles. Matt, whose taste and thoughtfulness obviously outstripped his pocket, tearfully told the girl to forget it and was about to return the can to the shelf, when a middle-aged man standing behind him said, "Wait, here's five bucks. Any kid who would think of buying his mother truffles for Mother's Day deserves to be subsidized!" We still have the tiny empty can on a shelf in our kitchen.

Truffles are underground fungi, subterranean relatives of puff balls that grow 8 to 24 inches under the earth in symbiosis with the roots of trees. The truffle extracts sugars from the tree roots and in return offers them minerals, especially phosphorus, which it produces more efficiently than the tree can. It grows in symbiosis with a relatively few species of trees, which include oaks, lindens, and hazelnuts in Europe, but also these and the Douglas fir in North America.

None of the varieties of truffles ever break aboveground (even the sand truffle appears as a little bump in the desert sands) and must be smelled out by trained dogs, pigs, or goats. Truffle hounds (not a breed, most are mongrels) are the most favored by farmers because they can be trained to sniff out the fungus but are not hell-bent on devouring it, as are pigs and goats. The dogs can be distracted by a dog biscuit before they eat up the profits.

Recently it has been discovered that truffles produce a musky chemical aroma that is also in male pigs' saliva and induces mating behavior in sows. The sex pheromone is also secreted in the human male's underarm sweat, a nice tidbit to pass along with the Strasbourg pâté. Here's some other trivia to ponder: the rich, meaty-nutty flavor of the fungi and their ability to intensify the flavors of dishes is due to a very high content of glutamic acid—or natural monosodium glutamate.

Truffles were eaten by Babylonians and, later, by Romans—although neither knew that they were eating fungi. The peoples of medieval Baghdad ate truffles from the Arabian desert known as *Terfez* (the sand truffles mentioned above). These are closely related to the European truffles and can only be distinguished from them by botanists. Some grow in southern Europe, but they are really plentiful in North Africa and the Middle East. One of the richest known sources is the Kalahari Desert in Botswana. Inferior in taste and aroma to the European varieties, they often find their way into cans marked French or Italian.

In France truffles remained relatively unknown until the fourteenth century, and the Italians only began serving them at royal banquets in the sixteenth century. Although the great gastronome Pierre François de la Varenne had very nice things to say about truffles in the seventeenth century, it wasn't until the nineteenth century that the French and Italians treated them like the rare delicacy they are.

The dispute over which is better, the French black or the Italian white, will probably never end. Brillat-Savarin did say that the white Piedmont truffle was superior; he retained his French citizenship in spite of this and is considered by the Italians to have some of the most discriminating taste buds that ever existed.

The center of black or French truffle harvest is a town called Périgueux, some eighty-five miles northeast of Bordeaux. They are also found up the Rhône valley in the hills as far north as Burgundy. (Italy and other parts of southern Europe yield a tiny crop of blacks but they are not as pungent as those from Périgord.) This truffle is coal black and covered with wartlike protuberances that make it difficult to clean. It has a strong perfume and almost no flavor raw. Canned truffles in general have little of the aroma of the fresh and should be used to "decorate" and, perhaps, only to impress.

The "black diamond" of French cuisine is gathered in smaller quantities than ever these days, but even so the annual production is in the millions of pounds. Because of their high price they are often used to lend their aroma to other foods — consequently they can be stored with things like rice or potatoes and their perfume will penetrate and flavor them. Even the peelings are used, especially to infuse oil and vinegar with the elusive truffle flavor, and are available canned. So strong is the truffle fragrance that it can pass through the shell of a fresh egg overnight and flavor a dish made with the egg the next day.

The center of white truffle or Italian truffle production is a town called Alba in the northwestern Piedmont region of Italy, whose northern border is shared by France. Alba is about forty miles southeast of Turin and is a wonderful place to visit in October, when the truffle season begins and a truffle fair takes place. Here you'll find fresh truffles celebrated in innumerable dishes from carpaccio with truffle shavings to creamy risotto flecked with delicate morsels of the fungus. The white truffle is also found in the foothills of the mountains that ring the south side of the Lombardy plain and on the north side of the Apennines southward to Modena. They are also gathered in France and Yugoslavia. The harvest season usually ends when snow begins to fall.

The white truffle has the size, shape, and the appearance of a whitish-yellow new potato without its scaly skin. Smaller and larger specimens of course prove the rule, but all have such an intense aroma that they can be detected rooms, and even floors, away from where they are stored. The smell is said to be like that of garlic and the taste sort of peppery.

While the French black truffle is usually cooked, the Italian white truffle is usually sliced or shaved raw directly onto a dish, such as pasta, right at the table. The server uses a specially devised truffle shaver for the purpose, which produces razor-thin pieces enabling one small truffle to serve a large dinner party without anyone feeling deprived. It is the aroma rather than the flavor, again, that pleases the diner and is why they are invariably served raw. Canned white truffles lose much of their distinctive perfume and will disappoint a true truffle lover.

Because few of the other common European, North American, South African, West African, North African, and Middle Eastern truffles are available commercially, especially in American markets, most people assume that truffles only grow in Italy and France. However a mycologist from the U.S. Forest Service has claimed that truffles taken in the Douglas fir forests extending north from San Francisco into British Columbia are equal in taste and perfume to the famous European varieties; *Tuber gibbosum,* quite abundant in that region apparently, looks to be the most promising to take its place along with American caviar as a gourmet's delight.

Varieties

White truffles available commercially are Italian. Black truffles are French.

Availability

Fresh white truffles are available in specialty food stores from October to

January. The black truffle can be purchased fresh from November through early winter. Canned white or black varieties are always on "gourmet" food store shelves.

Storage

If you are not going to use fresh truffles immediately, don't invest in them. Although they keep in the refrigerator, they lose a lot of the taste and aroma you are paying for. If you have any left over, use them sparingly to flavor good-quality olive oil or vinegar or wine you intend to cook with—use the peelings to do the same.

Basic Preparation and Cooking Methods

Black truffles should be thoroughly scrubbed and peeled before using. Save the peelings to flavor sauces, stuffings, and pâtés. Slice truffles very thin with a knife or a truffle slicer. Cut patterns from the slices and use to decorate mousses, pâtés, aspics, hors d'oeuvre, etc., which are to be cooked. However, what should be a triumph of taste often turns out to be a pretty disappointment. Canned black truffles can be used directly from the can to decorate and flavor; it is not necessary to cook them. The French sometimes soak canned truffles in Cognac to make them more pungent. M.F.K. Fisher, the legendary food writer, suggests using dry white wine instead ". . . to bring out the perfumes . . . and leave a beautiful bit of dark juice to find its way elsewhere (in a sauce . . . or down the cook's omnivorous gullet?)." Save the precious truffle water they come in to flavor other things that absorb moisture in the cooking process. White truffles should be sliced or shaved fresh directly on the already-prepared dish right at the table. Canned whites lack the perfume of the fresh, so don't expect too much. Truffles in general owe most of their glamour to their rarity and expense.

nutrition

So little is consumed that nutrition is the last thing to think about. The cost is first, followed by the fact that some people find even a small amount of truffles difficult to digest. They may be the lucky ones.

CHEESE FONDUE WITH WHITE TRUFFLE SHAVINGS

Serves 4

If you feel compelled to spend your money on truffles, at least serve them in a dish that allows the "mushroom worth its weight in diamonds" to star—like this classic *fonduta* of northwestern Italy. A little Swiss, a little Italian, the Val d'Aosta area has some of the best cooking in a country already blessed with an excess of incomparable food. Accompany the *fonduta* with a full-bodied Italian red wine and be transported. Serve this as an elegant antipasto or light supper dish.

1 **pound imported Italian fontina**
   cheese, cut into ½-inch dice
1 **cup milk**
1 **small fresh or canned white**
   truffle

3 **large egg yolks**
12 **thin slices of Italian bread,**
   lightly toasted

In a small bowl, soak the fontina in the milk for at least 1 hour. Slice the truffle paper-thin with the blade side of your cheese grater.

In the top half of a double boiler or in a fondue pot, heat the milk and cheese mixture, stirring constantly, until the cheese melts and is combined with the milk. Add the egg yolks, 1 at a time, stirring constantly to incorporate after each addition, and continue to cook until the mixture is smooth and silky, about 3 or 4 minutes. Serve immediately in individual bowls showered with a few shavings of the truffle. Pass the toast separately.

NOTE: If you are using canned white truffle, add 1 tablespoon of the liquid from the can to the milk and cheese mixture before heating.

ULTIMATE SCRAMBLED EGGS

Serves 4

Another dish that gives the truffle its due is simple scrambled eggs. But scrambled eggs are anything but simple when some like them moist and some like them dry. Other than making a separate portion of eggs for each diner, we suggest cooking them over moderately low heat to keep them soft and creamy and serve those who like them dry *last,* no matter what their gender. Scrambled eggs continue to cook in their own heat even after they leave the pan, so remove them from the stove a little before they reach the "perfect" texture.

1 fresh or canned black truffle

4 tablespoons unsalted butter

8 large eggs

½ teaspoon salt, or to taste

½ teaspoon freshly ground pepper

2 tablespoons water (if using canned truffle, use the liquid in the can plus water, if necessary)

2 dashes Tabasco or other hot pepper sauce

Mince the truffle. (If using a fresh truffle, peel it first, reserving the peelings for another use.)

In a large skillet, melt the butter over moderate heat. Meanwhile, briskly beat the eggs with the truffle, salt, pepper, water, and Tabasco until frothy. Pour the egg-truffle mixture into the skillet and reduce heat to very low. With a fork, gently stir the mixture, lifting it from the bottom as it thickens and pulling it from the edges into the center of the pan. Continue stirring until just before the desired texture is achieved. Remove from the heat immediately and serve directly from the pan.

TURMERIC

[*CURCUMA DOMESTICA;*
CURCUMA LONGA]

You might be surprised by the inclusion of turmeric among the underground treasures in this book, especially if you are familiar only with the ground powder. But turmeric starts out as a rhizome that looks something like a stunted version of its cousin, ginger. We have seen it for sale in Indian markets in New York and at other Southeast Asian markets in little pinkie-sized fingers whose brown skin hides bright orange flesh.

Turmeric is used fresh in South Indian and other Southeast Asian cooking, sliced, chopped, or grated and added to the stews known as curries. Ground turmeric, the more universal version of the spice, is an essential ingredient of curry powder or *garam masala,* and is made by grinding the dried orange rhizomes into a fine, aromatic, yellowish powder that gives curries their characteristic yellow-orange color.

In medieval times turmeric was known in Europe as "Indian saffron." Marco Polo, writing in 1280, mentions that he saw turmeric growing in the Fukien region of China, ". . . a vegetable that has all the properties of true saffron, as well the smell as the color, and yet it is not really saffron." It was listed as a coloring agent in an Assyrian herbal dating from about 600 B.C. and was highly valued in ancient sacrificial and religious rites in both India and China. To this day in India a turmeric-dyed thread still binds together a Hindu marriage. Indonesians rub turmeric water on their bodies in the same way we use alcohol or cologne. In the Far East many women use turmeric on their faces as a cosmetic, like face powder or rouge.

Turmeric is what makes ballpark mustard so yellow and is used in *piccalilli,* and in many other pickles and relishes. But by far its main use is to give curries their yellow color and their distinctively pungent flavor.

Indian curry powder, as you probably know, is not made from a single "curry" spice (there is no such thing), but is a blend, most likely the cook's own, of different spices and herbs. Depending on the cook's budget the blend might include as few as three or upward of thirty seasonings. But it will almost always contain turmeric. The Indians also use it a good deal to color sweet dishes.

Incidentally, like ginger, you can grow your own turmeric plant at home. Just find a "finger" with a bud or node on it and sink it into damp soil. You just may have a 2- to 3-foot high houseplant eventually with 6 to 10 tall leaves and maybe even a yellowish white flower cluster.

Varieties

Turmeric is essentially the same whether imported from Haiti, Jamaica, Peru, or its native India.

Availability

The best fresh turmeric is found at Indian, Southeast Asian, and other ethnic markets in late spring and early summer. Powdered turmeric is, of course, available all year round. Although it has a long shelf life, it is best bought at a market where there is lively turnover. Indian markets sell the bright orange powder in plastic bags.

Storage

Fresh turmeric keeps best in the refrigerator first wrapped in a paper towel, then placed inside a plastic bag. The dried spice, as we said, keeps well, but if you are not using it in large amounts or often, transfer it to a tin or jar with a tight-fitting lid and keep it in a dark cupboard.

What to Look For

When buying fresh turmeric, look for very firm "fingers." Cut or broken ends will not affect the flavor.

Basic Preparation and Cooking Methods

Add fresh turmeric to curries and other stews along with other fresh ingredients. Chopped, sliced thin, or grated and added to chili, meat loaf, and some fish and seafood dishes, it adds an exotic and interesting flavor—not to mention its beautiful yellow-orange color.

---

nutrition

The fresh rhizome is high in vitamin C and potassium and low in calories. But so little of either form, fresh or powdered, is used in a recipe that its nutritional qualities are usually irrelevant.

CURRIED SHRIMP WITH CAULIFLOWER, POTATO, ONION, AND FRESH TURMERIC

Serves 4

We've adapted this recipe, quite freely, from one in our friend Madhur Jaffrey's first cookbook, *An Invitation to Indian Cooking*. Exotic, nutritious, and eminently delicious, it's a one-dish meal that's so simple to prepare and so flavorful that we fall back on it often. It also tastes just as good cold or at room temperature. We discovered this by mistake, when our daughter, Abby, who likes to eat anything left over from dinner—cold from the fridge for breakfast—insisted we taste it. Ever since, it has become a warm-weather standby. We even make it *just* to serve cold. But not for the first meal of the day.

4   all-purpose or boiling potatoes (about 1 pound), peeled and cut into ½-inch dice

1   pound shrimp, peeled and deveined
    Salt and freshly ground black pepper

1   medium or large onion, coarsely chopped

2   tablespoons coarsely chopped garlic

1   2-inch piece fresh gingerroot, peeled and coarsely chopped

1   2-inch piece fresh turmeric, peeled and coarsely chopped, or ½ teaspoon ground turmeric

4   tablespoons water

1   large head fresh cauliflower, or 2 small heads

4   tablespoons peanut, corn, or canola oil

1   medium fresh ripe tomato, peeled and chopped, or 2 canned Italian plum tomatoes, chopped

2   tablespoons chopped fresh coriander (cilantro) or more to taste

1   fresh hot green chile, seeded, deveined, and finely chopped, or ¼ teaspoon cayenne pepper

2   teaspoons ground coriander

1   teaspoon ground cumin

1   teaspoon *garam masala* (available at Indian and specialty food shops) or curry powder

1   tablespoon freshly squeezed lemon juice

½   cup warm homemade chicken stock or canned broth or warm water

Boil or steam the potatoes for 10 minutes; set aside.

Meanwhile, rinse the shrimp under cold running water and pat dry. Sprinkle with salt and pepper to taste and set aside.

In a food processor or blender, process the onion, garlic, ginger, and turmeric with the water until it becomes a paste.

Break the cauliflower into small florets, rinse in a colander, and set aside to drain.

In a large sauté pan, bring the oil to rippling over moderate heat, add the shrimp and stir until they just become opaque. Remove with a slotted spoon and reserve. In the remaining oil in the same pan, fry the onion paste over moderate heat, stirring, for 5 minutes. Add the tomato, 1 tablespoon of the fresh coriander, and the chile and cook, stirring often, 5 minutes more (add a teaspoon or so of warm water or chicken broth if the mixture begins to stick). Stir in the cauliflower, ground coriander, cumin, *garam masala,* 1 teaspoon salt, and the lemon juice. Add the warm stock or warm water, stir well, cover, reduce heat to a simmer, and cook, covered, for 10 minutes. Add the reserved potatoes, stir, cover, and cook 10 minutes more. Stir in the reserved shrimp and cook 5 minutes. Transfer the mixture to a warm serving dish and serve sprinkled with the remaining chopped coriander. Or cool to room temperature and chill for 10 minutes before serving.

NOTE: If the shrimp accumulate liquid while waiting to be added to the cauliflower mixture, substitute this for all or part of the chicken stock.

Sometimes this dish will be more soupy than at other times. If there is too much liquid, mash enough of the potatoes into the gravy to thicken it. This dish may be served with plain boiled rice, in which case you might want more liquid.

If serving chilled, a good deal of the liquid will be reabsorbed by the potatoes, so it can be served on a bed of lettuce leaves, or on a mound of cooled plain boiled rice, or on rice that has been combined with thinned mayonnaise (using some of the gravy or a few teaspoons of chicken stock to thin it).

TURNIPS

[*BRASSICA RAPA*]

white turnip

navet (Fr.)

nabo (Sp.)

rube (Ger.)

rapa (It.)

*I*t was probably a woman, who, with a little luck and some intuitive feeling, sowed the first turnip seeds five or ten thousand years ago. For thousands of years before, her ancestors had been foraging for food and found turnips to be a nourishing, satisfying root. She may have noticed that a new crop of plants came up in the same area in which she had foraged the season before, and realized this was not a miracle in the true sense but a natural phenomenon that she could help along if she could only discover how nature did it.

Perhaps it was trial and error or just dumb luck or, as we prefer to think of it, maybe she was one of the first geniuses in the human evolutionary chain. A man, we're pretty sure, didn't start agriculture, not because he wasn't just as smart, but because his job was to provide meat. He was a hunter. In the division of labor it was the woman who foraged for fruits, nuts, and vegetables (mostly roots) and the woman who would have come up with this brilliant idea—an easier, more practical, surer way to supply her family with food than hit-or-miss searching. She might even have had some leftover produce to trade for other things—and so she probably developed commerce soon after she developed agriculture.

Is the Harvard MBA really evolved from a woman planting a turnip? Maybe not, but agriculture did make nomadic tribes stay around to collect the harvest. They began to settle into communities, develop ways to trade for things they didn't grow, and—not incidentally—begin a civilization. The MBAs came later.

Anyway, about five thousand years ago the cultivation of turnips and other food plants began. The turnip is one of the oldest of cultivated foods and a root man had relied upon for sustenance millennia before agriculture began. When kept in its natural underground home or its equivalent, it stored for months after it grew to maturity, so during the lean winter season women (short for woman) could still pull turnips out of the earth or take them from a primitive root cellar she had devised.

Turnips were the potatoes of ancient cuisines. They fed the poor and the rich as well, although the rich Romans, according to *The Pantropheon*, added so many pungent ingredients to them in the stewing that we can't imagine diners figuring out just what it was they were eating: "—after the water had been extracted from them [the turnips], they were seasoned with cumin, rue, and benzoin, pounded in a mortar, adding to it afterwards honey, vinegar, gravy, boiled grapes and a little oil. The whole was left to simmer and then served." The poor simply boiled their turnips or ate them raw (which is one way we like them—chilled and thinly sliced).

Even before the Romans, the Greeks must have developed several turnip varieties because Pliny discusses long turnips, flat turnips, and round turnips, some with Greek place names. He called them *rapa* and *napus*. *Napus* became *nepe* in Middle English, then *naep* in Anglo-Saxon. Combine *turn* (meaning, "make round," the shape of the root) with *naep* and you quickly get *turnip*.

Near Beijing in China there are some caves where evidence shows that in prehistory man ate turnips raw and, after fire was discovered, ate them roasted. In France, cave paintings show turnips being boiled in clay pots.

Many people turn up or wrinkle their noses when turnips are mentioned. We've always loved them—especially the mashed turnips once served and sold in cartons by Horn & Hardardt, the famous chain of "automats." Actually, turnips are widely grown here and are available year-round. The South grows them mainly for the green tops, taken while the plant is still young. The root is quite attractive, globular in shape, somewhat like a beet, pure white in color with a ring of bright purple around the crown. They can be eaten raw or cooked, used to enhance the flavor of soups (like the Italians do in minestrone), roasted with pork or birds, added to omelettes, made into soufflés, mashed, riced, glazed, pureed, fried like potatoes, added to stews, sliced, grated, or diced and added to salads.

One thing to keep in mind, if you add turnips to your garden, you, like Scarlett O'Hara, ". . . will never go hungry!"

- - - - - - - - - - -
Varieties
- - - - - - - - - - -

There is only one kind of turnip that shows up in produce markets in this country, the white turnip. In spring you'll usually find them in bunches with the greens intact. These are small, about 1½ to 2 inches in diameter, and tender. They are the new crop. In the fall and winter, turnips are usually marketed without their greens. Late winter turnips can be slightly bitter and more pungent than their younger brothers. They're also a good deal larger, about 3 inches across or more. What some dealers identify as a "yellow turnip" is, in reality, a rutabaga, a relative of the cabbage, not a distinct species like the turnip (see page 243).

Availability

The best turnips are in the markets in cool weather, in spring and fall. Winter turnips are larger with a tougher, bitter skin, but they are just as delicious if chosen carefully.

Storage

Turnips can keep for weeks in a plastic bag in the refrigerator and sometimes can last for months if stored properly in a cold area or in a root cellar.

What to Look For

Choose fresh turnips with smooth, unwrinkled skins, without rust marks, and those that feel heavy in relation to their size. They should be globular in shape with a sometimes flattened stem end circled in purple. Toss back those that are misshapen, bruised, soft, or shriveled, or show signs of sprouting from the top.

Basic Preparation and Cooking Methods

Peel (the skins can be bitter) and cook small whole turnips or larger roots diced into ¾-inch pieces in boiling salted water until just tender. You can also steam them. Either way they take about 15 to 20 minutes. Almost anything you can do with potatoes, you can do with turnips short of baking them (others have been successful at this but not us). They make perfect companions braised with their own greens, can be added raw to salads, shredded to garnish soups or fish dishes. Some cooks like to cook turnips first and then peel them. We find it just as easy to use a swivel-bladed parer and get the job done up front.

nutrition

White turnips are low in calories (only 23 in 100g) and high in potassium (188mg). In 100g you'll also find: 0.8g protein, 4.9g carbohydrates, 0.9g fiber, 0 cholesterol, 22mg vitamin C, .04mg thiamine, .05mg riboflavin, .3mg niacin, 34mg sodium, 35mg calcium, 24mg phosphorus, and .4mg iron.

Pan-Roasted Turnips
with Garlic

Serves 4

Turnips can be roasted in the oven with meat or poultry just like potatoes, but if you're not making a roast and want a change from potatoes, this top-of-the-stove recipe is a tasty alternative.

2 large garlic cloves, peeled and thinly sliced

3 tablespoons unsalted butter or margarine

1 pound small turnips, peeled and cut crosswise into ¼-inch rounds

Salt and freshly ground black pepper to taste

In a small saucepan of boiling water, blanch the garlic for 2 minutes; drain and pat dry. Set aside.

In a skillet or sauté pan large enough to hold the turnips in one layer, melt the butter over moderate heat. When the foam subsides, cook the turnips, turning them frequently, for 10 to 15 minutes, or until they are golden and tender. Add the reserved garlic and salt and pepper to taste and cook the mixture, shaking the pan frequently, for 2 minutes. Serve immediately.

NOTE: For a more garlicky flavor, use 1 clove of garlic instead of 2, mince it rather than slicing it, and add it raw, not blanched, after the turnips are golden and tender; then cook for 2 minutes.

Turnip Soup Mellowed with Rice

Serves 6

Leave it to the Italians to come up with a soup that is simple, easy to prepare, and absolutely extraordinary. Reading the ingredients doesn't give you a clue as to how good this soup tastes; it's so good that it can be served to accolades at the most elegant dinner parties—not just kept for family applause.

2 tablespoons unsalted butter

1 tablespoon olive oil

1 pound small turnips, peeled and cut into ½-inch dice

6 cups canned chicken broth or homemade vegetable stock

½ cup unconverted long-grain rice
Salt and freshly ground black pepper to taste

2 tablespoons minced fresh parsley, preferably Italian flat-leaf

¾ cup freshly grated Parmesan

In a large saucepan, melt the butter with the olive oil over high heat. When the foam subsides, sauté the turnips, tossing frequently, for about 5 to 7 minutes, or until browned. Add the broth, bring to a boil, reduce heat to moderate, and cook, covered, for 10 minutes. Stir in the rice and cook the mixture, covered, until the rice is *al dente*, about 15 minutes. Add salt and pepper to taste. Just before serving stir in the parsley and ¼ cup of the Parmesan. Serve hot. Pass the remaining ½ cup Parmesan to be added at the table.

TURNIPS WHIPPED WITH POTATOES AND BUTTERMILK

Serves 6 to 8

Buttermilk is a pleasant alternative to the ubiquitous sour cream as an ingredient for mashed turnips and potatoes. Buttermilk has fewer calories and less fat and, let's face it, we all can do without those. Besides, if you are like us, we always have some buttermilk left over from baking a cake and, other than freezing it, this is a good way to use it up.

1 pound turnips, peeled and cut into ½-inch dice	1 cup buttermilk
2 pounds all-purpose potatoes, peeled and cut into ½-inch dice	1½ tablespoons minced shallots
2 tablespoons unsalted butter	1 teaspoon salt, or to taste
	⅛ teaspoon freshly grated nutmeg

Place the turnips and potatoes in a large saucepan with cold salted water to cover and bring to a boil. Reduce heat to moderate and cook for about 15 to 20 minutes, or until the potatoes and turnips are very tender. Drain the vegetables, return them to the pan, and steam over moderate heat for about 30 seconds. Transfer to a large mixing bowl.

Meanwhile in a small saucepan over moderately low heat, warm the buttermilk, butter, shallots, salt, and nutmeg over moderately low heat until the butter melts and the liquid is warmed through.

Pour the buttermilk mixture over the turnips and potatoes and, with a hand mixer or standing electric mixer, whip on low speed for 1 minute, or until the sauce is incorporated into the vegetables. Turn to high speed and whip 3 to 4 minutes more, until very smooth. Serve immediately in a heated serving bowl, or keep warm in the top of a double boiler.

NOTE: If shallots are not available, substitute 1 medium onion, cut in small chunks, and 2 garlic cloves, peeled and quartered.

Turnip Gratin with Potatoes and Dill

Serves 4

A gratin made with sliced turnips and potatoes could take from 50 minutes to an hour to bake. When the turnips and potatoes are grated first (a food processor does it quickest) and sautéed for 10 minutes, the baking time can be reduced by nearly two-thirds. This gratin is delicious, has a smoother texture akin to a puree, and the added bonus of quick preparation.

- 3 tablespoons unsalted butter
- 1 pound turnips (about 4 medium), peeled and coarsely grated
- ½ pound boiling potatoes (about 2), peeled and coarsely grated
- 1 tablespoon snipped fresh dill
- ¼ teaspoon freshly grated nutmeg
- Salt and white pepper to taste
- ½ cup heavy cream
- ½ cup homemade chicken stock or canned broth
- ½ cup fresh bread crumbs
- ½ cup freshly grated Gruyère, Swiss, or Jarlsberg cheese

Preheat the oven to 425° F.

In a heavy skillet or sauté pan, melt the butter over moderately low heat. When the foam subsides, cook the turnips and potatoes, stirring occasionally, for 10 minutes. Stir in the dill, nutmeg, and salt and white pepper to taste, heat briefly, and transfer the mixture to a buttered 15 x 2½-inch oval gratin dish. Smooth the surface with a spatula.

In a small bowl, whisk together the heavy cream and stock, and pour it over the turnip-potato mixture. Sprinkle with the bread crumbs and the Gruyère.

Bake the gratin on a baking sheet in the middle of the oven for 20 to 25 minutes, or until the top is golden. Serve from the gratin dish.

NOTE: Substitute parsnips for the potatoes for an even more earthy, piney taste with a touch of sweetness.

Alternatively, if fat intake is a concern, replace the heavy cream with lowfat milk or lowfat plain yogurt and bake 5 minutes longer.

TURNIP AND ROOT VEGETABLE STUFFING

*Makes about 12 cups; enough for a 14- to 16-pound turkey
serving 12 to 18*

To stuff or not to stuff—this seems to be the question these days, due primarily to all the scare talk about dangerous bacteria that can develop if hot stuffing is placed in a cold turkey and allowed to sit before roasting. We've been stuffing birds for years and have had no disasters. Of course, we stuff the bird just before it goes into the oven and the stuffing is always at room temperature or even slightly chilled. An unstuffed bird roasts faster and more evenly than a stuffed one, so you might want to bake the stuffing separately in a casserole. In any event, this stuffing is fragrant, delicious, and even healthful. If you elect not to stuff your turkey, pack the stuffing into a casserole or two, dot with butter, and bake for about 40 minutes in a preheated 350° F. oven.

2 pounds turnips, peeled	1 tablespoon freshly ground black pepper, or more to taste
2 celeriac (celery root) (about 1 pound each), peeled	½ cup (1 stick) unsalted butter
4 or 5 large carrots (about 1 pound), peeled	1 large onion, finely chopped
1 large parsnip (about ½ pound), peeled	8 large garlic cloves, peeled and thinly sliced
2 pounds baking potatoes, peeled	2 cups stale bread cubes, or 8 slices stale bread torn into small pieces
2 cups homemade chicken stock or canned broth	4 scallions, white and green parts, thinly sliced
1 tablespoon salt, or to taste	

Cut the turnips, celeriac, carrots, parsnip, and potatoes into coarse chunks. In a food processor, in batches, pulse the vegetable pieces several times until coarsely grated, transferring each batch to a large sauté pan or soup kettle. Pour the stock over the grated vegetables, add 1 tablespoon salt and 1 tablespoon pepper, and bring to a boil over moderately high heat. Reduce heat to a simmer and cook, stirring occasionally, for 5 minutes.

Meanwhile, in a skillet, melt the butter over moderately high heat. When the foam subsides, add the onion and garlic, reduce heat to moderate, and sauté the mixture for about 3 minutes, or until the garlic just turns golden. Add the butter-onion-garlic mixture to the cooked vegetables in the sauté pan and cook, stirring often, for 2 minutes more. Add the bread cubes and scallions and stir to combine well. The mixture should just about hold together. If too moist, add more bread cubes. If too dry, add more stock by the tablespoon. Taste and adjust seasoning, adding more salt and pepper if needed. Let cool completely before stuffing turkey.

STIR-FRIED TURNIPS AND CABBAGE SPIKED WITH CUMIN

Serves 4

- - - - - - - -

Some simple combinations, some earthy combinations are never tasted by dinner guests, which is their loss. If you keep this one to yourself, you're denying your friends a real treat.

2 tablespoons olive oil	½ teaspoon ground cumin, or more to taste
1 medium onion, thinly sliced	Salt and freshly ground black pepper to taste
4 cups coarsely chopped cabbage	
1 pound turnips, peeled and cut into ½-inch dice	

In a heavy skillet or sauté pan, bring the oil to just short of smoking over moderately high heat. Add the onion slices and cook, stirring, for 3 minutes, or until they are limp. Stir in the cabbage, turnips, cumin, and salt and pepper to taste. Reduce heat to moderate, and cook, stirring frequently, for 8 to 10 minutes, or until vegetables are just tender. Transfer to a warm bowl and serve hot.

TURNIP, HERRING, AND ROAST
BEEF SALAD

Serves 8

Whoa! Wait up here. We can almost hear you thinking, that's a combination I never heard of. That's something I don't think I'd like to have pass my lips. Herring? Roast beef? Turnips!! Please, don't knock it until you have at least read through the recipe. It's good. It's interesting. It's savory. And it's unfamiliar only because it's hardly ever served outside of northeastern Europe. We've included it in this compilation of recipes because it utilizes the very vegetables we are concerned with—and offers yet another facet of their many-faceted possibilities.

1½ pounds turnips, scrubbed

2 all-purpose potatoes (about ½ pound), scrubbed

1 cup sour cream

¾ cup mayonnaise

1 tablespoon snipped fresh dill

1 tablespoon Dijon mustard

1 pound cooked, leftover roast beef, steak, or grilled beef, cut into ¼-inch dice

12 ounces pickled herring, cut into ¼-inch dice

1 cup chopped sour gherkins, or more to taste

1 cup homemade or bottled chopped pickled beets

1 cup chopped red onion

Salt and freshly ground black pepper to taste

In a large saucepan, cover the turnips and potatoes with cold salted water and, over moderately high heat, boil the vegetables for 10 minutes. With a slotted spoon remove the turnips, set aside to cool, and continue boiling the potatoes for 5 minutes more, or until they are tender. Drain and let cool.

Peel the turnips and potatoes, and cut them into ¼-inch dice.

In a small bowl, combine the sour cream, mayonnaise, dill, and mustard until well blended.

In a large bowl, combine the turnips, potatoes, roast beef, herring, gherkins, pickled beets, and onion, and add the sour cream dressing. Toss the mixture to combine well. Add salt and pepper to taste. Chill the salad for at least 4 hours or up to 24 hours, then transfer to a salad bowl and serve with pumpernickel or other dark bread and butter.

NOTE: Some old-country cooks like to add a peeled, cored, and chopped apple or substitute sweet gherkins for sour, or even add ½ cup raisins or currants to the salad. We resist these additions and substitutions only because we prefer the salad savory rather than sweet. The one addition we might make is 1 to 2 teaspoons drained bottled horseradish.

TURNIP AND DAIKON SALAD WITH RUSSIAN DRESSING

Serves 4 to 6

The turnip is a humble vegetable that is most often eaten cooked but is crunchy and tender raw. Combined with daikon and Russian dressing, a salad emerges that packs real punch. Turnips and daikon are easy to julienne: just pile up ⅛-inch slices and cut through them vertically at ⅛-inch intervals. You'll end up with perfect little matchsticks.

1 pound small turnips, peeled and cut into ⅛-inch julienne
1 pound daikon, peeled and cut into ⅛-inch julienne
1 small onion, minced
1 cup homemade mayonnaise (page 107) or good-quality bottled mayonnaise
½ teaspoon Worcestershire sauce

3 tablespoons ketchup
1 tablespoon freshly grated or drained bottled horseradish
3 tablespoons minced sweet gherkins
1 tablespoon chopped drained capers
Salt and freshly ground black pepper to taste

Toss the julienned turnips and daikon and minced onion together in a salad bowl. In a small bowl, whisk together the mayonnaise, Worcestershire, ketchup, horseradish, gherkins, and capers. Add salt and pepper to taste. Pour the dressing over the turnip-daikon mixture and toss gently until combined thoroughly. Taste and adjust seasoning.

WATER CHESTNUTS

[*ELEOCHARIS DULCIS*]

ma tai (Ch.)

kurokuwai (Jap.)

Water chestnuts, the underwater stem tips of a form of rush or water grass, have been grown by man for a long, long time. At "Spirit Cave" in Thailand near the Burmese border, archeological expeditions reported having found the seeds of peas, beans, cucumbers, and water chestnuts that were *probably* cultivated by man as early (by carbon dating) as 9750 B.C. That's two thousand years before it can be *proven* that agriculture began in the Near East or Central America.

The Chinese have cultivated water chestnuts in rice paddies and around streams and ponds for centuries. They are considered *yin,* or cooling, are eaten to sweeten the breath, and are still valued for medicinal purposes in some parts of the Far East. One interesting and odd use for them is administering a paste made from the dried and ground chestnuts to a child who has accidentally swallowed a coin!

Water chestnuts do look like chestnuts except for a little tuft on one side of their roundish, flat-based bodies where the grasses sprout. The scalelike leaves with which they're covered can be dull or glossy, brown or ebony-colored. The flesh is firm, crisp, and white.

Varieties

Until very recently only canned water chestnuts were available in this country, but now you can find them fresh as well. Although fresh water chestnuts are worth making a special trip to find, the canned varieties packed in water and imported from Hong Kong or Japan are more than adequate because the brief cooking they receive during the canning process does not diminish their crispness and nutty flavor.

Availability

Fresh water chestnuts can be found in Oriental markets and some specialty food stores from early summer through late fall.

Storage

Fresh water chestnuts can be stored in the refrigerator for weeks, loosely wrapped in paper towels and placed in a plastic bag. Or they can be peeled, covered with tap water, placed in a tightly sealed container, and refrigerated. This will keep their flavor and texture intact for weeks at a time.

What to Look For

When buying fresh water chestnuts, pick through them and choose only those that are rock-hard and have a glossy look.

Basic Preparation and Cooking Methods

After rinsing and peeling (the fresh) or draining (the canned), the little rounds may be either sliced thin, quartered, or diced for a long list of famous Chinese and Japanese dishes. With brief blanching (about 5 minutes) fresh water chestnuts can be added to salads, or skewered with chicken liver and bacon for that once-ubiquitous cocktail favorite, *rumaki*. Fresh or canned, their crunch is also welcome in many other Western dishes, preferably added toward the end of the cooking time to retain crispness. They're particularly nice diced into consommés or creamed soups.

nutrition

Rich in minerals, 100g of peeled or canned water chestnuts contain 106 calories; 1.4g protein; 23.94g carbohydrates; .8g fiber; 11mg calcium; .6mg iron; 22mg magnesium; 63mg phosphorus; 584mg potassium; 14mg sodium; 4.0mg vitamin C; .14mg thiamine, .2mg riboflavin; and 1.0mg niacin. And, of course, no cholesterol.

CRUNCHY SAUTÉED WATER CHESTNUTS IN CREAMY RICE

Serves 4

- - - - - - - - -

Sautéed water chestnuts add a welcome crunch to our favorite rice recipe. We've given it an extra bit of seasoning to contrast it with the bland water chestnuts.

2 tablespoons unsalted butter

1 1-inch piece fresh gingerroot, minced

1 medium onion, finely chopped

1 tablespoon minced garlic

1 teaspoon salt, or to taste

1 cup unconverted rice

1 tablespoon light olive oil or vegetable oil

1 8-ounce can sliced water chestnuts, drained and rinsed

⅛ teaspoon cayenne pepper
   Salt and freshly ground black pepper to taste

In a medium saucepan, melt the butter over moderate heat. When the foam subsides, add the ginger and onion and cook, stirring frequently, until the onion begins to soften, about 2 or 3 minutes. Add the garlic and cook, stirring, for 1 minute more. Mix in 1 teaspoon salt and the rice and stir until each grain of rice is coated with the butter. Pour 2¼ cups of water over the rice and bring to a boil. Reduce the heat to low and cook, covered, 17 to 20 minutes, or until almost all the liquid has been absorbed and the rice is glistening.

Meanwhile in a medium skillet bring the oil to rippling over moderate heat and add the water chestnuts. Reduce heat to moderately low and sauté, tossing frequently, until lightly browned, about 5 minutes. Add the cayenne and season with salt and black pepper to taste.

Toss the water chestnuts with the rice and serve.

SHRIMP AND WATER CHESTNUTS IN A FRAGRANT CREAM SAUCE FOR FETTUCCINE

Serves 4 to 6

This is not an Italian sauce. Neither is it Oriental. It borrows a little from both worlds and comes up with a provenance all its own. The pink shrimp and the crisp, sweet water chestnuts, the unique combination of spices, and the smooth texture of the pasta all combine to make a truly international dish.

1 pound small shrimp, peeled, shells reserved

¼ teaspoon salt, or to taste

¼ teaspoon freshly ground white pepper, or more to taste

¼ teaspoon ground cardamom

¼ teaspoon ground nutmeg

1 cup bottled clam juice

½ cup water

1 can (8-ounce) sliced water chestnuts, drained

½ cup heavy cream

1 tablespoon unsalted butter

2 scallions, minced, white and green parts reserved separately

1 tablespoon medium-dry sherry

1 teaspoon cornstarch

1 pound fresh fettuccine

In a medium bowl, toss the shrimp with ¼ teaspoon salt, ¼ teaspoon white pepper, the cardamom, and nutmeg, and set aside.

Place the shrimp shells in a medium saucepan over moderately high heat. Add the clam juice and ½ cup water; bring to a boil and cook for 5 minutes. Strain, reserving the stock and discarding the shells. Return the stock to the pot, add the water chestnuts, and simmer over moderately low heat for 3 minutes. Remove the water chestnuts with a slotted spoon and set aside.

Add the cream to the stock and bring to a boil over moderately high heat; reduce heat to low just to keep hot.

In a medium skillet, heat the butter over moderate heat. When the foam subsides, add the minced white part of the scallion and cook, stirring, until softened, about 1 or 2 minutes. Add the reserved shrimp with any liquid that has accumulated in the bowl and the reserved water chestnuts and toss to combine. Add the cream-stock mixture, reduce heat to a simmer, and cook, stirring frequently, until the shrimp turn opaque, about 3 minutes.

Meanwhile, in a large stockpot bring 4 or 5 quarts of water to a boil. Add 1 tablespoon salt.

In a small bowl, stir the sherry into the cornstarch, and add it to the shrimp mixture. Raise heat to moderate, stir, and cook until the sauce boils and thickens slightly, about 3 minutes. Taste and adjust the seasoning with salt and white pepper. Keep warm over low heat.

Add the fresh fettuccine to the boiling water all at once. Stir constantly. Test for doneness every 30 seconds until *al dente*, about 3 minutes. Drain immediately by pouring, water and all, into a colander placed in the sink. Transfer the fettuccine at once to a heated serving bowl, add the shrimp and water chestnut sauce, toss gently but completely, sprinkle with reserved scallion greens, and serve immediately.

YAMS

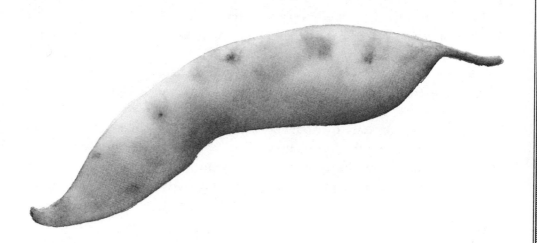

[*DIOSCOREA*]

Chinese yam

winged yam

potato yam

igname de Chine (Fr.)

P otatoes are tubers, sweet potatoes are roots, yams are rhizomes.

The true yam is related to the lily and the amaryllis; the sweet potato is of the morning glory family. We are discussing *true yams* here, not the "moist" red sweet potatoes often mislabeled as yams at your market. Though designated as "moist," the sweet potato is drier, less juicy than the true yam, and one hundred times less sweet.

The taste of the true yam and the "moist" sweet potato is very much the same, but the similarity stops there. Yams can grow up to a gigantic 30 pounds, with some specimens 6 to 8 feet long and weighing in at close to 100 pounds! The creeping vine that produces these monsters can form them both above and below ground—but only in a humid, tropical environment. They are one of the few plants native to both the Old and the New World (the African continent, Southeast Asia, and the tropical regions of the Western Hemisphere).

Yams were first cultivated in Africa about 11,000 years ago, in Southeast Asia about 10,000 years ago. Asian migration took the yam to Polynesia about 3,500 years ago, at about the same time South American Indians started to cultivate them there.

The white yam of Africa has been called the "potato of Africa" most likely because it has helped many West Africans to survive. There it is boiled, peeled, and sliced and served plain; or pounded into a paste and made into croquettes or deep-fried balls. African cooks also puree it with crushed pepper or fresh nutmeg; thinly slice and fry it like potato chips; chunks find their way into stews and ragouts, and are cooked with onions. In some parts of Africa, yams are so revered that consuming them is almost a religious rite. Yams are often eaten at ceremonies commemorating deaths, and celebrating marriages and the recovery from sickness and disease.

Yams grow in our Deep South, but rarely find their way to northern markets. You do find them, at times, in Hispanic markets (where almost every underground vegetable is called, generically, a yam, to further confuse the situation), and in Oriental markets. Comparatively few acres are devoted to yams in this country compared to almost 6 million acres in Africa, where 90 percent of the world's yams are cultivated.

True yams may be bigger and sweeter than the sweet potato, but they are much less nutritious. They contain only a trace of carotene (which the body converts into vitamin A), while the sweet potato is one of nature's richest sources. And though they were used to curb scurvy on long voyages, they have only one-third the vitamin C of sweet potatoes. Certain varieties of yams are used to extract substances that are valuable raw materials in the production of birth control pills, cortisone, and other medicines.

If you do come across a true yam and bring it home, treat it in recipes just as you would a sweet potato.

---

nutrition

In 100g there are 116 calories; 27.89g carbohydrates, 17mg calcium, .54mg iron, 21mg magnesium, 55mg phosphorus, 819mg potassium, 9mg sodium, 9mg zinc, .24mg copper, .18mg manganese, 17.1mg vitamin C, a trace of thiamine and riboflavin, .76mg niacin, .3mg vitamin B_6, 23mg folacin, and no cholesterol.

INDEX

Appetizer
Burdock and Mushroom Pâté
with Yogurt-Dill Sauce, 20
Carrot Beignets Flecked with
Scallions and Jalapeño,
Spicy, 28
Horseradish, Tuna Sauvage
with, 112
Leek Pie, Savory, 146
Leeks Sautéed with Scallops
in Ginger Cream, 151
Parsnip Chips, Crisp Herbed,
180
Potato and Farmer Cheese-
Filled Pirogi in Sour Cream
Dough, Russian, 206
Rutabaga and Potato Terrine
Striped with Scallion Puree,
250
Scallion, Creamy Blue Cheese
and Toasted Almond Sand-
wich Filling, 268
Shallot Mousses Bathed in
Stilton and Walnut Sauce,
Hot, 274
Socca with Garlic and Cumin,
79
Wasabi Mayonnaise Dip,
Batter-Fried Vegetables
with, 110

Beef
Brisket, Baked with Carrots,
Fruit and Sweet Potatoes,
36
Corned, Tomato and Chile
Filling, Cassava Roulade
with, 46
Roast, Turnip and Herring
Salad, 322
Stir-Fried with Lotus Root,
Spicy, 156
Beet(s) (beetroot), 2–15
about history and lore, 2–3
availability, varieties, etc., 3–
4; nutrition, 4
Beetific Chocolate-Nut Torte,
14

and Coriander Soup,
Creamed, with Orange
Juice, 8
Fresh, in Lime Butter, 13
Grated Raw Salad Vinaigrette
with Dill, 9
and Green Beans with Scal-
lion Vinaigrette, 12
Parslied Sweet, with Two Pi-
quant Flavorings, 10
and Pearl Onions Pickled in
Raspberry Vinegar and
Wine, 11
and Salsify Salad under
Horseradish Cream, 256
Sweet-and-Sour Soup with
Caraway and Yogurt, 5
Ukrainian Winter Borscht, 6
Borscht, Ukrainian Winter, 6
botanical families (of vegeta-
bles), xiii
Brioches, Chive-Potato, 60
Burdock (beggar's button), 17–
21
about, 17
availability, varieties, etc., 17–
18; nutrition, 18
and Mushroom Pâté with
Yogurt-Dill Sauce, 20
Sautéed with Chicken Breasts,
Black Sesame Seeds and
Apple, 19
Butter
Brown, Garlic and Capers,
Salsify with, 257
Lime, Fresh Beets in, 13
Rosemary, Baked Sweet On-
ions with, 169
Scallion, Flavored with Curry,
265
Shallot for Sauces, 272

Cake
Beetific Chocolate-Nut Torte,
14
Carrot, Orange-Glazed, 40
Cheesecake, Four-Ginger, 100
Chocolate Mashed Potato, 230

Frosted Spiced Parsnip, 182;
with Cream Cheese Frost-
ing, 183
Ginger Angel Food, with Bit-
tersweet Chocolate-Ginger
Icing, 92
Ginger Bundt, 96
Pound, Buttery Ginger-Pear,
94
Carrot(s), 23–41
about beta-carotene in, 23–24
about history and lore, 23–25
availability, varieties, etc., 25–
27; nutrition, 27
Beignets, Spicy, Flecked with
Scallions and Jalapeño, 28
Cake, Orange-Glazed, 40
Curried Vichyssoise, Cold, 33
-and-Daikon Blanket for
Fried Fish Fillets, Pickled,
65
Fruit and Sweet Potatoes,
Brisket of Beef with, 36
International Intoxicated, 35
and Pistachio Custard Dessert
Pudding, Sweet, 39
Puree, Vanilla-Scented, 30
Salad, Moroccan Minted, 32
Savory Spiced, with Yogurt
and Currants, 38
Sherry-Glazed, with Dill, 31
Soup, Skillet-Charred Puree
of, 29
Turnip and Scallion Gratin,
Crusty, 34
Cassava (manioc, tapioca,
yucca, etc.), 43–47
about history and lore, 43–44
availability, varieties, etc., 44–
45; nutrition, 45
Roulade with Corned Beef,
Tomato and Chile Filling,
46
Celeriac (celery root, céleri-
rave), 49–57
about, 49
availability, varieties, etc., 49–
50; nutrition, 51

Jicama and Unpeeled Apple
Slaw with Yogurt Dressing,
127
Parsnip and Horseradish Pu-
ree, 56
Potato and Onion Salad,
214
Potato and Parsnip Soup,
Pureed, 53
and Potato Pie Filled with Sea
Scallops and Sautéed Cab-
bage, 224
and Potatoes, Naked Mashed,
55
Rémoulade, 54
Soup, Cream of, Hot or Cold,
52
Turnip and Gruyère Pancake,
57
Cheesecake, Four-Ginger, 100
Chicken Breasts, Burdock Sau-
téed with Black Sesame
Seeds, Apple and, 19
Chicken and Jerusalem Arti-
choke in Mustard May-
onnaise, 118
Chive(s), 59–61
about, 59
-Marinated Chilled Shrimp,
61
-Potato Brioches, 60
and Red Caviar, Leek and
Baked Potato Vichyssoise
with, 141
Chocolate
Bittersweet, Ginger Icing,
93
Bittersweet, and Ginger
Terrine with Gingered
Custard Sauce, Frozen,
98
-Ginger Chunk Cookies, 97
Mashed-Potato Cake, 230
-Nut Torte, Beetific, 14
Cookies, Ginger-Chocolate
Chunk, Gigantic, 97
Cream Cheese Frosting, 183
Croutons, Garlic, Brown-and-
White, 81
Crystallized Ginger, Homemade,
102

Daikon (Asian radish, Chinese
turnip, etc.), 63–66
about, 63
availability, varieties, etc., 64;
nutrition, 64
-and-Carrot Blanket for Fried
Fish Fillets, Pickled, 65

Snow Pea and Bell Pepper
Salad with Sesame-Ginger
Dressing, 66
and Turnip Salad with Rus-
sian Dressing, 323
Dessert. See also Cake; Pie
Frozen Ginger and Bitter-
sweet Chocolate Terrine
with Gingered Custard
Sauce, 98
Log, Spiced Sweet Potato
with Cream Filling, 292
Sweet Carrot and Pistachio
Custard Pudding, 39

Eggs. See also Savory Pie;
Soufflé Roll
Fried Onions and, 174
Potato and Onion Spanish
Omelette, Fragrant with
Dill and Fennel, 218
Ultimate Scrambled (with
truffles), 306

Fennel and Onion, Cream of
Parsnip Soup with, 186
Fennel, Radish and Endive
Salad with Mustard Vi-
naigrette, 237
Fettuccine, Shrimp and Water
Chestnuts in a Fragrant
Cream Sauce for, 328
First course. See Appetizer;
Salad
Fish. See also Herring; Salmon;
Sardines; Sole; Tuna
Fillets, Fried, Pickled Daikon-
and-Carrot Blanket for, 65
Frosting, Cream Cheese, 183

Garlic, 68–83
about history and lore, 68–72
availability, varieties, etc., 72–
74; nutrition, 74
Brown Butter and Capers,
Salsify with, 257
Caramelized, 83
Croutons, Brown-and-White,
81
Kohlrabi, Raw, with Hot An-
chovy Sauce and, 132
Marinade, Barbecued Pota-
toes in, 201
Mayonnaise, Provençal, called
Aïoli, 76
Pan-Roasted Turnips with,
316
Pasta with Oil, Capers and,
78

Pickled Squid with Root Veg-
etables, 80
Potato Wisps, Golden-Fried,
Dusted with, 199
Potatoes, Great Mashed, with
Onions and, 200
and Red Onion Applesauce,
Savory, 77
-Roasted Potatoes with Kala-
mata Olives Provençale,
219
and Salsify Sauce for Lin-
guine, Peppery, 259
Sardines, Chilled Fried, with
Vinegar, Raisins, Pignoli
and, 82
Socca with Cumin and, 79
Soup, Double, 75
Ginger (ginger root), 85–102
about history and lore, 85–87
availability, varieties, etc., 87–
89; nutrition, 89
and Bittersweet Chocolate
Terrine with Gingered Cus-
tard Sauce, Frozen, 98
Bundt Cake, 96
Cake, Angel Food, with
Chocolate-Ginger Icing, 92
-Chocolate Chunk Cookies,
Gigantic, 97
Cream, Sautéed Leeks with
Scallops in, 151
Crystallized, Homemade, 102
Four, Cheesecake, 100
Jerusalem Artichoke and
Pork Stew with Olives and,
122
and Onions with Curried
Cabbage, 171
-Pear Pound Cake, Buttery,
94
and Vodka Shrimp over Snow
Peas, 90
Gingered Raw Scallops with
Shredded Root Vegeta-
bles, 91
Gingered Sweet Potatoes with
Sherry and Walnuts, 289

Herring, Turnip and Roast
Beef Salad, 322
Hors d'Oeuvre. See Appetizer
Horseradish, 104–13
about history and lore, 104–5
availability, varieties, etc.,
105–6; nutrition, 106
-Bread Crumb Sauce, 108
Celeriac and Parsnip Puree,
56

Cream, Salsify and Beet Salad under, 256
-Mustard-Orange Sauce, 109
-Sour Cream Salad Dressing, 113
Tuna Sauvage with, 112
Wasabi Mayonnaise Dip, Batter-Fried Vegetables with, 110
-Yogurt Mayonnaise with Capers, 107

Jerusalem Artichoke(s) (sunchokes), 115–23
about history and lore, 115
availability, varieties, etc., 116–17; nutrition, 117
and Chicken Salad in Mustard Mayonnaise, 118
Cucumbers and Peppers, Sauté of, 119
Pickles, Marion Wiener's Louisiana, 120
and Pork Stew with Olives and Ginger, 122
Jicama, 125–28
about, 125
availability, varieties, etc., 125–26; nutrition, 126
Celeriac and Unpeeled Apple Slaw with Yogurt Dressing, 127
Hash Browns, 128

Kohlrabi, 130–34
about, 130
availability, varieties, etc., 130–31; nutrition, 131
and Celery Gratin, 133
-Leek Soup with Potato and Parsley, 134
Raw, with Hot Anchovy and Garlic Sauce, 132

Leek(s), 136–51. *See also* Onions
about history and lore, 136–37
availability, varieties, etc., 138–39; nutrition, 139
and Baked Potato Vichyssoise with Red Caviar and Chives, 141
Colcannon-Stuffed Potato Shells with Bacon and, 226
Crackling Deep-Fried Shoestring, 140

and Fresh Coriander Sauce, Panfried Salmon Steaks with, 150
with Grated Nutmeg, 148
-Kohlrabi Soup with Potato and Parsley, 134
Pie, Savory, 146
Risotto, 149
and Roots Soup, Cream of, 142
and Sausage Soufflé Roll, Savory, 144
Sautéed with Scallops in Ginger Cream, 151
Linguine, Peppery Salsify and Garlic Sauce for, 259
Lotus Root (water lily, duck acorn, etc.), 153–56
about history and lore, 153
availability, varieties, etc., 154; nutrition, 154
Salad in Oriental-Style Vinaigrette, 155
Spicy Beef Stir-Fried with, 156

Mayonnaise
Dip, *Wasabi*, Batter-Fried vegetables with, 110
Horseradish-Yogurt, with Capers, 107
Provençal Garlic, called Aäoli, 76
Quick Method, 107
Mussel and Potato Salad with Basil Vinaigrette, 216

Noodles, Buttered, Crisp Browned Shallots Showered on, 276

Onion(s), 158–75
about history and lore, 158–61
about varieties (Bermuda, green, pearl, red, Walla Walla, etc.), 160–63
availability, etc., 163–65; nutrition, 165
Baked Sweet, with Rosemary Butter, 169
Caramelized, Creamed, Rutabagas with, 248
Creamy Potato and Celeriac Salad, 214
Dilled Golden Creamed, 170
and Fennel, Cream of Parsnip Soup with, 186

Fried, and Eggs, 174
and Garlic, Great Mashed Potato with, 200
and Ginger with Curried Cabbage, 171
Pearl, and Beets Pickled in Raspberry Vinegar and Wine, 11
Potato, Cauliflower and Fresh Turmeric, Curried Shrimp with, 310
and Potato Spanish Omelette, Fragrant with Dill and Fennel, 218
Red, and Garlic Applesauce, Savory, 77
Rings, Fried, in Mustard-Beer Batter, 168
Sauce, Golden, Orecchiette with, 172
Soup, Paris Market, 167
Soup, Pink Velvet, 166
and Taro Soufflé Pie, 298
and Tomato Relish with Jalapeño, 175
Orecchiette with Golden Onion Sauce, 172

Parsnip(s), 177–86
about history and folklore, 177–78
availability, varieties, etc., 178–79; nutrition, 179
Celeriac and Horseradish Puree, 56
Celeriac and Potato Soup, 53
Chips, Crisp Herbed, 180
Frosted Spiced Cake, 182
Maple Pie with Pecan Crust, 184
without Ornamentation, 182
Puree with Peas and Scallions, 181
Soup with Fennel and Onion, Cream of, 186
Pasta. *See also* Fettuccine; Linguine; Noodles; Orecchiette; Penne
with Garlic, Oil and Capers, 78
Pearl Onions. *See* Onions
Penne Vella, Potato Sauce on, 222
Pickles, Jerusalem Artichoke, Marion Wiener's Louisiana, 120
Pie. *See also* Savory Pie; Soufflé Pie

Parsnip Maple with Pecan Crust, 184

Sweet Potato-Orange Custard, 291

Pirogi, Potato and Farmer Cheese-Filled, 206

Pork and Jerusalem Artichoke Stew with Olives and Ginger, 122

Potato(es) (Irish potato, spud), 188–231. *See also* Sweet Potato

about history and lore, 188–93; slang, 192–93

about varieties of, 191–92; new, 194; old, 195; chips, fries, etc., 191–92

availability, etc., 194–97; nutrition, 197–98

Baked, and Leek Vichyssoise with Red Caviar and Chives, 141

Barbecued, in Garlic Marinade, 201

Broiler-Fried, with Fresh Basil and Olive Oil, 202

Cakes Flavored with Mace, 212

and Celeriac, Naked Mashed, 55

Celeriac and Parsnip Soup, Pureed, 53

and Celeriac Pie Filled with Sea Scallops and Sautéed Cabbage, 224

Chip Soup (Yes, Potato Chip Soup), 205

-Chive Brioches, 60

and Farmer Cheese-Filled Pirogi in Sour Cream Dough, Russian, 206

French Fries, Crusty, 203

Garlic-Roasted, with Kalamata Olives Provençale, 219

Great Mashed, with Garlic and Onions, 200

Mashed, Choclate Cake, 230

Mashed, Dinner Rolls, Flavor-of-the-Day, 228

and Mussel Salad with Basil Vinaigrette, 216

Onion, Cauliflower and Fresh Turmeric, Curried Shrimp with, 310

and Onion, Spanish Omelette Fragrant with Dill and Fennel, 218

Pancakes, Everybody's Favorite, 210

and Parsley, Kohlrabi-Leek Soup with, 134

Pie with Smoked Salmon, Scallions and Cream, 220

Ramp Champ or Ramps Mashed with, 242

Rösti-Traditional Swiss Fried Potato Cake, 208

and Rutabaga Terrine Striped with Scallion Puree, 250

Salad, Celeriac and Onion, Creamy, 214

Sauce on Penne Vella, 222

Shells, Colcannon-Stuffed, with Leeks and Bacon, 226

Soup with Dill and Scallions, 204

and Sweet Potato Gratin, Two-Toned, 284

and Tomato Stew with Pancetta, 223

Turnip Gratin with, and Dill, 319

Turnips Whipped with, and Buttermilk, 318

and White Bean Salad with White Bean and Roasted Pepper Dressing, 213

Wisps (chips), Golden-Fried, Dusted with Garlic, 199

Radish(es) (black, red, white), 233–38

about, 233

availability, varieties, etc., 233–35; nutrition, 235

Fennel and Endive Salad with Mustard Vinaigrette, 237

Red, Chilled Crushed Scallion and Sour-Grass Soup with, 266

and Scallions with Raspberry Vinegar Glaze, 236

and Snow Peas, Sole with, in Lime Vinaigrette, 238

Ramp(s) (wild leek), 240–42

about, 240

availability, varieties, etc., 240–41; nutrition, 241

Champ or Ramps Mashed with Potatoes, 242

Relish, Onion and Tomato, with Jalapeño, 175

Rice, Crunchy Sautéed Water Chestnuts in Creamy, 327

Risotto, Leek, 149

Rolls, Browned-Butter Sweet Potato Cloverleaf, 286

Rolls, Dinner, Flavor-of-the-Day Mashed Potato, 228

Root Vegetable(s)

about, xi–xvi; bulbs, corms, fungi, rhizomes, roots, tubers, xiv–xv

Garlic-Pickled Squid with, 80

Gingered Scallops with, 91

and Leek Soup, Cream of, 142

and Turnip Stuffing, 320

Rutabaga(s) (Swede, yellow turnip, etc.), 244–51

about, 244–45

availability, varieties, etc., 245–46; nutrition, 246

Creamed with Caramelized Onions, 248

Gratin of, with Fresh Rosemary, 247

and Potato Terrine Striped with Scallion Puree, 250

and Watercress Puree, 249

Salad

Beet, Grated Raw, Vinaigrette with Dill, 9

Beets and Green Beans Chilled, with Scallion Vinaigrette, 12

Carrot, Moroccan Minted, 32

Celeriac Rémoulade, 54

Daikon, Snow Pea and Bell Pepper with Sesame-Ginger Dressing, 66

Jerusalem Artichoke and Chicken in Mustard Mayonnaise, 118

Jicama, Celeriac and Unpeeled Apple Slaw with Yogurt Dressing, 127

Lotus Root, in Oriental-Style Vinaigrette, 155

Potato, Celeriac and Onion, Creamy, 214

Potato and Mussel, with Basil Vinaigrette, 216

Potato and White Bean with White Bean and Roasted Pepper Dressing, 213

Radish, Fennel and Endive with Mustard Vinaigrette, 237

Salsify and Beet under Horseradish Cream, 256

Turnip and Daikon, with
Russian Dressing, 323
Turnip, Herring and Roast
Beef, 322
Salad Dressing, Sour Cream-
Horseradish, 113
Salmon. *See also* Smoked Salmon
Steaks, with Leek and Fresh
Coriander Sauce, 150
Salsify (oyster plant, vegetable
oyster), 253–60
about history and lore, 253–
54
availability, varieties, etc.,
254–55; nutrition, 255
and Beet Salad under Horse-
radish Cream, 256
with Brown Butter, Garlic
and Capers, 257
and Garlic Sauce for Lin-
guine, Peppery, 259
Gilded, 258
Sautéed with Two Peppers,
260
Sandwich Filling, Scallion,
Creamy Blue Cheese and
Toasted Almond, 268
Sardines, Chilled Fried, with
Garlic, Vinegar, Raisins and
Pignoli, 82
Sauce(s). *See also* Butter; May-
onnaise
Anchovy and Garlic, Hot,
Raw Kohlrabi with, 132
Horseradish-Bread Crumb,
Creamed, 108
Horseradish-Mustard-Orange,
109
Potato, on Penne Vella, 222
Shallot Butter for, 272
Stilton and Walnut, Hot
Shallot Mousses Bathed in,
274
Vinaigrette, Caramelized Shal-
lot, 277
Yogurt-Dill, 21
Sausage and Leek Soufflé Roll,
Savory, 144
Savory Pie. *See also* Soufflé Pie;
Soufflé Roll
Leek, 146
Potato and Celeriac, Filled
with Sea Scallops and Sau-
téed Cabbage, 224
Potato, with Smoked Salmon,
Scallions and Cream, 220
Scallion(s) (cibol, green onion,
stone leek, etc.), 262–68.
See also Ramps

about history and lore, 262–
63
availability, varieties, etc.,
263–64; nutrition, 264
Butter Flavored with Curry,
265
Creamy Blue Cheese and
Toasted Almond Sandwich
Filling, 268
and Dill, Potato Soup with,
204
and Peas, Parsnip Puree with,
181
Puree, Rutabaga and Potato
Terrine Striped with, 250
and Radishes with Raspberry
Vinegar Glaze, 236
Scorched, 267
Smoked Salmon and Cream,
Potato Pie with, 220
and Sour-Grass Soup with
Red Radish, Chilled, 266
Scallops
Gingered Raw, with Root
Vegetables, 91
Sautéed Leeks with, in Ginger
Cream, 151
Sea, and Sautéed Cabbage,
Potato and Celeriac Pie
Filled with, 224
Seafood. *See* Mussels; Scallops;
Shrimp; Squid Shallot(s)
(eschalots, Spanish gar-
lic), 270–77
about, 270
availability, varieties, etc.,
270–71; nutrition, 271
Butter for Sauces, 272
Caramelized, Vinaigrette
Sauce, 277
Creamed, and Endive Soup
with Bacon, 273
Crisp Browned, Showered on
Buttered Noodles, 276
Mousses Bathed in Stilton
and Walnut Sauce, 274
Shrimp
chilled, Chive-Marinated, 61
Curried, with Cauliflower,
Potato, Onion and Fresh
Turmeric, 310
Ginger and Vodka, over Snow
Peas, 90
and Water Chestnuts in a
Fragrant Cream Sauce for
Fettuccine, 328
Smoked Salmon, Scallions and
Cream, Potato Pie with,
220

Socca with Garlic and Cumin,
79
Sole with Radishes and Snow
Peas in Lime Vinaigrette,
238
Soufflé Pie, Taro and Onion,
298
Soufflé Roll, Savory Leek and
Sausage, 144
Soup
Beet, Creamed, and Corian-
der, with Orange Juice, 8
Beet, Sweet-and-Sour, with
Caraway and Yogurt, 5
Carrot, Curried, Vichyssoise,
Cold, 33
Carrot, Skillet-Charred Puree
of, 29
Celeriac, Hot or Cold Cream
of, 52
Celeriac, Potato and Parsnip,
Pureed, 53
Garlic, Double, 75
Kohlrabi-Leek, with Potato
and Parsley, 134
Leek and Roots, Cream of,
142
Leeks and Baked Potato
Vichyssoise with Red Cav-
iar and Chives, 141
Onion, Paris Market, 167
Onion, Pink Velvet, 166
Parsnip with Fennel and On-
ion, Cream of, 186
Potato Chip (Yes, Potato
Chip), 205
Potato with Dill and Scal-
lions, 204
Scallion and Sour-Grass, with
Red Radish, Chilled 266
Shallot, Creamed, and En-
dive, with Bacon, 273
Sweet Potato with Yogurt and
Caraway, 288
Turnip, Mellowed with Rice,
317
Ukrainian Winter Borscht, 6
Squid, Garlic-Pickled with Root
Vegetables, 80
Stuffing, Turnip and Root Vege-
table, 320
sunchokes. *See* Jerusalem Arti-
chokes
Sweet Potato(es) (white sweet
potato), 279–93
about history and lore, 279–
80
availability, varieties, etc.,
280–82; nutrition, 282

Bourbon-Spiked, and Apricot Puree, 283
Brisket of Beef Baked with Carrots, Fruit and, 36
Cloverleaf Rolls, Browned-Butter, 286
Dessert Log with Cream Filling, Spiced, 292
Gingered with Sherry and Walnuts, 289
-Orange Custard Pie, 291
Orange-Lemon Puree with Pecan Topping, 285
and Potato Gratin, Two-Toned, 284
Soup with Yogurt and Caraway, 288
Spiced with Apple, Pear and Currants, 290

Taro, 295–99
about history and lore, 295–96
availability, varieties, etc., 296–97; nutrition, 297
and Onion Soufflé Pie, 298
Panfried, Italian Style, 299
Truffle(s), 301–6
about history and lore, 301–3

availability, varieties, etc., 303; nutrition, 304
Ultimate Scrambled Eggs, 306
White Shavings, Cheese Fondue with, 305
Tuna Sauvage with Horseradish, 112
Turmeric, 308–11
about history and lore, 308
availability, varieties, etc., 309; nutrition, 309
Fresh, Curried Shrimp with Cauliflower, Potato, Onion and, 310
Turnip(s) (white turnip), 313–23
about history and lore, 313–14
availability, varieties, etc., 314–15; nutrition, 315
and Cabbage Spiked with Cumin, Stir-Fried, 321
Carrot and Scallion Gratin, Crusty, 34
Celeriac and Gruyère Pancake, 57
and Daikon Salad with Russian Dressing, 323
with Garlic, Pan-Roasted, 316

Gratin with Potatoes and Dill, 319
Herring and Roast Beef Salad, 322
and Root Vegetable Stuffing, 320
Soup Mellowed with Rice, 317
Whipped with Potatoes and Buttermilk, 318

Wasabi Mayonnaise Dip, Batter-Fried Vegetables with, 110
Water Chestnuts, 325–29
about, 325
availability, varieties, etc., 325–26; nutrition, 326
Crunchy Sautéed, in Creamy Rice, 327
and Shrimp in Cream Sauce for Fettuccine, 328

Yams, 331–32. See also Sweet Potatoes
about, history and lore, 331–32; nutrition, 332
Orange-Lemon Sweet Potato Puree with Pecan Topping, 285